The Words and Music of Paul Simon

THE PRAEGER SINGER-SONGWRITER COLLECTION

The Words and Music of Paul Simon

James Bennighof

James E. Perone, Series Editor

PRAEGER

Westport, Connecticut
London

782.4216
Ben

Library of Congress Cataloging-in-Publication Data

Bennighof, James.
    The words and music of Paul Simon / James Bennighof.
        p.   cm. — (The Praeger singer-songwriter collection, ISSN 1553–3484)
    Includes bibliographical references (p.   ), discography (p.   ), and index.
    ISBN 978–0–275–99163–0 (alk. paper)
    1. Simon, Paul, 1941—Criticism and interpretation.   2. Popular music—United
States—History and criticism.   I. Title.
ML420.S563B46 2007
782.42164092—dc22   2007026125

British Library Cataloguing in Publication Data is available.

Library of Congress Catalog Card Number: 2007026125
ISBN: 978–0–275–99163–0
ISSN: 1553–3484

First published in 2007

Praeger Publishers, 88 Post Road West, Westport, CT 06881
An imprint of Greenwood Publishing Group, Inc.
www.praeger.com

Printed in the United States of America

The paper used in this book complies with the
Permanent Paper Standard issued by the National
Information Standards Organization (Z39.48–1984).

10   9   8   7   6   5   4   3   2   1

For Dori, Elspeth, and Samuel

Contents

Acknowledgments

I appreciate the many friends who encouraged me through (or at least listened to me talk about) the writing of this book. I also wish to acknowledge Baylor University, which provides equipment and materials for my work as a member of the faculty. Specific thanks go to Sha Towers of the Crouch Fine Arts Library at Baylor for helping me to find several elusive sources, and to Ruthann McTyre and Ellen Jones of the University of Iowa Libraries for helping Towers on one crucial occasion.

Among several websites that contain helpful bits of information, two warrant particular mention. Rich Kent's *The Simon and Garfunkel Homepage* (http://freespace.virgin.net/r.kent/index.html) usually proved to be the most efficient route to guitar tablature; while I take responsibility for all of the observations about guitar technique in this book, the ready availability of these tablatures often expedited the process of initial orientation to a song's key and so forth. A similar role was played by Melinda Hesbacher's site, *The Unofficial Capeman Website* (http://members.aol.com/Pretybelle/enter.html), which is devoted to the 1998 musical; again, while all the points made in the book about the songs in *The Capeman* are my own, the synopses and other information on Ms. Hesbacher's site provided me with a very useful point of departure for interpreting these songs within the context of the narrative.

A.M.D.G.

Introduction: Paul Simon as an Artist and Composer

Born October 13, 1941, in Newark, New Jersey, Paul Simon was to become one of the most popular singer/songwriters in the second half of the twentieth century. Simon was like many of the other performers to whom the label "singer/songwriter" was first applied, including such luminaries as Bob Dylan and Joni Mitchell, in several important respects. Unlike many of the most successful songwriters of the generation before them, these artists usually performed their own songs and, although many others also recorded versions of these songs, those produced by the singer/songwriter were usually the best-known. Furthermore, unlike many of the other popular-music performers of their own day, the singer/songwriters tended to be "solo acts"—that is, while they often worked with other musicians, these took the role of accompanists or occasional collaborators, rather than sharing equal status as members of a permanently established band. In Simon's case, of course, both of these characteristics are qualified in one important way—in the initial part of his career, he performed most of his songs not solo, but as part of a phenomenally popular duo with Art Garfunkel.

As a teenager, Simon began to write and perform songs, often in collaboration with Garfunkel, in the rock and roll style of the late 1950s. The duo first attained lasting success, though, with songs that were identified with the newly popular folk styles of the early 1960s. They recorded five studio albums together: *Wednesday Morning, 3 A.M.; Sounds of Silence; Parsley, Sage, Rosemary and Thyme; Bookends;* and *Bridge over Troubled Water.* Several songs from these albums found a permanent place on the landscape of American popular culture, including "The Sound of Silence," "I Am a Rock," "Scarborough Fair/Canticle," "Homeward Bound," "The 59th Street Bridge

Song (Feelin' Groovy)," "America," "Mrs. Robinson," "Bridge over Troubled Water," "Cecilia," and "The Boxer."

These early hits took advantage of the wide variety of styles that were available to the American popular songwriter of the 1960s, including "folk" sounds as well as others. Known for valuing thoughtful, literary lyrics, Simon has consistently sought musical resources that can most effectively complement his textual ideas. As he began to make solo albums, he frequently collaborated with musicians whose specific stylistic strengths provided additional grist for his creative mill. In albums from the 1970s, such as *Paul Simon, There Goes Rhymin' Simon,* and *Still Crazy after All These Years,* for example, this approach yielded songs like "Mother and Child Reunion" with Jamaican studio musicians; "Duncan," with Los Incas; "Kodachrome," with the Muscle Shoals Rhythm Section; "Loves Me Like a Rock," with the Dixie Hummingbirds; and "Gone at Last," with Phoebe Snow and the Jessy Dixon Singers.

This eclectic sensibility is even more clearly demonstrated by the works of the following decade. The somewhat idiosyncratic *Hearts and Bones* included a variety of instruments (including contrabass guitar, vocoder, and synclavier) and collaborators as varied as classical minimalist composer Philip Glass, jazz guitarist Al DiMeola, and the doo-wop vocal group the Harptones, but its popularity didn't match its broad range of resources; its best-known song was probably the relatively obscure title track. (The preceding album, *Still Crazy after All These Years,* had included not only the title track, but also the other hits "My Little Town," "50 Ways to Leave Your Lover," and "Gone at Last.") More significant, though, was the next album, *Graceland.* Drawing heavily on material that Simon culled from various African traditions, this production took a giant step into world music (creating a worldwide furor over issues related to apartheid at the same time). Following this, *The Rhythm of the Saints* similarly explored Brazil, and *You're the One* shows the influence of these global forays. Finally, Simon's most recent album, *Surprise,* is probably most distinctively characterized by the combination of a generally simple instrumental texture with a "sonic landscape" credited to Brian Eno; again, though, the album draws stylistically on a variety of influences.

It is clear that Simon's central strength is writing popular songs and creating the albums that they inhabit. He has written songs in other contexts as well, though, most notably in two dramatic efforts. Following the inclusion of a few of his songs in *The Graduate* in 1968 and a bit of his music in *Shampoo* in 1975 (as well as a small acting role in Woody Allen's *Annie Hall* in 1977), in 1980 Simon wrote and starred in a feature film, *One-Trick Pony,* which contained 10 original songs. Then in the 1990s he collaborated with the Nobel Prize-winning poet Derek Walcott to write a Broadway musical, *The Capeman,* which ran briefly in the fall of 1997.

Throughout his career, Simon has written relatively slowly, and so the catalog of his work is smaller than one might expect for a career that now spans 50 years. Nevertheless, his achievements and influence have been formidable.

Eight Grammy awards from the Simon and Garfunkel years were followed by two in 1975 and two more in 1986–87, and 14 of his songs have reached the top 10 on the Billboard charts. Most recently, he was awarded the first annual Gershwin Prize for Popular Song by the Library of Congress. This style-spanning achievement is reinforced by perhaps one of the most significant indications of Simon's impact on the music world: the wide range of performers who have recorded his compositions. These include icons as varied as Bob Dylan and Joan Baez, Frank Sinatra and Rosemary Clooney, Aretha Franklin and Roberta Flack, Perry Como and Tom Jones, Bill Evans and Paul Desmond, Chet Atkins and Floyd Cramer, Yes and Wings, and the Bangles and Annie Lennox. It is clear that Simon's fellow musicians have found much of value in his work, and it seems equally certain that listeners will find his music rewarding for years to come.

THE SCOPE AND ORGANIZATION OF THIS BOOK

Almost all of Paul Simon's mature work is readily available on his albums and collections. In almost all cases these recordings feature him as a performer, and in the few exceptions (solos by Garfunkel and songs from *The Capeman*), he was centrally involved in the production process. In this volume I present a thorough study of this body of work.

Because there are relatively few songs, each that appears on an album can be discussed in this survey. This examination will proceed chronologically, addressing not only the individual songs, but also important observations about the albums that they comprise. In addition, it will include, insofar as it bears upon the listening experience, information about Simon's personal circumstances and the musical and cultural milieu in which he created these works.

The survey will examine how each of Simon's songs integrates text and music into a unified work of art. Usually the central issue will be the way the musical setting relates to the textual ideas: What form or forms are applied to the music and text? Upon what styles does the setting draw? How does its melodic and harmonic structure define, complement, or comment upon the text? How do other factors, such as instrumentation, arrangement, recording techniques, and so on contribute to the work?[1] I might note here that, while the primary purpose of these discussions is not to specify exactly *how valuable each song may be*, I hope that much of the information they contain may apply to the reader's appreciation of *how each song may be valuable*.

Each discussion of a song is most informative if the reader is listening to the song as well as reading about it (or if the reader at least has a vivid memory of the way the song sounds). For even more detailed study, the reader may wish to consult a sheet-music publication of the music. (Most of these include piano parts that relate to the actual recorded performance—the object of this study—in deceptive ways; for many purposes, a simpler lead-sheet format, which provides just the sung melody, words, and chords, may be more useful.

This version of almost all the songs except those on the recent *Surprise* is provided in *The Definitive Paul Simon Songbook* [New York: Amsco Publications, 2005].) It is also worth noting that the discussions often include specific technical chord names. This level of detail is intended to provide specific information for the musically trained reader who will benefit from it. However, when knowledge of how a particular chord is constructed is crucial in understanding the point being made at the time, I attempt to clarify this information. In any event, additional information about the construction of simple chords is provided in the appendix, and a brief explanation is also provided along with the glossary that follows this section.

I conclude my discussion with a brief assessment of Simon's creative identity that is based on the analyses of individual songs in the book. Here in particular I draw conclusions about his aesthetic perspective as revealed in the compositional methods, and the results of those methods, that these songs reflect throughout the evolution of his career.

I have included at the end of the book two sections that may enhance the reader's understanding. The first of these, the appendix, discusses the general principles that apply to the musical languages and styles upon which Simon draws. Taking major-minor classical tonality as its point of departure and drawing on examples from Simon's work, this material may be particularly helpful for readers without formal music-theoretical training, but it should also provide an interesting survey for others as well.

The section following the appendix is a brief discography of Simon's albums and songs. Those interested in a much more extensive discography (including cover versions of Simon's work by other artists), videography and filmography, and bibliography may consult *Paul Simon: A Bio-Bibliography* by James E. Perone (Westport, CT: Greenwood Press, 2000). Finally, the book concludes with an index of songs and important names and terms discussed in the text.

Glossary and Brief Guide to Chord Structure

Aeolian mode: A diatonic scale with the following pattern of whole- and half-steps ascending from the tonic note to the tonic note an octave higher: whole-half-whole-whole-half-whole-whole. The white keys on a piano from A to A exemplify this pattern. (See Appendix for more information.)

arpeggio: A chord played one note at a time, ascending or descending.

bridge: A section of a song that conveys the sense of connecting between two sections that are more thematically primary.

capo: A device used by guitarists to raise the sounding pitch of the strings. Ordinarily each string can vibrate along its entire length, from the "nut" at the end of the neck to the bridge below the soundhole on the body of the guitar. When the capo is clamped onto the neck of the guitar behind a fret, all of the strings can only vibrate between that fret and the bridge, thus producing higher notes. The effect of this is to create a guitar at a higher pitch, so that a chord that would ordinarily sound as D major, for example, would sound as E♭ major if a capo were to be placed at the first fret, E major at the second, and so forth.

chromatic: Not belonging to the fundamental diatonic scale of a piece. (See Appendix for more information.)

coda: A section of music that occurs after the main portion of a piece has concluded (from a Latin word meaning "tail").

diatonic: In music based on seven-note scales, having a pattern of whole and half steps in which a group of two whole steps is separated from a group of three whole steps, above and below, by single half steps. The white keys on a piano exemplify this pattern. (See Appendix for more information.)

dominant: In a major or minor scale, the fifth scale step (such as G in the key of C major or C minor), or a chord that uses this note as its root. (See Appendix for more information.)

doo-wop: A style of rhythm-and-blues singing popularized during the 1940s and 1950s, often featuring a soloist and accompanying vocal ensemble.

Dorian mode: A diatonic scale with the following pattern of whole- and half-steps ascending from the tonic note to the tonic note an octave higher: whole-half-whole-whole-whole-half-whole. The white keys on a piano from D to D exemplify this pattern. (See Appendix for more information.)

fret: One of several metal low metal barriers embedded across the neck of a guitar or similar instrument; a string depressed behind a fret can only vibrate between the fret and the bridge, thus sounding a higher note than it would if it were allowed to vibrate along its entire length.

hammer-on: The production of a note on a guitar or similar instrument by striking the string with a finger of the left hand that remains on the string behind a fret; this differs from the more common method of plucking the string with the right hand using a finger or plectrum (pick).

hook: A distinctive musical figure in a popular song, often considered an essential ingredient because of its attractiveness and/or memorable nature.

interval: The distance between two notes.

legato: Played smoothly, with minimal separation between notes.

lick: A characteristic, brief musical figure played in a prominent way as an embellishment in a performance of a piece; the term is usually used in the context of popular or vernacular music.

Mixolydian mode: A diatonic scale with the following pattern of whole- and half-steps ascending from the tonic note to the tonic note an octave higher: whole-whole-half-whole-whole-half-whole. The white keys on a piano from G to G exemplify this pattern. (See Appendix for more information.)

modal: Relating to the diatonic modes, as contrasted with major or minor scales. (See Appendix for more information.)

obbligato: A prominent musical line that accompanies the primary line, often with a sense of improvisation and/or ornamentation.

ostinato: A repetitive, usually accompanimental musical pattern.

pedal point: A note that is sustained or repeated while other parts or harmonies change against it.

riff: A characteristic musical figure that recurs throughout a piece; the term is usually used in the context of popular or vernacular music.

scat: A style of jazz singing characterized by improvisational, instrumental-sounding nonsense syllables.

syncopation: Rhythmic emphasis that falls off the strong beat or part of the beat, rather than on.

subdominant: In a major or minor scale, the fourth scale step (such as F in the key of C major or C minor), or a chord that uses this note as its root. (See Appendix for more information.)

submediant: In a major or minor scale, the sixth scale step (such as A in the key of C major or A♭ in the key of C minor), or a chord that uses this note as its root. (See Appendix for more information.)

tonic: The central note of a key, that is, the note toward which other notes gravitate, and which provides the most stable point of arrival; or a chord that uses this note as its root. In major and minor keys, and in most other scales, this is the note after which the key or scale is named. (See Appendix for more information.)

vamp: A repetitive accompanimental pattern; the term is often used to describe a pattern that can continue indefinitely, for example while waiting for a soloist to begin playing or singing.

vocalise: An exposed, improvisatory-sounding vocal line.

BRIEF GUIDE TO CHORD STRUCTURE

This guide describes the structure of chords discussed in this book. The chords are usually named by a note name and other letters, numbers, and/ or symbols. Most of these are explained below, with each section preceded by the symbols to which it applies (using as an example the note-name *C*). References to chords as they function in keys, using words like *subdominant, tonic,* and so forth, are explained briefly in the preceding glossary, and more extensively in the Appendix. The very rare references by Roman numerals are explained in the Appendix.

Most chords, and most chords discussed in this book, contain a *root* after which the chord is named, a *third* (two steps above the root), and a *fifth* (two steps above the third). A C major chord, then, contains the root C, the third E, and the fifth G. These three basic notes constitute a *triad*.

C, Cm, C minor (major and minor triads): Major triads are usually named in this book with only the note of their root, so this would be called a *C chord*. The exact size of the intervals among these notes determines whether a chord is major or some other *quality*; if the E is changed to an E♭, this chord becomes minor, and would be called *C minor* or *Cm*.

C7, Cm7, Cmaj7 (seventh chords): Other notes can be added to the triad, most typically a *seventh*, two steps above the fifth, which in this case would be a B or B♭. Chords that would result in this case could be major seventh chords (C-E-G-B, called *Cmaj7*), minor seventh chords (C-E♭-G-B♭, called *Cm7*), or major-minor seventh chords (C-E-G-B♭, called *C7*).

C9, Cadd9, C6, Cm6, C11, Cm11 (added-note chords): Less commonly, a ninth could be added (this would be a D if the root is C, making a *C9* chord—sometimes called *Cadd9*), a sixth could be added (some kind of A, resulting in a C-E-G-A (*C6*) or C-E♭-G-A♭ (*Cm6*)), or even an eleventh could be added (an F, making a *C11* or *Cm11* chord).

Csus4, C+, Cm7♭5, C diminished 7 (alterations of triad): Finally, the basic triad can be altered in ways other than lowering the E to an E♭, as described above with reference to minor chords. The E could be replaced with an F, usually regarded as a *suspended* note that wants to resolve back down to the E; since the F is a fourth above the C, this chord is commonly called a *Csus4*. The fifth of a major chord could be raised; the resulting C-E-G♯ chord is called *augmented,* and is symbolized with *C+*. Or the fifth of a minor chord could be lowered to make a *diminished* chord—C-E♭-G♭. Such chords in this style usually contain a seventh, either B♭, making a C-E♭-G♭-B♭ chord, commonly identified here by *Cm7♭5*; or B♭♭, making a C-E♭-G♭-B♭♭ chord, commonly identified here by *C diminished 7*.

The Urban Folk Influence

Paul Simon and Arthur Garfunkel, three weeks his junior, came to know each other well as schoolboys in Forest Hills, New York, and it was at this time that they began to perform together at school, as well as at venues such as private parties and bar mitzvahs. As they grew into their teen years, they listened to the early rock and roll music that was popular in the late 1950s—with one notable influence being the Everly Brothers—and Simon became interested in writing his own songs. They began to frequent the music publishers' offices in New York, and at the age of 15, performing as "Tom and Jerry," they actually had a Top 40 hit, "Hey Schoolgirl." This led to an appearance on American Bandstand, and then to not much else in the way of fame. The duo recorded a few more songs without further commercial success, and Simon continued to write songs, some of which were recorded by other performers. Almost all of these efforts disappeared quickly.[1]

After graduating from high school, Simon and Garfunkel matriculated at college (Garfunkel at Columbia to study mathematics, and Simon at Queens to study English literature), but each continued his involvement in the music business. For Simon, in addition to continuing to write, this meant recording demos for other writers (sometimes in the company of Carole Klein—later to become known as Carole King) as well as other occasional activities. One of the most important benefits of this period of time for the aspiring musician was the thorough knowledge that he gained of the popular music industry, including both business practices and technical studio procedures.

WEDNESDAY MORNING, 3 A.M.
AND THE PAUL SIMON SONGBOOK

After college (and a brief stint at law school), Simon continued his musical pursuits. No doubt influenced by his studies of English literature, he was becoming increasingly interested in the literary potential of his songwriting work. He found that the aesthetic environment and musical traditions of the early urban folk movement provided fertile ground for nurturing this impulse. Beginning to incorporate these styles into his own writing, he performed, sometimes with Garfunkel, in clubs in New York and England. A positive reaction to their music on the part of Tom Wilson, a producer of Bob Dylan's early work at Columbia records, resulted in their recording their first record album (LP), *Wednesday Morning, 3 A.M.*, in 1964. Intended to capitalize on the folk-music boom, the album combined five of Simon's songs and an original Simon-and-Garfunkel arrangement of a sixteenth-century sacred work with six more "proven" songs by other writers. It did not enjoy significant commercial success, however, and Simon returned to England.

There, his contact with a supporter named Judith Piepe led to his recording 12 of his songs, accompanied only by his guitar, to make an album called *The Paul Simon Songbook* (originally released only in the United Kingdom, but now available in the United States as well) in 1965. He was continuing to perform, write, and produce music in England and Europe when a song from *Wednesday Morning, 3 A.M.*, "The Sound of Silence," began to attract attention. In response to this, and unbeknownst to Simon and Garfunkel, Wilson added new instrumental tracks to the recording in order to give it a "folk rock" sound, and the reconstituted single was a huge success.

Simon was rushed back to the United States, and he and Garfunkel quickly recorded an album, *Sounds of Silence*, around the new version of the song, using the existing Simon compositions (along with one instrumental, "Anji," written by the British guitarist Davey Graham) that were felt to complete the album most effectively. *Sounds of Silence*, released in 1966, sold extremely well and established the duo in the public consciousness; the rest of their studio albums, each tremendously popular, followed in regular succession. *Parsley, Sage, Rosemary and Thyme*, also released in 1966, was the first of these and was the first opportunity that Simon and Garfunkel—along with recording engineer Roy Halee—had to exercise artistic control over the production of an album as a whole.

Of course, Simon and Garfunkel had had enough experience in the business even by the time *Wednesday Morning, 3 A.M.* was produced that they (or just Simon in the case of *The Paul Simon Songbook*) would have had some influence on the way the first three albums were assembled. All the same, each of them was shaped largely by external circumstances—the label-influenced "assembly" of *Wednesday Morning, 3 A.M.* and *Sounds of Silence* was discussed earlier in this chapter, and the haste with which *The Paul Simon Songbook* was recorded gives it more the character of a live set than that of a carefully produced album. These first four albums were in some ways the result of sorting out how to release quite a few songs that had accumulated, and in fact, all but two of the songs on *The Paul Simon Songbook* appear in different versions on at least one of the duo albums (and "The Sound of Silence" actually appears on the first two duo albums[2]). Because of this, it is not essential to consider the composition of each album as a whole as a reliable reflection of Simon's creative process. More revealing of his development will be a discussion of the songs on *Wednesday Morning, 3 A.M.*, along with the two that appear only on *Songbook*, as they show how some of Simon's initial urban folk efforts led up to the landmark "The Sound of Silence."

Probably the earliest-composed of these songs, "He Was My Brother," appears on both *Wednesday Morning, 3 A.M.* and *The Paul Simon Songbook*.[3] (It is credited to a Simon pseudonym, "Paul Kane.") Its theme and style are clearly products of Simon's interest in the urban folk movement, as it tells the story of a civil-rights worker who dies in the struggle to bring about racial equality. Simon implied at one point that it had been written in response to the devastating news that an acquaintance of his, Andrew Goodman, had suffered just such a fate.[4] However, according to notes that Garfunkel wrote for *Wednesday Morning, 3 A.M.*, the song had been composed by June 1963, a year before Goodman's death, although the *Songbook* version does change a reference to "this town" to "Mississippi" in order to refer more specifically to Goodman.[5]

The four verses of the song use a simple antecedent-consequent structure. In the first half of each, the progression of simple folk-guitar chords, strummed in "boom-chick" alternation with bass notes, first prolongs the tonic chord (D) and then moves to the dominant chord (A): D-C-D-Bm/F#-G-A. The second half repeats the same series with a final resolution to the tonic: D-C-D-Bm/F#-G-A-D.[6] The modal (Mixolydian in this case) nature of the C chord recalls the use of modal scales in rural folksongs. The melody follows a similarly parallel structure in the halves of the verses, moving from a sustained A down to an E in each verse's first half, and then completing the journey from the A to a concluding D in the second.

The verses unfold the story directly, first introducing the listener to the brother who died at age 23, then describing the antagonistic reaction to his civil-rights work, then relating his murder, and finally mourning his death, but declaring that "he died so his brothers could be free." The simplest recording of the song, the Simon-plus-solo-guitar version on *Songbook*, reveals four ways that the repetitive verse pattern is brought to a convincing conclusion. Two of these are typical folk-song formulas—the melody of the last line moves triumphantly to a new, higher register, and the last line is repeated. But two are more subtle.

First, the "brother" idea, when introduced in the titular first line, seems to be meant literally, or at least to indicate intimate companionship, and thus it encourages the listener to empathize with the narrator. But at the end, the idea is inverted to indicate the martyr's embrace of many "brothers" (and, implicitly, especially those of a different race), thus praising his generosity of spirit. Second, the sustained word "free" at the end rounds out the song by connecting with the sustained syllables "He" and "Free-" at the beginnings of the verses.

This song's virtues as an essay in the newly popular folk style had actually been crucial in leading Tom Wilson to produce *Wednesday Morning, 3 A.M.*[7] The version of the song that appears on that album includes added instruments that create a fuller, more jangly sound. Garfunkel provides a high harmony line throughout until the end, at which point he takes the newly ascended melody and Simon sings a lower harmony. This version is thus a bit sweeter than that on *Songbook,* but essentially the same structurally.

The next of the recorded songs to have been written is the little-known "The Side of a Hill." This song appears only on *The Paul Simon Songbook,* although almost half of the "Canticle" text from *Parsley, Sage, Rosemary and Thyme*'s "Scarborough Fair/Canticle" is drawn from its lyrics.

The simple poetic structure of the song's three four-line stanzas is emphasized by an identical melody (with very minor variations) for each. The first verse tells of a boy lying "asleep" in the earth on the side of a hill while a war is fought in the valley below "in a land called 'Somewhere,'" the second reveals that a soldier killed the boy and describes a cloud watering his grave "with its silent tears," and the third describes continued, senseless fighting, while recalling the image of the weeping cloud.

This text, with its political commentary expressed in the context of a narrative implied by a few vivid images, is quite typical of the urban folk genre. Its musical setting makes full use of the resources available to a singer with a single acoustic guitar. Simon fingerpicks his accompaniment in the guitar-friendly key of G major (capoed three frets to sound in B♭), and uses all six major and minor chords within the key (GM, Am, Bm, CM, Dm, Em) and none outside of the key, and his playing is full of typical folk-guitar elements such as hammer-ons and runs.

The music presents several interesting subtleties, though. Most importantly, Simon manipulates the sense of stability in the key to reflect the unsettled nature of the text. The first verse is preceded by a brief interlude that strongly implies the key of A minor, and this leads to the A minor chord that begins the verse. This "sideways" beginning sets the text "On the side of a," and then the real tonic chord, G major, arrives on the stable word "hill." The last word of each of the first three lines is set with a G chord but avoids closure with a non-G melody note (either B or D). Then, in the first two verses, the last line finally concludes with G in the melody, but this arrival is undercut with a deceptive cadence to an E minor chord.

Only in the third verse does the last word receive a stable G melody note and G chord. This final stability is underscored by a brief guitar coda that solidly emphasizes the G harmony (in contrast to the A minor introduction). Simon further achieves closure by ending the third verse with the phrase "on the side of a hill," which opened each of the first two verses but was withheld until this point from the third.

Other touches might also be appreciated. A guitar run echoes the melody after the first lines of the first and last verses but is omitted in the second verse when the melody has just a single note on the word "weeps"; the run is echoed in the interludes between verses and expanded in the coda. Perhaps the most bitter line-ending idea occurs at the end of the third line of each verse, and the G harmony here is immediately undercut by a "sad" Bm/F♯ harmony. On the other hand, the song is not perfect—for example, the connection between the war and the boy's death is not made clear, making the latter seem a bit gratuitous as a poignant image that is meant to support an antiwar argument. Nonetheless, the intricacies and elegance of the song's structure, at a time when many superficially similar songs would have lacked such craftsmanship, reflect a classical compositional aesthetic on Simon's part.

Both of these songs are quite topical, and the same can also be said of the other song that appears only on *The Paul Simon Songbook*. As was the case with "He Was My Brother," "A Church Is Burning" addresses the civil-rights movement. It is anchored by a chorus that describes a church that has been set ablaze by racists. Its text describes the flames rising in the sky and compares them to praying hands. The idea of prayer is then amplified by attributing words to the flames, as the fire is said to be declaring freedom despite the destruction.

The melody supports this progression of thoughts by gradually ascending throughout the chorus. The song is played in the key of D (capoed up one fret to sound in E♭), and the lines of the chorus concentrate on successively higher notes in a D chord. The first emphasizes the low D, decorated by the E above it, and the second similarly treats the F♯ and G♮. The third reaches the A and B but falls back to the E, and then the fourth and fifth leap to the high D before finally returning to the low one.

This melodic process is firmly stabilized by tonic D chords at the beginnings and ends of most of the lines, and this emphasizes both the factual reporting of the incident and the claim about the flames' message. In contrast to this treatment in the chorus, the three verses introduce destabilizing events or ideas by beginning each line with a nontonic chord and emphasis on a melody note of E or G; each line then moves once or twice to the tonic chord and a more stable note (F♯ in the first two lines and D in the last two). The first verse describes the arsonists' approach to the church and the triumphant singing that had taken place there previously; the second describes the act and its aftermath, and the third brings encouragement for the civil-rights movement while acknowledging the challenges inherent in pursuing it.

The harmonic language in this song is similar to that in "He Was My Brother" and "The Side of a Hill." As a rule, the verses and choruses use five of the six major and minor chords in the key, omitting only B minor. Contrasting exceptions to this practice define two key moments in the song, though. An extra line is inserted in the first verse, and here a modal C chord highlights the fact that "just hours" separated the exuberant singing and the act of arson. And the triumphant declaration at the end of the final chorus is emphasized by a melodic rise to the high F♯, accompanied by a harmonic detour through the heretofore-missing B minor chord.

This song is not well-known, since it does not appear on any of the duo albums, and it is not a particularly notable aesthetic achievement on Simon's part. But it does provide one additional example of Simon's adoption of a typical urban folk premise, and the way that he shaped the idea that he chose to explore.

The third-composed song is "Sparrow," which appears on *Wednesday Morning, 3 A.M.* The core of the folk-combo accompaniment is an acoustic guitar that alternates bass notes and strums in a style evocative of Appalachian folk music: the Aeolian mode is established in the key of E (capoed three frets to sound in G), with bass hammer-ons stylistically complementing the urgent tempo. The basic structure is, again, simple, with four verses essentially identical in metrical structure and musical setting.

Each verse first asks who will love the sparrow by providing some resource, and then gives an answer. In the first three verses, an oak tree, a swan, and wheat refuse to provide shelter, verbal encouragement, and food, respectively. In the fourth, the earth consents to provide a eulogy.

Musically, every verse is essentially the same, with only two significant variations. The earth's affirmative answer is heralded by an extra guitar kick, and its final, benedictory comment, "From dust were ye made and dust ye shall be," is embellished by the return of an atmospheric vamp that precedes the first and third verses. Apart from these, though, it is mainly within each verse that Simon shapes musical elements to support the text.

In each verse, the sparrow's plight as conveyed in the opening question is underscored by a modal progression away from and back toward the tonic harmony of E minor (Em-D-C-D). Three simple lead-guitar interjections further set the plaintive tone, and Garfunkel indicates the sparrow's frailty with a simple high harmony line.

The brief answer is stated by Simon alone with a return to the E minor chord, and then the character that is speaking is identified with an A major chord that breaks out of the mode. This harmony emphasizes the character's pride (haughty and selfish in the first three cases, and more authoritative in the last) and continues to dominate, decorated by D major and B minor chords, throughout the character's explanation (with Garfunkel now on low harmonies that support the character's smug lack of generosity), until E minor returns at the end of the verse. The melody, though, which has mainly focused on a very narrow range from E to G, concludes on an open-ended G, implying a continuing need for resolution in the first three verses, and a universal endless cycle in the last.

Each of these four songs deals, more or less directly, with social ills, a topical focus typical of the urban folk movement. In fact, a negative outlook on life pervades the first four albums, with few respites. ("Kathy's Song" and "Homeward Bound" find some solace in a lover—inspired by Kathy Chitty, Simon's English girlfriend—as does "For Emily, Whenever I May Find Her";

"A Simple Desultory Philippic," "We've Got a Groovey Thing Goin'," and "The Big Bright Green Pleasure Machine" are at least somewhat light-hearted; and "The 59th Street Bridge Song (Feelin' Groovy)" is completely upbeat.) Such a perspective is not surprising, not only because of the general mood at the time, but also because it is easier for many writers to write the kind of literary lyrics that interested Simon about painful topics than about more positive ones. In any event, Simon developed a reputation for alienation in his writing during these years—a reputation that apparently did not pose difficulties for him.[8]

The fourth song, "Bleecker Street," continues in this vein. It paints a portrait of despair at this apt-sounding Greenwich Village locale, with each of the four verses depicting a specific scene. Some hints of hope are offered throughout by images of Christianity—a realm to which Simon refers often in his early work—but this is presented as being remote. The fog that covers Bleecker Street like a shroud hides the shepherd from the sheep; the holy sacrament, which is the poet's rhyme, is also crooked, and the fact that rent is 30 dollars, echoing Judas Iscariot's 30 pieces of silver, suggests some sort of betrayal on his part; the church bell's chime is soft; and "it's a long road to Canaan."

Garfunkel's liner notes for *Wednesday Morning, 3 A.M.* provide a "listener's guide" to the album's five original Simon songs in the form of a purported letter to Simon that mentions the artistic and intellectual value of the songs and chats about some of the details of gigging and recording.[9] In his discussion of "Bleecker Street," Garfunkel says that the song was "too much for [him] at first" (elsewhere he has been quoted as saying that he found it "too dark"), and he goes on to explain the "extremely challenging" symbolism that makes it "difficult to understand." It is unclear to what degree Garfunkel felt that all this was true (as opposed, say, to his writing it as a kind of apologia and/or encouragement for listeners who might otherwise be put off by their own difficulty in understanding the lyrics), but the series of images does not seem nearly as incomprehensible as he intimates when viewed by today's standards.

Be this as it may, some elements of the song provoke more thought than do others. As the lyrics make their way from a general description of the scene to a depiction of futile interaction, the poet, the divine hint of the "church bell," and finally a hummed fifth verse, the music is essentially the same for each verse. As was the case in "The Side of a Hill," the harmonies include, and are limited to, the six major and minor chords within a key (played in C major, sounding in E major). The arrangement as a whole is rather sweet for the level of despair that the song depicts, although some might find that this conveys a sense of poignancy.

The song is particularly free in its large-scale metrical structure. Whereas the most typical pattern would be phrases that use four or eight measures, the stressed syllables in each verse of "Bleecker Street" suggest phrase lengths of five, seven, four, and six measures respectively (with four-measure interludes). Although this pattern is consistent throughout the song, its irregularity within each verse creates an attractive, conversational, rambling quality that enhances the song's ruminations on the various images that it presents.

Finally, one might observe that this song refers to a creative writer (the poet). As is the case with the references to Christianity, this somewhat self-conscious topic is to be common in Simon's songwriting. One previous example has already been observed in "Sparrow," with the question of who will write the sparrow's eulogy.

The title song of the first album, "Wednesday Morning, 3 A.M.," resembles "Bleecker Street" as it uses a pleasant sound to tell a sad story. In fact, a completely different perspective is taken on the same story in "Somewhere They Can't Find Me," a song on the *Sounds of Silence* album that combines much of the same text with a driving, electric beat. "Wednesday Morning, 3 A.M.," however, is an acoustically based ballad, played in the key of C (capoed up 5 frets to sound in F).

Like the other songs discussed thus far, its formal structure is simple. In this case four verses, essentially identical musically, alternate with a simple C-Dm-C figure that serves as introduction, interlude, and coda. The narrator/protagonist begins by telling of his lover sleeping peacefully beside him, and the sweet tone of this description is supported by the music. All of the harmonies are diatonic; that is, they incorporate only notes within the key rather than any more tension-filled chromatic pitches. (Once again, though, Simon makes full use of this harmonic palette by including all six major and minor chords in the key.) Furthermore, the harmonies outline a very classical structure, although not every succession is typical of classical procedures. As was the case in "He Was My Brother," the first half of each verse starts on the tonic harmony and ends with a well-prepared dominant, and the second half retraces this kind of path but continues to a concluding tonic.

Both Simon and Garfunkel sing throughout "Wednesday Morning, 3 A.M.," and the vocal arrangement is essentially the same (with slight variations accommodating varying numbers of syllables) in each verse. Garfunkel always sings above Simon (except on occasional unison notes), but the most prominent melody line shifts from one to another throughout the verse. This attractive folk-like melody mirrors the simple, classical shape of the harmonic progression. In each half of a verse, it begins by circling near the tonic note C, skips to the C an octave above, and works its way back down, concluding on the D in the first half of the verse, and on the C at the end of the second half. Garfunkel adds a high harmony part, identical in each verse, throughout. Despite all these appealing features, the lyrics soon introduce less positive elements. In the second verse, we learn that the narrator will soon need to leave forever. The third verse explains that this is because he has robbed a liquor store, and the fourth verse expresses regret, but also resignation, at his plight.

The song fits in the folk-song tradition in its storytelling presentation of a tragic situation. But it doesn't always do so gracefully. Much of this results from the fact that it is difficult to obtain a clear sense of the narrator's character. The prettiness of the music and the gentleness of his syntax suggest an innocent nature that is not easily reconciled with his crime, especially in the absence of any explanation of his need for the money. And, whether he is essentially a naive youth or a street-tough punk, some of his turns of phrase seem out of character. The two most obvious of these are actually *in* character for Simon himself—the narrator refers, more literarily than one might expect, to "pieces of silver," recalling again Judas Iscariot of Christian tradition, and to creative writing with "a scene badly written / In which I must play." These incongruities are particularly obtrusive in this rather transparent setting, as are a couple of oddly accented phrases: the evocative word "mist" is glossed over in the musical presentation, and the second word of "a hard liquor store" is stressed in an unnatural way. (Whether or not these particular details troubled Simon, the reworking of the song that resulted in "Somewhere They Can't Find Me" eliminated all of them except the dramatic reference.)

For whatever reason, those involved in the production of *Wednesday Morning, 3 A.M.* chose to use this ballad as the title track. As implied earlier, however, another song from the album was destined to achieve much greater popularity and longevity. And, while it is certainly not the case that greater popularity always reflects greater value, a close examination of "The Sound of Silence" reveals some elements that may have contributed to achievements of both sorts.

"The Sound of Silence" is played in the key of A minor. On *The Paul Simon Songbook,* Simon capos up two frets so that the song sounds in the key of B minor, and on the duo version, with Garfunkel taking the melody while Simon sings a lower harmony part, the song is capoed up six frets to sound in the key of E♭ minor. A very brief and simple (but now famous nonetheless) melodic guitar figure leads into the opening verse, which quietly tells the darkness that the singer wants to describe a vision that he has received. In this vision, which is recounted over the remaining four verses, he sees thousands of people who are unable to communicate in a genuine way. In their lives, significant communication is defeated by "the sound of silence." It is not heard, or it is not understood, or it inspires no interest, or at best it is merely whispered. Oddly, a neon light that they worship instead of communicating with each other tells them about the messages that they are missing. And even when the singer himself tries to warn them about the silence, they do not hear him.

Each verse contains first a stage-setting couplet, second a couplet that moves the action forward, third an asymmetric (long-short) couplet that presents the climactic thought of the verse, and finally a line that refers to the silence. After the first couplet establishes the A minor tonal center with the Aeolian progression Am-G-Am, the second and third emphasize the relative major tonality, C major, with neighboring F major chords, and then the harmonies return to a G-Am progression for the final line.

The melodic contour of each verse very clearly supports this pattern of establishment, motion to a climax, and return to a stable idea. The first couplet pairs an arpeggiated A-C-E-D figure with its echo a step lower, G-B-D-C. The motion of the second couplet is then underscored by repeating the arpeggio at a higher level, stretching each time above the top note: C-E-G-A-G, C-E-G-A-G. The climactic third couplet's long first line leaps up from the C to the newly achieved A and travels further to the higher C before retreating back to the A, and the short second line and the final line return (incorporating a reversal of the arpeggiated figure along the way) to the lower A.

As has been seen in earlier songs, the harmony line (sung in this case by Simon) is essentially the same in each verse. It does not significantly shape the verse, simply adding to the harmonic outlines and enhancing the texture throughout. Because it does not vary from verse to verse, the vocal arrangement is not capable of shaping the song as a whole. This is generally done through variations in instrumental texture, which tends to thicken (even if, in the solo version, this simply means a fuller strumming style) throughout the song. One other detail, though, does contribute to this large-scale shaping. In the fourth verse, the third couplet's short line is cut off to illustrate the failure to hear even the singer's warning. In a very neat detail, rather than depriving the long line of a rhyme, for the word "fell," Simon simply provides the rhyme late by substituting "well" for "sound" in the last line.

As was the case for many prophetically angst-ridden songs of the time, the specific object of these lyrics' anxiety is left undefined, and the universality of application that this makes possible is no doubt partly responsible for the song's popularity. Listeners can interpret the source of the breakdown as being whatever they choose it to be, or (perhaps equally importantly) they can vaguely sympathize with the negative tone without consciously choosing any source. Be this as it may, there are other ways that this song both typifies and transcends Simon's earlier work.

For one thing, it combines a very distinctive folk sound with a classical sensibility. The folk sound is established not only by the prominence of the guitar work, but also by the purity of the modal language. This modal approach tends to soften the focus on the A minor tonic harmony. Specifically, in this case, the chord that leads to A minor is always G major, rather than the E-major harmony that, with its G♯, would lead strongly to A in a pure A-minor setting. In addition to this, during much of the verse the focus shifts to C major rather than A minor, and even that harmony is decorated by F-major chords, rather than the stronger G major option. At the same time, the way that text, melody, and harmony combine to create an elegant approach to and descent from the climax of each verse is quite classically conceived.

The text itself refers to Simon's favored themes at this point in his work of Christianity (or at least religion) and creativity. Religious references include a vision, a halo, the "neon god," and prophets, and the references to communication that are central to the text most specifically cite creative work in "people writing songs that voices never share." Perhaps the most striking textual gambit, though, comes in the opening lines, in which the singer begins a conversation, not with the listener, or even with another character in the song, but with the anthropomorphized "darkness, my old friend." In addition to setting up the multiple references to light throughout the remainder of the song, this conceit creates a sense of intimacy, as the listener is made privy not only to the singer's inner thoughts, but to a conversation with hints of long-term psychological distress.

Establishing the Voice of "Simon and Garfunkel"

SOUNDS OF SILENCE

In its electrified incarnation, "The Sound of Silence" was placed at the beginning of Simon and Garfunkel's second duo album, *Sounds of Silence*. As mentioned above, all the songs that follow on this album (but not the instrumental "Anji") were composed by Simon. Of these nine songs, five are also found on *The Paul Simon Songbook*, and the other four had not previously appeared on an album (although, as has been noted, "Somewhere They Can't Find Me" is a reworking of the "Wednesday Morning, 3 a.m." theme). While the urban folk sensibility dominates the album as a whole, the songs exhibit a considerable degree of stylistic variety, in many cases drawing on prominent trends in folk-rock and pop music at the time.

The second song on the album, "Leaves That Are Green," had appeared on *Songbook*, and its text and music are consistent with the folk-bard persona that that album showcases. Both versions of the song feature rather upbeat arrangements. The *Songbook* version uses a busily fingerpicked D major texture (capoed up two frets to E). The arrangement on *Sounds of Silence* not only incorporates Garfunkel's vocal harmonies but also amplifies the folk-jangly sound with added instruments, most prominently including jaunty harpsichord intro, interjections, and outro.

Upbeat though the musical texture might be, the four verses of the text itself convey a pessimistic perspective on life (again, typically for the "folk bard"). Each of the first three verses presents a brief scene but concludes with a refrain that observes that the titular leaves turn to brown, wither, and crumble. A similar fate is thus indicated for the various vignettes—the progression of the singer's life, a romantic relationship, and the ripples caused by a pebble tossed in a brook. The last verse echoes this positive-negative progression with repeated "hello"s followed by repeated "good-bye"s.

The lyrics of the song support its thesis in a rather straightforward way and include one or two typical references to creative communication—the girl fades like an unwritten poem, and the ripples sadly "never [make] a sound." The whole song is shaped a bit by the placement of Garfunkel's harmonies (in the duo version)—they start later in the first verse than they do in the others, allowing the bard to begin his conversation with the listener in an intimate way—and by a truncated refrain in the last verse and unresolved dominant harmony at the end of the outro. More remarkable, though, is the way the musical motion in each of the full verses reflects the progression of the text.

Some of this is accomplished by the melody. Although its rhythm is interestingly varied, its pitch structure is quite simple, staying almost entirely within a perfect fifth, and most often moving from each note to a neighboring note, rather than skipping or leaping across notes. It sets the six phrases with a series of small arches, with high points on F♯, A, G, F♯, E, and G, respectively. The highest point—the A in each verse—is approached by a skip and accompanies the last word before the positive image is undercut with two descending skips.

At the same time, the harmonies also reinforce this sequence of emotions with a judicious placement of modal chords. The first phrase is set with a standard diatonic D-Em-A-D progression, and the tonic D harmony remains for the positive first half of the second phrase. The negative half, though, is colored with a modal C major harmony. After a standard diatonic half cadence in the third line, the appearance of the wistful "leaves that are green" in the refrain also uses the C chord. This time the harmony falls to a G chord before returning through A to D, and the refrain then sets the withering idea with the submediant B-minor chord before "crumbling" on an open-ended dominant A harmony.

If some of the songs on this album emphasize the "folk" aspect of folk-rock, the third song, "Blessed," definitely leans in the other direction. The prominent electric-guitar sound recalls some of the more electrified arrangements of the Byrds, and the phrasing and form of the song are quite different from the rather fluid progression of, say, "The Leaves That Are Green." Each of the three verses is comprised of two parts. In the first part, three Beatitude-like lines state that various entities are "blessed," and a fourth says, "O Lord, why have you forsaken me?" In the second part, the singer describes his pitiful situation.

This song addresses Christianity in the most direct way yet, but, as was the case in "Bleecker Street," the faith is not found to be an effective solution. The bitterness of the singer, in fact, contributes to the disjunct form of the song. Each of the four lines that comprise each verse's first part is presented as more of an independent outburst than a part of a continuous development of thought. The first line begins to tell who is blessed on the high F-sharp and D, over the tonic D major harmony, skips down to A, and finishes the thought by descending through G, F-sharp, E, and D; these last four notes are accompanied in monolithic rock fashion by the chords of which they are the roots, G major, F-sharp minor, E minor, and the tonic D major. The second line repeats this pattern. In each verse, both of these strident declarations cite as "blessed" people or entities traditionally respected by the church—respectively, the meek, the lamb, the land and kingdom, the devout man, stained glass, and the church service.

In contrast, the third line of each verse softens its tone musically by starting lower, accompanied by a subdominant G chord that provides a respite from the tonic D chord, and being sung more softly. Textually, though, this line claims blessing also for nontraditional recipients—the despised, junkies, and devotees of various cheap values. The following outcry to the Lord returns, however, to the formula of the first two lines, merely changing the order of the final notes and chords a bit.

Throughout this first section of each verse, Simon sings this principal melodic line, and Garfunkel sings the words in harmonies above him, usually following the contour of his line (often at the interval of a third). After the concluding question establishes the plight of the singer, however, the words of his private lament are sung only by Simon, with Garfunkel providing wordless harmonies on sustained high notes. (These harmonies seem to incorporate two voices, presumably involving overdubbing of one of the singers.) These second sections vary more widely from verse to verse than did the first sections. In each case an A minor harmony is decorated by B minor, all above a D pedal point, and the melody explores the same notes, but in each succeeding verse the singer has less to say, with only the first verse providing two movements to the B minor harmony. On a large scale, the piece is brought toward a conclusion by this diminishing process, and the conclusion is punctuated as well by cacophonous percussion sounds at the end of the last verse.

The album shifts abruptly from the instrumentation, topic, and emotional tone of "Blessed" with "Kathy's Song," a love song written, as mentioned in the previous chapter, for Simon's English girlfriend, Kathy Chitty. This is sung by Simon alone, accompanied by his guitar, and is very similar to a performance of the same song on *The Paul Simon Songbook*. The song is played in G major (both recordings sound in approximately G♭ major, presumably because the guitar is tuned low), and, as was the case with "The Side of a Hill" in the same key, showcases the possibilities inherent in that key for elaborate fingerpicking.

As with the other songs of this period in Simon's career, the overall form is simple. The six verses are essentially identical musically, and they are preceded by an introduction, give way to brief interludes after the second and fourth verses, and are followed by a coda that is based on the melody of the verses. Each verse consists of four lines, and each line extends a simple four-measure sung phrase with a measure of guitar. The melody combines flexible rhythms with a simple, classical contour: the first line ascends from G to B, the second rises to C and descends to A, the third reaches the climax on D before subsiding to C, and the last descends from there to the beginning G. The tonic G major harmony firmly supports the first line, the climactic note at the beginning of the third line, and the concluding note, but less stable harmonic passages lead from the end of the first line to the beginning of the third, and then from the beginning of the third to the end of the fourth. (As was the case with several songs discussed earlier, Simon makes full use in these passages of the major and minor chords in the key of G, although E minor is only somewhat implied in passing.)

Both the simplicity of the formal structures and the flexibility of the rhythms lend themselves to a conversational tone as the singer addresses his lover. He says that the rain has gently evoked memories of "England, where my heart lies"; specifically, his thoughts are with Kathy. His distraction makes him unable to write his songs convincingly, because the beliefs that he ordinarily expresses in them pale in comparison to her. He returns to the image of the rain, observing that the drops die, and that similarly "there but for the grace of you go I."

"Kathy's Song" is a typically attractive love song, not only because of the depth of romantic devotion that it expresses, but also because of the warm, rich interaction of guitar and voice within a fairly simple structure. At the same time, it provides a good example of the way that Simon incorporates the themes of creative expression and Christianity into a song whose main theme is neither of these. Kathy supersedes each of these, as she makes the singer's creative efforts pale by comparison with her, and she replaces not only his beliefs in general, but specifically replaces God in the concluding line quoted above. In this song, of course, this attests to the depth of the singer's love for Kathy, but the fact that Simon chose these two ideas as significant points of comparison indicates the importance that they held in his perspective.

As noted in the previous chapter, "Somewhere They Can't Find Me" is a reworking of "Wednesday Morning, 3 A.M." Both this instance and the earlier modification of "The Sound of Silence" moved in the direction of electrification. However, while in the case of "The Sound of Silence" electric instruments were simply dubbed over the original acoustic master, this transformation constitutes a completely new conception of the central lyrical idea. As such, this is a rare specimen, and it is interesting to examine exactly what elements were retained from the original song, and what features were added.

From the text of the four verses of "Wednesday Morning, 3 A.M.," "Somewhere They Can't Find Me" keeps most of the first, third, and fourth verse, and adds a chorus that is sung after each verse. The chorus tells of the singer's forthcoming flight, ending with the title line. This addition, along with the driving beat, tends to underscore the "bad-boy" side of the singer, and this emphasis is reinforced by the treatment of the verses: the omitted second verse had contained some of the more sensitive text, a minor change to the original third verse removes some hand-wringing, and the last verse is also toughened up.

The music for "Somewhere They Can't Find Me" is completely different from that for "Wednesday Morning, 3 A.M." Rather than being conjunct and fluid, the melody pounds away on relatively few notes—B for much of the verse, skipping down to F♯ at the end of the first half and stepping up to C♯ at the end of the second, and concentrating on the high F♯ and E, and then the B in the chorus before ending on the low F♯. Harmonically, the verse consists of two motions from B major to F♯7, mostly supported by a stepwise—each note the neighbor of the previous one—descent in the bass.

This stepwise descent embodies an irony. On the one hand, it is very compatible with the driving rock beat. But it is actually explicitly derived from an acoustic source. Simon opens "Somewhere They Can't Find Me" by playing the beginning ostinato figure from "Anji," a solo instrumental composition for acoustic guitar written by the English guitarist Davey Graham—which, in fact, appears in its entirety as the next track of the album, the only instrumental track on any of the duo albums.[1] The figure (played in A minor but capoed up two frets to sound in B minor) is based on a stepwise descending line, one step per half note, and when the first verse starts, the line is picked up by the bass, slowed down to one step per two measures, and slightly altered. The faster motion is resumed following each chorus, which at the end makes explicit the connection with "Anji."

The beginning of the first verse is also accompanied by a whole band. Throughout the piece, numerous sixties-rock devices are used—prominent organ, piano, and electric guitar licks, orchestration including stark violin lines and horn parts, and a suitably desperate-sounding harmony line for Garfunkel on the chorus. The result is more clearly focused than that of "Wednesday Morning, 3 A.M.," but still less than totally satisfying—the rock style seems contrived and is not helped by new text in the last verse that seems not to make sense while including the phrase "up tight."

In writing "Somewhere They Can't Find Me," Simon drew on a variety of sources in order to take an alternate approach to a basic idea. These two traits are also exemplified by the next two songs on *Sounds of Silence*, "Richard Cory" and "A Most Peculiar Man." Each of them is drawn rather directly from another source—the former from the 1897 poem of the same name by Edwin Arlington Robinson, and the latter from a newspaper article that Simon read in England that concluded that the subject was "a most peculiar man."[2] Each of them describes a man who commits suicide. Furthermore, each provides two parallel perspectives on the character with an oddly similar outcome. In each case, facts about the man and his tragic death are provided, but at the same time the singer editorializes about him in ways that seem to represent the opinions of many other observers. The assessment clearly misses some of the most crucial conclusions—respectively, that there is something about Richard Cory's life that is not enviable, and that the most important reaction to the "peculiar man" is sympathy for a fellow human, rather than an overriding consciousness of his peculiarity. And, most remarkably, the reiteration of the assessment at the end of each song indicates that it remains the dominant perspective for the singer and those he represents.

Notwithstanding these similarities, the two songs differ sharply from one another with respect to the personal circumstances of their title characters and to the musical styles that they employ. "Richard Cory" consists of three verses, alternating with three choruses. A pounding rock beat throughout serves to underscore both Mr. Cory's sophistication, described in the verses, and the singer's bitterness as a member of the working class, described identically in each chorus. Only a few of the words at the end of the third verse (most notably the concluding "put a bullet through his head") are drawn directly from Robinson's poem, but the rest of the lyrics effectively express the original ideas, with the choruses drawn from the end of the poem's third stanza and the beginning of the fourth.

The musical structure of each verse is essentially the same and supports the lyrics in similar ways. A conversational observation about Richard Cory in the first line incorporates some jaunty rhythms, but a fairly inactive melody, as the tonic C♯ minor chord is modally decorated with a B major harmony. The second line expands on this observation and uses upward leaps and a more focused G♯ major and G♯7 chord at the end to support the expansion. The third line maintains this energy by adding to the idea (including a low-brow hard "g" in the word "orgies" in the second verse) and staying in the high melodic register, and the last draws a conclusion as the melody returns to the lower register. (In the third verse, the third line begins a new idea with equal energy and the fourth starkly delivers the surprise of the suicide.) Register is used similarly in the chorus, as the melody starts low, reaches up a bit to report that the singer works in Richard Cory's factory, and then moves more decisively upward as the singer repeatedly expresses his desire to be Richard Cory.

"Richard Cory" is not extensively shaped on the large scale; the similarity of the verses to one another supports its premise of simply recounting the facts and commenting on them. However, the instrumental embellishments vary somewhat throughout, and Garfunkel's voice part becomes a bit more prominent as the song progresses. A sense of punctuation is achieved at the end of the last chorus, somewhat underscoring the irony of the singer's obstinate desire, with a slight extension before the last "Richard Cory," and a particularly important vocal contribution by Garfunkel, including a brief, sharply dissonant D♯ over Simon's concluding C♯.

Although electrical instruments are also used in "A Most Peculiar Man," the tone is much softer than that of "Richard Cory," mimicking that of the solo-plus-solo-acoustic-guitar version on *The Paul Simon Songbook*, and Garfunkel's vocal contributions throughout support this feeling. Each verse is constructed on a very simple harmonic framework, but, again in contrast to "Richard Cory," the verses vary greatly in the ways that they are distributed over this scheme. The first verse sets the harmonic pattern, which progresses in standard classical fashion. First, as the lyrics describe the man, the tonic D chord is followed by a progression through Em and the dominant A7 back to D (the song actually sounds in D♭ major, again, at least on the solo version, presumably because the guitar is tuned a half-step low). Then, as the lyrics reiterate that he was a most peculiar man, the harmonies take one more quick trip, this time through G and A7 back to D.

The verse is a standard 16 measures long. The beginning D harmony occupies a natural-sounding four measures, and each of the other D harmonies also starts at the beginning of a four-measure unit (on measures 9 and 13, respectively). Apart from this, though, the length occupied by a given harmony is somewhat unpredictable; usually each harmony is associated with a specific melodic figure that is used as long as Simon chooses to supply it with words. For example, the E minor harmony in the first verse lasts three measures, each one of which sets a phrase of text with a small melodic descent to E. In the second and third verses, E minor gets four measures (with one descent to E in each measure), and in the fourth, E minor gets *eight* such measures, in this case emphasizing the proliferation of details about his suicide and his unhappy life. (In the solo version, Simon does not always devote a full measure to each phrase when a harmony is extended, simply chanting the phrases while vamping on the E minor chord, and moving to the A7 chord when he's finished with them. This gives an effect of blurting out the information, while the duo version, presumably constrained to a regular measure assignment because several people are playing and singing at once, conveys more of a sense of an inexorable drumbeat of depressing information.)

This temporal flexibility creates a ruminative mood as the man and his death are described. Simon uses this premise to set up his conclusion nicely. Specifically, right before the last phrase of the last verse, he inserts a brief additional harmonic cycle—G-A7-D-Bm—with harmonies changing twice as fast as before, to emphasize the glib lip service of the observers ("And all the people said, 'What a shame that he's dead'") before they reiterate their overriding conclusion about his peculiarity.

As was the case with "Kathy's Song," "April, Come She Will" is performed by a single singer (Garfunkel this time) accompanied by Simon's solo guitar. This song, too, was included in an essentially identical version on *The Paul Simon Songbook*. It is also played in the key of G major, although it sounds in G♭ major (as does "Kathy's Song") on the low-tuned guitar of *Songbook*, while being capoed up to A♭ major to suit Garfunkel's voice on *Sounds of Silence*.

In the text of the song, each of the six months from April to September is associated with a stage in a relationship—one that is ultimately doomed, as in April "she" comes, in May she stays, in June she changes her tune, in July she flies, in August she "dies," and in September "a love once new has now grown old." Each of the three verses includes four lines, with two lines assigned to each month. The melody is graceful and free, not conforming to two- or four-measure groupings, but the music is essentially the same in each verse.

In the first line the melody rises from D to G while a tonic G harmony is emphasized. The second line begins higher, on C, and descends to G over a darker E minor harmony. In the third line the melody arches up to B before returning to the G, again on E minor. The fourth line, like the second, begins on the C, but descends this time all the way to E, emphasizing even more the inconclusive E minor harmony.

Both of the first two verses follow this pattern, and the third is very similar, but it is altered to bring the song to a conclusion. Here, instead of rising to B in the third line, the melody leaps up to D, creating a new climax pitch, and only descends to B (but still over the E minor harmony). The last line, like that of the earlier verses, starts on C, but, although it is extended by a measure, it only descends to G, finally against the tonic G harmony. The new melodic high point, by transcending what has come before, effectively sets the overview words "I'll remember," and the tonic ending brings the song to an effective musical conclusion, but it seems a bit incongruous to reach such a neat, major ending over the resigned concluding words.

"We've Got a Groovey Thing Goin'" is something of an anomaly in Paul Simon's catalog. While his early songwriting attempts had been focused on imitations of current hits, none of his other songs dating from the *Wednesday Morning, 3 A.M.* album or later is this formulaic. Over a pop/rock combo, complete with guitars, burbly organ, and, eventually, strings and brass, the singer protests his baby leaving him in three frantic verses, reiterating in each chorus that he and she have "got a groovy thing goin', baby." As in "Somewhere They Can't Find Me," the song begins by decorating its minor tonic chord (C minor in this case) modally with the major triad a whole step lower (Bb major here). Over various typical changes for the style, the singer moves rapidly from register to register in his distress, with aerial support from Garfunkel from the middle of each verse to the middle of each chorus, ending each chorus on the dominant G chord before the instruments introduce the next verse with the "groovy thing" motive. After the third verse, the last two lines repeat and fade.

The concluding song on *Sounds of Silence*, "I Am a Rock," makes considerably more compelling use of the band, electrifying another of the songs that had first been recorded on *The Paul Simon Songbook*. On the earlier version, in accompanying a rougher, more Dylanesque vocal performance with a single acoustic guitar, Simon shaped the overall form by varying picking and strumming patterns and by changing the dynamic level. On the duo recording, much more could be varied. The introduction and first two phrases are played by Simon alone with the acoustic guitar, and then drums kick the band in. Electric guitar lines appear prominently, Garfunkel joins in, and eventually an organ part develops and becomes increasingly frenetic throughout the course of the song. These, along with the bass and drums, dominate the texture throughout the remainder of the song until the very end, when the forces drop back to Simon and the acoustic guitar for a very brief, ironic coda, and a return to the opening guitar vamp.

In the text of "I Am a Rock," Simon adopts the persona of a self-absorbed, self-insulated individual. The singer describes ways that he has physically and emotionally isolated himself, and it is clear that he is doing this in order to prevent himself from being vulnerable to the pain that may result (and has apparently already resulted) from establishing friendships or being in love. Each verse begins with three lines that establish a particular feature of the singer's attitudes or actions; each of these lines is slightly separated from the others, each has a higher climax note than the one before, and each is lent a sense of immobility by ending with a melodic descent that concludes on the tonic chord of G major (capoed up five frets to sound in C). The next three lines repeat a short melodic figure as the singer's words build momentum in describing his perspective; throughout this passage, the motion is also enhanced by the lack of a tonic chord (as with several of the songs discussed earlier, this song uses all the major and minor triads in its home key). Finally, a brief refrain ascends to declare, "I am a rock, I am an island," concluding on the high tonic note against a tonic chord.

While the text presents the perspective of the singer's persona, it makes clear, not particularly subtly, that his approach is not a viable one. The singer says that he disdains laughter and loving, indicates that his position has arisen from pain that he has suffered, and overtly contradicts John Donne's famous poetic dictum that no man is an island. And, finally, in another reference to the Simonesque theme of creative writing (and, in this case, its limitations), his emotional state reaches an apex as he uses higher notes than usual to begin the last verse with a claim that his books and poetry will protect him.

PARSLEY, SAGE, ROSEMARY AND THYME

As was mentioned in the preceding chapter, *Sounds of Silence* was hastily assembled so that its release could take advantage of the popularity of the electrified version of "The Sound of Silence." For this project, existing Simon compositions were drawn upon as needed in order to fill out the album with the mix of folk-rock, folk, and pop-rock described above. Judging by sales figures, this effort was successful in launching an extremely popular album from the platform of a hit single. But the hurried process of assembling it was less than satisfactory for the duo. It was the following album, *Parsley, Sage, Rosemary and Thyme,* that afforded them, along with Roy Halee, the producer and recording engineer who came to take the role of an almost equal partner in the recording process, the time to create a collection of songs in the way they wanted to do it. Garfunkel, in fact, commented in 1990 that "I think of *Parsley, Sage* as the first real album in doing what we do."[3] The album begins, in fact, with a song that was both extremely popular with the listening public and an excellent example of Simon and Garfunkel "doing what they did," "Scarborough Fair/Canticle."

As did several of the songs that have already been discussed, this one draws on preexisting material. It is actually a marriage of two songs. "Scarborough

Fair" is a traditional text and melody that was sometimes performed by the folksingers in the circles that Simon, and occasionally Garfunkel, had traveled in England and elsewhere, and some of the guitar accompaniment that Simon uses was probably also derived from these performers' work; he has said that "[his] arrangement was like [his] memory of [Martin Carthy's] arrangement."[4] Set against this song as a countermelody is another, "Canticle," which is an original tune, but (as mentioned earlier) draws almost half of its text from the earlier Simon song "The Side of a Hill."

Four elements contribute to the impact of this song. Most obvious among these is its pure sound quality, as established by the gracefully fingerpicked guitar accompaniment, delicate chimes, harpsichord embellishments, and the vocal blend. This last is enhanced both by the effective deployment of Garfunkel's striking voice, and by overdubbing that sometimes includes at least two parts on each song simultaneously.

The second engaging characteristic of the song is the nature of the texts that are juxtaposed. In the first verse of "Scarborough Fair," the singer asks if the listener is going to the fair, and then asks him or her to "remember [him] to one who lives there" who was once his lover. Over the course of the next three verses, the singer gives the listener a series of instructions for the girl (always inserting the chanted names of herbs that form the album's title), in each case saying that these actions will result in her being his true love. Then he concludes by repeating the first verse.

In each of the middle three verses, this wistful text is offset by the lines of "Canticle." Each of these follows on the end of a line from "Scarborough Fair." The text incrementally reveals the same picture of war that had been presented by "The Side of a Hill"—in its first verse one only understands that "the child of the mountain" is somehow blanketed; the second mentions a grave, then a soldier, gun, and clarion call; and the third returns to the text from "The Side of a Hill" for the vivid description of generals leading their troops to fight for a long-forgotten cause. The overall effect is one of gradually revealing the dissonance between the tone of "Scarborough Fair" and that of "Canticle." This discovery is made into a process for the listener, not only because "Canticle" develops its scene very gradually, but also because it uses the same delicate musical tone as "Scarborough Fair," and because many of its words are difficult to understand on the first hearing.

The third striking feature of this song is the way it places a strong melody in a thoroughly and distinctively modal setting. The central harmony is A minor (capoed up seven frets to E minor), but the piece derives a distinctive character from its consistent use of the Dorian mode. Rather common in traditional folk song (although used in few well-known songs, "What Shall We Do with a Drunken Sailor" being an oft-cited exception), this mode is distinguished from the Aeolian mode that dominates "Sparrow" and "The Sound of Silence" by a raised sixth scale degree—in this key, the sixth note in a scale ascending from A is F♯, rather than F♮, so that the entire scale is ABCDEF♯GA, rather than ABCDEF♮GA. First introduced in the guitar introduction, and then appearing in the melody on the last syllable of "rosemary," and also occasionally present in the "Canticle" material, this note gives the song a particularly luminescent flavor. Furthermore, the general antique quality of the piece is well-established by adherence to the mode throughout the piece—all the harmonies are composed of notes in the mode, and the G♯ that would typify a classical piece in A minor is always eschewed in favor of the modal G♮.

The final notable ingredient of the song is the way that it is shaped across the five verses, gradually growing as the song progresses before subsiding toward the end. This is a very common large-scale arranging strategy, but it is executed here in a particularly effective way, as elements are layered on top of one another throughout the course of the song. Most obviously, this process includes the addition of "Canticle" (the tune of which was apparently mainly written by Garfunkel[5]). But it is amplified by the activation of other forces—first the solo guitar begins, the voices start "Scarborough Fair," and the chimes emerge. In the second verse, the appearance of "Canticle" is heralded by the addition of the harpsichord and bass. Although there is an overall increase in textural density as the song proceeds, it ebbs and flows with the phrase structure of the verses; vocal parts multiply and sometimes incorporate dissonance, and repeated-note harpsichord figures support the increasingly evident military theme. Finally, the return to the first verse, without "Canticle," decreases the density, and the song is brought to a conclusion.

Three of the songs on *Parsley, Sage, Rosemary and Thyme*—"Patterns," "Flowers Never Bend with the Rainfall," and "A Simple Desultory Philippic"—had also appeared on *The Paul Simon Songbook*. (Interestingly, they are the last three songs on *Songbook*—apparently a coincidence.) The second song on *Parsley* is "Patterns." On *Songbook*, the four verses of this song are set in a minor folk-blues style—actually using the Aeolian mode—played in D (but sounding in D♭ because of the low tuning of Simon's guitar). Simon flavors the piece with several guitaristic techniques, for example, a bottom string retuned down from E to drone on D, high "bent" notes, a brief flat-picked interlude, and a repeated low F leading to the D on occasion.

The four verses are essentially identical to one another musically. They use the Aeolian mode throughout—the dramatic melody in the first half of each verse ascends from a lower D to the D one octave higher and then moves to G against a C chord. The second half essentially retraces the path of the first, but this time concludes with a descent to D against the modal cadential progression Dm-C-B♭-C-Dm. The text describes the singer observing patterns of light and shadows and grimly concluding that his life is compelled to follow constricting, predetermined patterns from his birth to his death.

On *Parsley, Sage, Rosemary and Thyme*, Simon and Garfunkel accentuate the desperate mood of the original with various instrumental and vocal colors. Many of the original guitar licks remain (although the key is now a true D rather than D♭), but the overall sound is more percussive. String snaps are prominent in the guitar part, and a syncopated bass and frenetic bongo part are added. Garfunkel inserts urgent vocal harmonies on the brief opening words or phrases of lines before allowing Simon to finish them alone. In the second verse, an almost Middle-Eastern flavor is created with chime-like sounds and sitar-inspired guitar interjections. Garfunkel becomes more prominent, while still intermittent, in the third verse, which is followed by a sitar-sounding interlude (a similar passage was to be heard a couple of years later in the Lemon Peppers' "Green Tambourine"). The texture subsides a bit in the fourth verse before an instrumental outro recalls the introduction.

The third song on the album, "Cloudy," strikes quite a different mood and uses a breezy, almost jazzy musical style unlike any of the songs already discussed. Its title serves as a point of departure for a scattered, whimsical text that describes the singer's musings as he hitchhikes aimlessly around California. The listener can readily hear how the instrumentation establishes an easygoing atmosphere: descending series of triplet turns on the acoustic guitar are interspersed between lines of text, and a jaunty bass line and percussive clicks move the song along while chimes and a wordless vocal descant are layered above the principal vocal line. More subtle, but also more remarkable, is the way that musical structure supports the lyrics' untethered mood.

In the first two verses, the melody, set in D major, floats within a very narrow range, concentrating at first on A and G before descending to D. It rises to A before landing twice again on D, and then rising to A to set up the beginning of the next verse. This structure differs from a more directed melodic form in that it is not defined by clear motion to climax notes, nor is there a resolution on the tonic note D at the end.

This lack of resolution is supported by the harmonies, which start by vacillating between idiomatically guitar-generated D and D suspended 2nd (a D chord with an added E—which creates a clash or dissonance within the chord—created simply by raising one finger and thus almost identical to the D) chords, rather than using a chord that creates a sharper contrast with the tonic. More significantly, only the last phrase ends on a tonic or dominant chord (in this case the open-ended dominant A7). None of the melodic arrivals on D is accompanied by a D major harmony (D diminished 7—a very unstable chord—Bm, and E7 are used instead), and the mid-verse motion to A uses an F♯ minor harmony.

The beginning of the third verse makes a gesture toward breaking out of this stasis, replacing the earlier verses' opening descent from A to F♯ with leaps from A up to D and back. Not only do these explorations of new pitch territory occur earlier in the verse than words had appeared in the others, but the words are sung in harmony for the first time here. Still harmonized, the next phrase moves from D down to B, in contrast to earlier verses' concentration on A and G. But, as is the case with the portentous bass motion that accompanies the D♭7 chord in each verse, this activity leads nowhere, as the rest of the verse returns to the patterns of the first two. This time, the concluding A7 harmony leads to a coda that borrows figures from the beginnings of the verses to fade out on a G chord, thus permanently avoiding resolution.

"Homeward Bound," the fourth track on *Parsley, Sage, Rosemary and Thyme*, is one of the most popular songs that Simon and Garfunkel recorded. Simon began to write the song, as its lyrics suggest, on the railway platform at Widnes while thinking about Kathy Chitty.[6] (While he surely continued to refine the song—his fellow musician Al Stewart reports hearing him work on it at Judith Piepe's flat in the East End[7]—the event has been commemorated with a plaque installed on the platform.)

Although it does not appear on *The Paul Simon Songbook*, "Homeward Bound" is very much a solo-singer-with-guitar work in concept. All of its musical ingredients can be executed quite effectively by a solo performer, and its lyrics describe the singer's life as a lone, traveling singer/songwriter. The three verses develop the picture of the singer's day-to-day life, with each verse more disillusioned than the previous one, and the refrain tells of his yearning to be headed to his home and his love. Because the singer is even more explicitly a songwriter than was the case in, for example, "Kathy's Song," "Homeward Bound" develops to the extreme the idea that the rewards of creative work pale in comparison to romantic fulfillment.

The acoustic-guitar foundation of the song is prominently retained in Simon and Garfunkel's recording. It is played in the key of G (capoed up to B♭), and the opening bars make use of this key's potential for two-voiced hammer-ons and stepwise bass lines. At the same time, the production and arrangement are very attractive and effective in supporting the structure of the lyrics. (Garfunkel has said that the production team had intended for "Homeward Bound" to be a very popular follow-up single after "The Sound of Silence," and in that spirit an initial recording was abandoned as inadequate so that the entire song could be recut.[8])

After a solo-guitar introduction, Simon starts singing alone, joined by a low-key bass, drums, solitary piano notes, and subtle guitar reinforcements. Garfunkel adds a high harmony on the second line of the verse. The instruments lend fluidity to the straightforward verse-refrain structure by dovetailing the connections between the sections. Toward the end of each verse, the drums kick the energy into a new gear that supports the refrain's "homeward bound" plea, and toward the end of each refrain, the texture subsides to the quieter level of the beginning of the verses. While this pattern applies to each verse, some elements change throughout the course of the song—the lead guitar becomes more active, and Garfunkel joins Simon at the beginning of the third verse, rather than waiting for the second line. After the energy subsides on the words "silently for me" at the end of the third refrain, the words are repeated, the instruments fall away, and the solo acoustic guitar concludes with its opening figure.

Just as the verse-refrain form of this song is straightforward, and yet effectively enhanced by the arrangement, the melodic and harmonic structure is simple but gains energy from a couple of subtleties. A low register (mainly around B-D) is used to describe the singer's description of his actual situation in the verse, but, similarly to the way the instruments increase their activity, it moves up at the end to a different register (G-B) that is used to describe the homeward images in the refrain. (In the refrain, the lower register is used for a quick return to reality—"I wish I was"—and for the concluding return to the verse.) And an interesting interplay between melody and harmony propels each verse forward: The melody for the first line dwells on D over a G harmony, and in the second line the harmony is raised to A minor, while the same melodic idea is *lowered* to dwell on C; this time, however, as the singer becomes increasingly absorbed by his plight, the energy is redoubled by an extension of the melodic line with a return to the opening D-over-G configuration.

The succession between "Homeward Bound" and the following track is, in tone at least, a textbook case of going from the sublime to the ridiculous. "The Big Bright Green Pleasure Machine" is a satirical appropriation of an electric, organ-heavy psychedelic rock style. In each verse, the singer rattles off a list of possible woes that the listener might be experiencing in personal, business, or romantic life, and then assures him that his distress can be readily eased by purchasing the titular device. The examples of problems are clever, and cleverly expressed, and syntax and rhyme schemes are amusingly manipulated to play off one another.

The broad central joke of the song is supported by straightforward musical devices, as the rock style is exuberantly employed—typical rock guitar interjections and churning organ licks are prominent, and the voices affect a Brit-pop sound. The three verses are relieved only by a brief bridge that encourages the listener to hurry to buy a Pleasure Machine before the supply is exhausted. At the beginning of each verse, questions about the listener's difficulties are expressed with sweeping, paired melodic lines and modal moves from the tonic D chord to a C harmony. After the second of these progressions, the harmonies descend through B♭ to A and G while more gradually ascending melodic lines help the singer—now momentarily solo—to summarize sympathetically. Finally, the singer (having been joined again by his vocal partner) descends to make his sales pitch as the G harmony moves down to F and then C to set up the return to D for the next verse. The typically major-chord-heavy sound for this particular rock style is further preserved by A, G, and E chords in the bridge.

The next two songs on *Parsley, Sage, Rosemary and Thyme* contrast sharply with one another in mood; although each exhibits considerable craft in its composition, they occupy opposite ends of the spectrum from lightheartedness to seriousness. "The 59th Street Bridge Song (Feelin' Groovy)" comes first. This song is probably based on less musical material than any other in Simon's catalog. The entire song (with the exception of a two-bar lead-in between the introduction and the first verse) is made up of variations on a two-bar ostinato figure, first presented in the introduction (four times) by Simon's fingerpicked acoustic guitar. Set in the key of G major (capoed up to B♭), the figure consists of four descending tenths—a melody line of E-D-C-B over a bass line of C-B-A-G, outlining a C-G/B-Am7-G chord progression.

Simon sings the lead vocal over the series of pairs of measures. In the first pair of the first verse he sings a decorated version of the E-D-C-B melody line an octave lower; in the second pair he starts the same way but ends by skipping up to G and down to D. The third pair, again, tracks the melody line, and the fourth pair skips up at the end, this time to B and back to G, on the words "feelin' groovy." While Simon thus concentrates on the melody line, Garfunkel sings harmony vocals above him that concentrate on the C-B-A-G of the guitar's bass line (but an octave above the guitar). During an interlude, the two echo the final words, "Badadadadadada, feelin' groovy," but now Garfunkel drops down to track the E-D-C-B melody line, while Simon drops to the bass line.

The second verse follows the same pattern, and the interlude is repeated, and then in the third verse the duo explores higher notes for most of the second and third pairs, accentuating this flourish with a barrage of triplet-quarter-notes. The song fades out with the ostinato continuing, the voices floating around on "ba-da" syllables, and a jaunty pennywhistle sound piping over the whole musical texture.

The whole song lasts barely more than one and a half minutes. The constant repetition of a brief musical fragment, combined with almost improvisatory-sounding elaborations, creates a kaleidoscopic sense of abandon. This is reinforced by the bass and drums (played by former Dave Brubeck sidemen Gene Wright and Joe Morello, respectively), which propel the song forward from the introduction on. And all of this, of course, is at the service of the lyrics, which rhapsodize about a carefree morning in a way that contrasts rather sharply with most of Simon's songs. The singer includes some fanciful images—addressing a lamp-post, feeling "dappled," and imagining the morning dropping petals on him—and does manage to include one reference to creative writing, the lamp-post's lack of rhymes. All in all, one might say that the song strives to say very little, both musically and philosophically, but that all its ingredients combine to do so quite effectively.

On the other hand, "The Dangling Conversation" strives for considerably more. It is linked to "The 59th Street Bridge Song (Feelin' Groovy)" in an interesting way that, ultimately, accentuates the differences between the two songs. It, too, is acoustic-guitar-based, and it is also played in the key of G, capoed up to B♭. The explicit link is created at the very beginning of the song; the guitar introduction starts with a prominent bass descent on precisely the same pitches that had just been heard repeatedly in the bass ostinato of "Feelin' Groovy," C-B-A.[9]

This connection recalls that found on *Sounds of Silence* between "Somewhere They Can't Find Me" and "Anji." Significantly, though, in this case, the first descent does not continue all the way down to the tonic note G. It is echoed by a line that starts one step lower and thus does reach the G, but now the note is accompanied by an unstable C harmony. Three measures later, both the tonic note *and* the tonic harmony finally create a point of stability from which the first verse can begin, but even here the note is not reached by the stepwise descent that had already been established, and it arrives off the downbeat.

All of this lack of musical stability serves to introduce a text that, as the title suggests, conveys a similar lack of satisfactorily fulfilling interpersonal relationships. The primacy of the acoustic guitar notwithstanding, this text is not fundamentally cast in the mold of traditional folk songs, as had been the case with many of Simon's compositions up to this point. Here he strives for a different level of literary subtlety. While the topic, a failing relationship, is not uncommon, its treatment is unusual in comparison with (even urban) folk songs of the time in at least two ways that relate to the sophistication of the principals. First, this sophistication is conveyed through images and themes not usually found in contemporaneous singer/songwriter songs, and second, the couple's cultural background somehow enables them to remain together even in the absence of genuinely rewarding communication.

In order to paint the picture of this desolate relationship, Simon ranges from the inclusion of very specific details of the couple's domestic life (the topics of their serious but disengaged discussions and the poetry that they're reading) to more poetic description ("and shadows wash the room") as well as similes that compare them with shells in which one can hear the ocean roar and badly written poems. This depiction sets the stage for the singer's observations that, in the midst of their sophisticated thoughts and discussions, he and his partner are not in harmony, and he can't really touch her, as they're trapped in the "dangling conversation" that helps to form the "borders of their lives."

Beyond the instability first conveyed by the introduction, the musical setting supports this text in various ways. In each verse, while the first four lines describe the scene, the melody lies rather low, set against a harmonic progression based on that of the introduction. The next four lines comment on the relationship, and the melody ascends to a high point from which harmonies outside the key help it to descend sequentially in dismay. Finally, a three-line refrain, using the lower register and the original harmonic scheme, delivers the verdict about the dangling conversation.

The genteel setting and the poignancy of the couple's plight are underscored by liberal use of sweet vocal harmonies (embellished by one instance of text-painting, when Garfunkel echoes the text "syncopated time" with a syncopated vocal fill). Moreover, the instrumental arrangement contributes substantially to this effect, as the foundation laid throughout the song by the acoustic guitar is overlaid by string lines and swells, as well as judiciously placed harp notes and flourishes, chimes, and timpani. But the unrest at the core of the song is subtly supported by the phrase lengths: in the place of the normative two- or four-measure groupings, three-measure phrases stammer through each verse's opening and closing sections; this pattern, in turn, gives the two-measure groups of the central melodic sequence a tumbling, headlong feeling.

Supported by these musical devices, the textual approach used in "The Dangling Conversation" made it Simon's most progressive effort up to that point. The following song on *Parsley, Sage, Rosemary and Thyme*, "Flowers

Never Bend with the Rainfall," which had also appeared on *The Paul Simon Songbook*, is somewhat simpler. In each verse of its text, the singer confesses that he is unable to discern reality. The chorus, though, declares that in the face of this difficulty he will still persevere in pretending that his life is under control, "and flowers never bend with the rainfall."

The singer's dilemma is conveyed in each verse by two lines that are essentially identical musically. The guitar part is played in G (sounding in that key on *Songbook*, but capoed to A on *Parsley*). In each of the verse's lines, the melody dwells obsessively on D with just one decorating E near the end of the line, and a leap up to G at its conclusion. A hint of the singer's out-of-kilter reality is given by the harmonic pattern. Although it is firmly grounded in G major, and the eight-measure line parses neatly into two- or four-bar phrases, a three-chord sequence cycles out of phase with the measure groupings; that is, when each chord in a G-Bm-C-G-Bm-C-G succession lasts for one measure, the tonic G chord accompanies the strong first measure of the first half of the line, but the B minor chord accompanies the fifth measure (the strong first measure of the second half). This effect echoes a similar device that occurs on a smaller scale in the intro and outro: at these times three-quarter-note groups cycle against the four-quarter-note-long measures.

While the verses dwell in this low register, the defiant declaration in the chorus starts on the higher D, against the hitherto unheard D chord, and works its way down again to the lower D before concluding with a leap up to G that echoes those in the verse. Much of this passage is characterized by regular two-bar groupings, but a bit of uncertainty may be inferred from the sustained notes sprinkled throughout.

As is the case with "I Am a Rock," this song makes clear that the singer is not to be envied. This outlook is complicated somewhat, though, by the style of the duo arrangement on *Parsley*. While Simon's solo version had been a typically unadorned, direct presentation, the later recording features a folk combo that produces a bright, almost bluegrass sound. Most prominent are a driving bass, tambourine, occasional lead-guitar fills, and rhythm guitar. Garfunkel adds his typical sweet vocal harmony lines, contrasting the static verse melody with descending scales. It may be that many listeners in the 1960s either heard this as a pleasant song without paying much attention to the lyrics, or had a vague impression of countercultural exploration fusing the images of dream states, the unsuccessful forces of "God and truth and right," and the references to King, pawn, joy, and sorrow. At any rate, perhaps to compensate for the bright setting, the duo version concludes with a D13sus4/A chord—the complexity of its structure, with, as its name indicates, an added 13th, and suspended 4th, all over an A bass note, reflecting its discordant sound.

"A Simple Desultory Philippic (Or How I Was Robert McNamara'd into Submission)" is the last track on one of the duo recordings that had appeared on *The Paul Simon Songbook*. The text is a satirical rant about the singer's confrontations with a wide variety of pop-culture personalities and phenomena. As one might expect for such an overtly and miscellaneously topical song, the two versions vary considerably in textual content. The fundamental large-scale textual form remains the same, though, as does the smaller-scale scheme of each of its component parts. In each recording there are three similar verses, and each of these is dominated by a series of names that have been "done" to the singer: "I been Norman Mailered, Maxwell Taylored...." Between the second and third verses, a contrasting section is inserted that tells about an "unhip" man the singer knew, and the *Songbook* version adds a coda-like partial fourth verse that recommends, when in London, finding oneself a "friendly haiku"—often thought to be a reference to Kathy Chitty.[10]

Given all these similarities, it is remarkable that the two versions differ completely from one another musically. On *Songbook*, Simon accompanies himself in G (actually G♭ because of the low tuning), playing bass notes and strumming his acoustic guitar with a flatpick. Each of the verses consists of two lines, the first ending on the dominant chord, D, and the second on the tonic G chord. The melody of each line starts the same, rising from G to dwell repetitiously on D in a way that emphasizes the singer's rattling off of item after item, and the first line ends on the D while the second concludes by descending to the G. The chanting nature of the tune lends itself to the main business of the song, which consists of Simon's using its topical premise as an opportunity to combine names and terms through clever rhymes, juxtapositions, and personal references.

The wordplay and brashness of the song, along with the unsubtle guitar work, would have unavoidably brought Bob Dylan to mind in any event, but this reference is cemented with the contrasting section. Using the talking-blues style often employed by Dylan, Simon vocally imitates him, refers to him (ridiculing the unhip man for thinking that "Dylan" is Dylan Thomas—who is, of course, the source of the folksinger's adopted name), and borrows his turn of phrase in reassuring the listener that "it's all right, Ma." Furthermore, in keeping with *Songbook*'s live-performance sound, Simon introduces the song by stating its title—interestingly, using Lyndon Johnson's name rather than Robert MacNamara's in this version.

The title is not stated on the recording of this song on *Parsley*. Here the acoustic guitar is replaced by an organ-drenched electric band. The key is now D, and the song is now dominated by a grinding electric-guitar riff. The chord changes and melody are new, and the first half of each verse is now broken into three short lines. (Garfunkel does not perform on this song.) About a third of the text in the first verse is new, as is about half the second verse; the third verse loses its first short line and undergoes a couple of changes toward the end. The central section, which is still spoken in a Dylanesque voice, retains almost all the text from that of the *Songbook* version, but focuses even more on Dylan—the most significant textual change is the last line, which is no longer a reference to England, but rather an additional quotation: "everybody must get stoned." This section now also imitates Dylan by including quick harmonica interjections, and the song takes this theme even farther at its conclusion, when

Simon intones "Folk Rock," and then is heard to whine, "I've lost my harmonica, Albert," in a reference to Dylan's manager Albert Grossman.

Parsley, Sage, Rosemary and Thyme is characterized throughout by sharp contrasts between successive songs, and following "Philippic" with "For Emily, Whenever I May Find Her" certainly exemplifies this. "Emily," sometimes thought to be named after Emily Dickinson (who also made an appearance in "The Dangling Conversation") is an ethereal showpiece for Garfunkel. He is accompanied only by an acoustic guitar, but the effect is still quite lush, partly because it is a 12-string guitar (which doubles the top two strings at the unison and the bottom four an octave higher), and partly because of the assistance of various studio techniques, including a lot of reverberation and unison overdubs to reinforce the vocals.

The song is played in D major (capoed up three frets to F) and lasts barely two minutes. A brief harmonic and melodic scheme forms the basis for five verses. In the first three, the singer uses ornate imagery to tell of his dream about seeking and then finding his lover. The fourth verse is an instrumental interlude, and in the fifth the singer tells of awakening and finding his lover with him, reiterating his love for her in a brief tag at the end. The mystical quality is created not only by the timbre of the guitar, but also by some of the rhythmic and pitch elements of the song. Most fundamental in this regard is the fact that the melodic structure is very flexible; Simon feels free to vary the syllable and accent pattern of the text lines within the verses, and he adjusts the rhythms and pitches in order to accommodate these alterations.

A sense of fluidity is established by this continuing variation, but also by the general rhythmic character of the song. Each verse establishes a norm of regular two-measure text phrases. This underlying pattern then serves to provide a context against which important notes and syllables can float off the important beats.

The contour of the melody similarly provides a norm that functions as a foil for variation. Each verse includes five brief phrases. The first three are based, respectively, on a descending series of thirds: A-F♯, G-E, F♯-D, and the fifth moves from D through G to an open-ended A against the dominant A chord. But not only do the exact rhythmic and melodic details of each phrase vary from verse to verse, as mentioned above, but the fourth phrase varies considerably and serves as the climactic point in each verse. Set against an C-major7 chord that lends an antique flavor by suggesting the Mixolydian mode, this phrase always includes the high B and also emphasizes various other members of the chord—the low C and E that would logically continue the descent of thirds to the D, as well as the G that forms thirds with the B and the E. Finally, the coda reaches past the B to the high C, reemphasizing the Mixolydian mode and leading to a last A, made all the more open-ended this time because of its harmonization by a Gsus2/F♯ chord.

"A Poem on the Underground Wall" resembles "Emily" in its overall brevity—lasting under two minutes—and in the brevity of its constituent parts (an intro and brief outro, five verses, and a contrasting section after the third verse), but its character is quite different. It tells the story of a man bent on scrawling a graffito on a sign in a subway station, and it depicts this furtive narrative with an urgent tempo, supported by a quasi-bluegrass texture.

The song is similar to "The 59th Street Bridge Song" in that much of it is based on a simple two-voiced contrapuntal figure. In this case the figure is unveiled one voice at a time in the introduction. The song is played in the key of E minor, with a secondary emphasis on G major (capoed up seven frets to B minor and D major, respectively). First (after a series of regular heartbeat-like thumps), the guitar plays two series of bass notes: C-B-G, G-F♯-E, landing on the tonic E minor chord as other instruments join. Then this pattern is repeated, with Simon humming the guitar notes while Garfunkel hums the second voice a third higher (shown in italics): C*E*-B*D*-G*B*, G*B*-F♯*A*-E*G*. Each of these six pairs of notes is now accompanied by a chord as follow (shown in parentheses): C*E* (C)-B*D* (C/B)-G*B* (G)-G*B* (G)-F♯*A* (G/F♯)-E*G* (Em).

Once the introduction has finished assembling this framework, the first verse begins to tell the story of the clandestine poet. The first two brief phrases are based on the two parts of the contrapuntal pattern, respectively (with the top voice sounding as the principal melody), and the same is true for the third and fourth phrases—each phrase pair executes a direct descent through the pitches and harmonies that have already been described. Then, in a fifth phrase, the principal voice rises to touch on D and E. This plan holds for the succeeding verses as well. The first three describe the man's restless waiting, the crayon that he holds, and the arrival of a train.

The interlude balances these descents with a steady ascent from B to G, building suspense as it describes the departure of the train and the man tightening his grip on his crayon. In the fourth verse he writes a poem consisting of a single unidentified four-letter word, and in the fifth he flees, exhilarated by his forbidden act; this verse, rather than concluding with the D-E melodic gesture, adds a final melodic descent.

Simon mixes into this narrative a variety of visceral and religious images. The man's resolve is tested by the arrival of the train (the last of the night). However, rather than accepting this "welcome" offer to the "groom" from the "womb," he listens to the "litany" of the departing wheels while clutching his "crayon rosary." Religious, creative, and visceral ideas coalesce in the final verse as the poem his rosary scrawled "resound[s]" and he leaves on foot "[t]o seek the breast of darkness and be suckled by the night."

The final song on *Parsley, Sage, Rosemary and Thyme*, "7 O'Clock News/ Silent Night," is really a simple collage with a simple point. As Simon and Garfunkel sing the first verse of "Silent Night" twice in two-part harmony over an arpeggiated piano part, a news announcer reads a series of reports on grim topics—civil-rights-related housing issues, the death of Lenny Bruce, the Richard Speck murders, and Vietnam. The result rather bluntly makes an ironic commentary on various social ills by juxtaposing them with tenderly expressed Christmas sentiments.

The Mature Simon and Garfunkel Albums

Art Garfunkel's feelings, quoted earlier, about the creative process involved in making *Parsley, Sage, Rosemary and Thyme* were informed by his reaction to the finished product; he found listening to the playback of the tape to be a "career high point."[1] While the experience had indeed enabled Simon and Garfunkel, for the first time, to take full advantage of their studio acumen in assembling a group of songs into an album, they were ready to explore new possibilities with the next attempt, which was to be titled *Bookends*.

While this album was being created, Simon was also involved in another project, one that more overtly explored new territory. He had been asked by Mike Nichols to provide background music for a movie Nichols was directing titled *The Graduate*. As it turned out, Simon's contribution to this project was to consist of four already-released songs—"The Sound of Silence," "Scarborough Fair/Canticle," "April, Come She Will," and "The Big Bright Green Pleasure Machine"—and only one new one—the hit "Mrs. Robinson." These songs were combined with incidental music that Dave Grusin contributed to the film to form a soundtrack album that was released simultaneously with *Bookends* (in 1968). Although most of the Simon material on the soundtrack album had already appeared (this was the *fourth* album for "The Sound of Silence"), and "Mrs. Robinson," which appeared on both albums, only appeared in its final form on *Bookends,* the soundtrack record album (LP) was phenomenally successful (as was the film itself).

BOOKENDS

Simon has said that "*Bookends* was our first serious piece of work."[2] The innovative element of the album is more readily obvious on the original LP format than it is on CD. This is because, while the second side of the LP is a typical collection of varied songs, the first side is intended to comprise a more purposefully unified whole. The side begins and ends with the appropriately named "Bookends Theme," a brief piece that is first played by an unaccompanied acoustic guitar, and then, at the end of the side, sung (accompanied by the guitar) by Simon and Garfunkel. The text refers to the passage of time, and to memories of a loved one, and thus fittingly concludes the series of intervening songs, which address interpersonal relationships at times of life that progress from song to song.

The opening, instrumental version of the "Bookends Theme" is followed by "Save the Life of My Child." This story song is similar in some respects to a much later song, "The Boy in the Bubble," which opens the *Graceland* album—it deals with individual crises in crowded urban settings, along with references to larger societal forces and at least a hint of some transcendent perspective. In both cases, these textual elements are variously supported by a churning groove, percussive and distorted electronic sounds created by a synthesizer, and a sense of a background conveyed by extramusical sounds or choral vocals.

In "Save the Life of My Child," four verses tell of a boy sitting on a high ledge and considering jumping. Each verse uses the same basic harmonic changes. Furthermore, each of the first three verses is followed by a chorus in which the boy's mother cries out the title of the song. But this relatively straightforward formal structure is varied and embellished in a number of ways in order to lend definition to the details of the story and, ultimately, to suggest a larger context.

The melody in each verse differs somewhat from those in the other verses, adopting distinctive contours in order to lend emphasis to particular words. In the first verse, the crowd's comprehension of the boy's peril is described. In the second verse, the police are summoned, someone speculates about drug use, and the *Daily News* reports on the incident. In the third verse, a policeman comments cynically on the youth of the day, and in the fourth darkness and a spotlight whip the crowd into a frenzy, and the boy jumps.

The melodic variations throughout the verses serve not only to set particular words effectively, but also, to a degree, to soften the regularity of the succession of verses: while the identical beginning of each chorus does serve as a clear marker in this regard, no two verses start identically, with the principal difference found in the length of time Simon dwells on the tonic note G. (The second and third verses' beginnings are actually quite similar to one another, but in this case regularity is softened by a longer-than-usual interlude before the third verse.)

Be all this as it may, the melodic variation is subtle compared to the other embellishments that are incorporated into the song. Crowd noises seep in, sometimes sounding like cheering, and they sometimes merge with wordless, ethereal choral passages. Spoken words from the unfolding drama can be heard, and Garfunkel intones the cynical policeman's words while Simon sings them, trailing off into a mocking "and 'blah, blah, blah.'"

Most striking of all, though, is the conclusion of the song. Instead of ending with the usual melody leading into the chorus, the fourth verse pauses, and then tells of the boy's leap by gently rising on the words "He flew away." The song then concludes with a new, simple melody that repeats the cryptic words, "Oh, my grace, I've got no hiding place," and fades without harmonic resolution.

Whether or not this ending suggests some sort of transcendent resolution to the scene at hand, "Save the Life of My Child" sets its grim depiction of contemporary youth firmly in the context of society as Simon saw it. The following song, "America," concentrates on a somewhat older couple. As the title implies, it also explicitly views its protagonists' personal concerns against the backdrop of the culture in which they travel. (In this way it continues the resemblance of *Bookends* to *Graceland,* as the second song on that album, the title track "Graceland," also tells of a culturally aware journey taken by emotionally needy people through a specified segment of the United States.)

While older than the suicidal youth, the couple in "America" nonetheless seems rather young. The singer adopts the role of the young man, describing in the first person an apparently impromptu romantic traveling alliance (he has recently hitchhiked alone in Michigan). The story is told in four verses, with an interlude after the second and a coda after the fourth. As in "Save the Life of My Child," Simon takes considerable melodic freedom from verse to verse. Most interesting, though, is the way that he varies the harmonic focus on the tonic to convey varying degrees of motion that are expressed in the text.

The beginning of each verse establishes the traveling idea effectively with a bass line that focuses clearly on the tonic by traveling resolutely, one step per three-beat measure, down the scale from the tonic note D to the subdominant note G. In the first verse, the singer's proposal of the journey is given a carefree tone with a melody that ascends and descends by skips in alternate measures. The focus on tonic is then diffused, with the harmonies vacillating among F#m7, B7, and B9 chords, as the travelers casually gather cigarettes and pies for provisions, only to return to the descending bass line as they depart "to look for America."

At the beginning of the second verse, the descending bass line gets the couple on a bus in Pittsburgh, but as the singer muses about how his time in Michigan now seems like a dream, he uses new melodic material and the harmonies vacillate between A and E. The interlude describes the lovers' idle passing of time as they make up identities for the people around them, and once again the harmonies vacillate in new territory, this time alternating various C chords with D chords.

The interlude is brought to a close by a slightly altered version of the descending bass line, and the third verse follows the pattern of the first as night falls. Now the F# and B harmonies accompany more time-killing after the couple determines that no cigarettes remain, but when the rising of the moon is described, the verse-closing bass descent emphasizes that time is passing once again.

In turn, the fourth verse generally follows the musical pattern of the second. This time the motion away from tonic focus follows the singer's admission (to a sleeping Kathy[3]) that he unaccountably feels lost. The emphasis on A and E chords accompanies him as he is reduced to counting cars on the New Jersey Turnpike, and imagining that they, too, have "all come to look for America." The descending bass line, with some varied harmonies, returns and cycles until it fades out. However, it doesn't begin until the singer stops singing, indicating that he remains in his state of uncertainty.

Bookends' chronological survey moves next, in "Overs," to a couple whose relationship has apparently run its course. The text is reminiscent in some ways of that of "The Dangling Conversation," by virtue of the genteel cohabitation that remains. Musically, "Overs" embodies a step into new territory for Simon. Up to this point, his work with verse-based forms had been characterized by increasing degrees of melodic flexibility from verse to verse, and his harmonic structures had revealed increasing independence from standard diatonic, major/minor, and/or modal rock- and folk-based styles. "Overs" displays a logical consequence of both of these trends: a more jazz-oriented style, including an extensive palette of chords, and a looser form defined more by recurrences of harmonic patterns and melodic motives than by a strictly strophic cycling of chords and melody. This approach lends itself well to the musings of the song, as (to the accompaniment of a single jazz guitar) the singer broaches the idea that the relationship might be over—his thoughts tend to come in small bursts, rather than the more carefully structured arguments that might fit well in a more systematically recurrent form.

The central musical idea of the song is a series of chords presented in the first 13 measures; these can be heard as a group of five, a group of six, and a group of two. In the group of five, the singer declares with a relaxed, flexible tempo that "the game is over." Then the music settles into a groove for the group of six, with chords initially carried along by stepwise descending bass motion, leading to a concluding turnaround in the final group of two. During this passage, the singer conveys a sense of resignation.

The same pattern then begins again. The harmonies in the opening five measures are slightly varied, while the following six remain the same. The melody is altered considerably—new motives mix with old or varied ones—as the singer declares that not much is left for the couple except for quiet pleasantness. The final two measures are replaced by an atmospheric interlude, sung by Garfunkel (otherwise present only in a few intermittent background vocals) about how time is calling attention to its passing.

When Simon begins again, he works his way through a third variation on the opening five measures. As he wonders how long he can continue in the relationship and contemplates his sadness, he begins the six-measure sequence. But this time the pattern is cut short after four measures as he hesitates to commit to leaving, and, as was the case with "Save the Life of My Child" and "America," the song ends without arriving at a musical resolution.

Simon concludes the text with a twist. In reconsidering his verdict that the relationship is "over," the singer decides that he must "stop and think it *over*." This kind of wordplay supports the urbane character of the song, as does Simon's use of the word "time"—early in the song he connects "good times" and "bad times" with *The New York Times,* and Garfunkel's interlude starts with the word "time" just as Simon's previous line ends with the same word.

Only one song remains before the vocal version of the "Bookends Theme" concludes side one of the LP: "Old Friends" completes the chronological tour by addressing relationships among elderly people. It is preceded by "Voices of Old People," a collage of tape recordings of elderly people made by Garfunkel in New York and Los Angeles. His subjects comment on treasured photographs, relationships, illness, living conditions, and other challenges of aging, and then "Old Friends" begins.

The text of this song is quite melancholy. It describes two old men sitting in the winter, "lost in their overcoats" on a park bench "like bookends," thus connecting with the title of the album, as sounds and litter float about. While they are described in the third person, the singer, apparently younger, observes that it's very strange to think of being that age, and concludes by referring to a fear that the men share.

The basic musical material is presented by Simon's voice and an acoustic guitar, with some harmony lines provided by Garfunkel. The song does not follow a strict form, but rather gently builds melodic ideas from a few reiterated motives; in particular, descending leaps on the words "old friends" tend to convey ends and/or beginnings of sections. A soft mood is conveyed by the song's harmonic language: only one harmony is nondiatonic, but more importantly the song is dominated by diatonic seventh chords, and important melodic notes often float on the sevenths of chords or nonchord tones, thus avoiding strong emphasis. (The song is played in the key of C major although sounding in E—the one nondiatonic harmony is a brief F minor chord. In fact, the song is reminiscent of some of Simon's early folk songs in that every major and minor chord in the key appears.)

Beyond the rather loose formal structure, these features—soft mood, acoustic guitar and typical vocal arrangement, poignant lyrics—comprise a fairly straightforward Simon-and-Garfunkel presentation. However, an additional element is crucially at work. An orchestral arrangement by Jimmie Haskell is overlaid on the song. As Simon and Garfunkel sing, it is dominated by strings, with a few xylophone notes, and its sighs generally sweeten the texture, with a few more distinctive musical gestures included to underscore text like "sounds of the city" and "settle like dust." However, when the duo stops singing, horns and other instruments are added, and the music becomes much more turbulent. The main motives of the song, the descending leap and stepwise melodic motion, are mixed in various rhythms and keys, with dissonance freely applied, and then the texture resolves to a single high, sustained F♯ played by the strings. Under this, the guitar plays the first four measures of the "Bookends Theme," implying an F♯ minor harmony. When the next harmony, E, is reached, the string note resolves down as well to E, the sounding tonic note of the new song, and disappears.

At this point, the "Bookends Theme" continues, this time including vocals. The musical outline of this theme is quite simple—a three-note pattern repeats for four measures over a D minor harmony (capoed to F minor at the beginning of the side and F♯ minor here at the end), and this resolves to a tonic C harmony (E♭ and E, respectively) for about three measures; this in turn is followed by two brief phrases against Dm7 and C. The whole theme is presented twice at the beginning of the side, and at the end it is presented twice by the guitar, then twice with vocal verses (with slight rhythmic variation), and then one last time by the guitar.

As mentioned earlier, the brief text addresses the general themes of memories and relationships that the preceding songs explored. It also explicitly mentions two ideas highlighted earlier—the repeated word "time" in the first verse connects with the use of that word in "Overs," and the mention of a photograph connects with some discussion in "Voices of Old People" of treasured pictures. "Bookends Theme" (and the entire suite) concludes with the resigned admonition to "Preserve your memories/They're all that's left you."

In contrast to the unified organization exhibited on the first side of the *Bookends* album, the second side consists of a more typical miscellany of five songs that are only related to one another as much as one would expect would naturally occur with a group of works written by a single person at around the same time. "Mrs. Robinson" had appeared in *The Graduate,* and "Punky's Dilemma" had also been submitted for that project, although it had ultimately not been used (the same was true of "Overs"). A satirical thread can be found in "Mrs. Robinson," "Punky's Dilemma," and perhaps "At the Zoo," and a touch of whimsy characterizes these last two as well as "Fakin' It." Stylistically, the side tends a bit more toward various flavors of rock than is the case with the first side, although "Punky's Dilemma" is an exception to this with more of an easy-listening jazz flavor.

The side begins with "Fakin' It," which uses a funky rock beat to convey the singer's insecurities. As in several earlier songs, Simon here establishes a clear verse structure that will be significantly varied through the course of the song. In this case, two specific features are developed throughout the course of the song that eventually underscore the singer's basic conflict.

In the first verse, he tells of a self-assured woman, in contrast to whom he feels that he's just "fakin' it." The rock sound, and the woman's confidence, are underscored by the first notable feature, a brightly tonicized C♯ major chord (in the key of E) in the middle of the verse, just after the end of a sung phrase. The second verse, in elaborating on his shortcomings, follows the same chord structure and general melodic outline, but melodic fragments are inserted, deleted, or substituted to suit the needs of the text (for example, a melody is extended into what had been the C♯ chord's empty measure to descend by step on the words "wears me down").

The third verse follows a similar procedure (the text refers hopefully, if not very convincingly, to thoughts of reliance on others), but it adds the second feature, an extension achieved by repeating the last four measures of musical material (using new text, however). The fourth explores yet another option. The singer fantasizes about an earlier lifetime, in which he was a tailor, and the music dissolves into a brief vignette: the C♯ chord is now expanded into a passage in C♯ major, and a jaunty tune is piped while a young woman greets the tailor (who is presumably more capable than the singer of the song). The singer insists that he is the tailor, but, again, more hopefully than convincingly—the C♯ material disappears as the music returns to E, and the ending material that had been extended in the third verse returns and is repeated several times as he concedes that he is still fakin' it; the music eventually fades out.

The main interest in "Punky's Dilemma" lies in the text. The music is pleasant enough—the melody frolics in improvised-sounding bursts as guitar, bass, and percussion lay down a soft-jazz-style accompaniment dominated by seventh chords. All the harmonies and sung notes are in the key of E major. As in other songs, some melodic variation accommodates the specific textual choices in each verse, but this case is unlike that of "Fakin' It" in that the variation has no substantial large-scale significance. Each of the three verses is essentially the same, and the form is augmented only by minimal intro and outro passages and a brief insertion after the second verse of the words "Ah, South California."

This breezy comment captures the spirit of the song, which somewhat improbably uses breakfast-food images to lampoon the Hollywood set. The singer fantasizes about being a cornflake in the movie business who talks to a raisin who performs in Los Angeles, or about toasting himself as an English muffin and then indulging in boysenberry jam. In the third verse, however, the text takes an abrupt left turn into territory that is, all the same, no more familiar than what it replaces. The singer now fantasizes about being an admired soldier, in contrast to "old Roger, draft-dodger," who sneaks around (accompanied by blundering and banging sound effects) in the basement.

The images that fill the hit song "Mrs. Robinson" are more rationally connected to one another and to the social milieu that they address, but they nevertheless range widely. Simon is clearly interested in collecting a variety of topics that can shed some light on the title character; this variety of perspectives notwithstanding, by the song's end it still remains unclear what exactly is going on in her life, as well as how this character relates to the one in the film.

The song achieves an attractive pop-rock sound with the instantly recognizable guitar hook—that memorable musical figure that serves as intro, interlude, and outro. This tone is maintained as it proceeds through four bright verses and choruses. Each verse starts by romping through an accelerating circle of fifth-related major and major-minor seventh chords (F♯7-B7-E7-A-D) before easing through a B minor chord to an F♯7-E7 turnaround that sets up the chorus to start on the tonic A harmony. The text in the first verse consists only of the syllables "dee-dee-dee" and "doo-doo-doo," enabling the first chorus to use this stable harmonic foundation to reassure Mrs. Robinson that Jesus loves her, God can bless her, and heaven can welcome her.

The harmonies in the chorus move forward in a strong classical pattern, favoring descending thirds, however, rather than fifths. The exceptions to the classical pattern are the treatment of the F♯ minor chord that accompanies Mrs. Robinson's name (and thus serves, with its minor quality, to imply that she is troubled, rather than to move forward) and the motion at the end of the chorus to the F♯ major harmony implied by the interlude.

The second verse (the first with actual text) suggests that Mrs. Robinson is mentally ill, encouraging her to talk about herself so that she can be helped, and to become comfortable with her surroundings. The third refers to some secret that must be hidden, and mentions typical domestic elements of her life: cupcakes in the pantry, and "the kids." These references are continued in the fourth verse, but a description of a Sunday afternoon and a political debate lead to ideas of choice, which in turn seem to be applied discouragingly to choices in Mrs. Robinson's life: "Every way you look at this you lose."

This verse is followed by the final chorus, whose words are now entirely different from those in the first three. Here Simon builds on the words of the verse in combining a perspective on the larger culture with the plight of the individual. He cites a cultural hero, Joe DiMaggio, but suggests the severity of Mrs. Robinson's difficulties by saying that "Joltin' Joe," to whom the nation has "turn[ed] its lonely eyes," "has left and gone away." This chorus concludes, as did the previous ones, with the repeated phrase, "Hey, hey, hey," followed by the guitar hook once again.

It may be impossible to specify the ingredients for a hit, even after a song is written, but perhaps some of the ways Simon's unique voice created this one are evident. Of course the song got a boost from its appearance (in an earlier version) in *The Graduate,* and it possesses a distinctive hook and attractive sounds. But it also benefited from a strong marriage of harmonic motion with textual purpose, *and* from the variety of Simon's lyrical efforts. These surely attracted some attention (even if, perhaps, often subconscious) by being unusual and imaginatively juxtaposed, and their variety also made them able to be identified with by a variety of listeners.

The last two songs on *Bookends* paint sharply contrasting pictures. In "A Hazy Shade of Winter," which had been written earlier, during Simon's days in England, the singer confronts a sense of hopelessness about his achievements in life. He may be a failed poet, as he has "manuscripts of unpublished rhyme," but, although "it's the springtime of [his] life," he has lost control of time. He feels that he might as well be a beggar as carry on his current empty existence.

The song is set in a fairly straightforward manner, with a rock beat in D minor and a verse-refrain structure. Both verse and refrain are dominated by a D-C-B♭-A bass descent; the D minor chord at the beginning of the refrain is approached modally by a C chord, while the one at its conclusion is preceded by an A7 chord. The refrain insists that the title expresses the singer's current state, while the first two verses describe his plight in more detail.

The third verse advocates more hope, leading into a refrain that, suitably, refers to spring. The next verse is altered by a brief interlude in which new musical material accompanies the singer's expression of hopes to be remembered in some way. The remainder of the verse, however, pulls him back into his despondent outlook.

The other side of the coin is represented by "At the Zoo," a whimsical-sounding song that concludes the album. The singer leads into the first verse by speculating that "it's all happening at the zoo." The music settles into a rock groove, and the key settles into G major for the verse, and he tells what fun it is to go to the zoo. After the introductory passage returns, the characters of the animals and the zookeeper are described in terms that may indicate that they represent particular people or kinds of people. As the title of the song repeats and fades, *Bookends* comes to a close.

BRIDGE OVER TROUBLED WATER

Simon and Garfunkel's final studio album, *Bridge over Troubled Water*, released in 1970, sold more copies than any of the others. It won five Grammy awards and contains four of the duo's best-known songs: the title track, "The Boxer," "Cecilia," and "El Condor Pasa." With good reason, Simon has called it their best album,[4] and Garfunkel has remarked that it "is the one with the most successful variety...[it is] kind of the richest, because it goes in so many different directions."[5] It is perhaps ironic that this album actually involved the least direct collaboration in its production. During much of the time that it was being created, Garfunkel was busy in Mexico with the filming of *Catch-22,* in which he was playing a role. He was thus available intermittently to sing his parts and occasionally contribute in other ways, but Simon took on the lion's share of the arranging and studio work.

This shift in interests and division of labor was symptomatic of a parting of ways for the duo. The process of splitting, and the period of time leading to the breakup, were apparently attended at times by some considerable interpersonal friction. On the other hand, at least two of the songs on the album, "So Long, Frank Lloyd Wright" and "The Only Living Boy in New York," are clearly affectionate gestures from Simon to Garfunkel. At any rate, the two were able to complete the work, and the result was one of the most popular albums ever produced.

The title song appears first on the album. Much has been written about "Bridge over Troubled Water"; both Simon and Garfunkel have discussed its writing and production in published interviews. The song was originally written in the key of G on the guitar but was transposed up to E♭ to fit Garfunkel's voice and given a piano accompaniment in order to achieve a gospel feeling that Simon envisioned. Simon had to convince Garfunkel that he was the right choice to sing the song, but later admitted to some jealousy when, in concert, Garfunkel would receive overwhelming applause when performing it alone.[6]

The piano accompaniment was created by the pianist Larry Knechtel, in consultation with Simon and Garfunkel, over the course of a few days. The song initially had only two verses, but during the recording process it was decided that it had the potential to be even more powerful if a third verse were added. Some instruments join the accompaniment in the second verse, and a fuller orchestral arrangement in the third verse brings the song to a grand climax. This small-to-large strategy, the graceful figures in the piano part, and the comforting, but not too specific, spiritual overtones of the text, are three general premises that were surely crucial factors in the song's tremendous appeal among listeners. At the same time, though, they form a framework within which specific interactions between textual content and melodic and harmonic structure work extremely effectively.

The first verse shows the way that this happens in three stages. The first part of the verse is subdued and tender, as the singer describes the girl's dismay and the way he will respond with comfort. In the second part, he firmly states his perspective and then returns to her plight in more absolute terms, leading to the refrain in which he uses the title of the song to declare his commitment most emphatically.

The melody during the first stage lies mainly in a low register—the high E♭ is touched once briefly and then reached more strongly to underscore the singer's closing response. (Garfunkel has reported that he initially omitted this octave leap when recording the song, and Simon objected to the revision[7]; although Garfunkel indicates that its inclusion is somewhat arbitrary, it may be significant—whether this was Simon's conscious intent—because of the way that it connects this passage with the later, higher affirmation of the refrain.) The harmonies are very simple—the tonic E♭ harmony is decorated with the subdominant A♭, avoiding the more strongly leading dominant harmony altogether. In addition, the first phrase introduces a crucial motive, the stepwise descent to the tonic G-F-E♭, which suggests at this point a sense of resignation on the word "weary." At the end of the section the motive gives some assurance as the singer says that he'll dry the girl's tears, but continued motion to the subdominant chord indicates that more is to be said.

The same motive begins the second stage, again conveying a sense of assurance, but now more direct engagement with difficulties is implied with the first use of the dominant B♭ chord as a foil for the tonic harmony. The high register is now reached more decisively as the G-F-E♭ motive is heard up an octave, in quarter notes, to express the girl's total inability to find companions—but now the E♭ is harmonized with a nontonic harmony, moving on to the third stage, the refrain.

At this point the motive appears once again on the emphatic words "like a bridge." The E♭ is still not harmonized with the tonic harmony, and in fact the refrain contains much more harmonic interest than was found in either of the earlier parts. A bright C7 harmony is reached by deceptive motion on the word "water," and it is followed by a cadence in C minor; when the refrain text is repeated, the same C7 chord appears, but this time it is followed by a final, dominant-to-tonic, cadence in E♭.

The text of the second verse follows the same pattern that the first did, and thus the effect of these musical features is the same. In the third verse, the singer no longer mentions the girl's distress, but simply encourages her to move forward and shine. (Some critics thought the phrase "silver girl" referred to a hypodermic needle, but Simon has said that it arose from his wife's discovery of her first gray hairs.[8]) While the musical elements still relate to one another in the same ways, then, their function with respect to the text now shifts slightly, but, for example, the low register and subdominant harmonies still apparently convey tenderness. (In fact, the low register might be perceived a bit differently in this verse because a simple harmony line is now added above the original melody.) The subtle shift in function and the transcendent "sailing" text, however, occur simultaneously with the addition of the strings and help to bring the song to its conclusion with a sense of a new dimension of emotional richness.

The next song on *Bridge over Troubled Water*, "El Condor Pasa," is an early example of a creative strategy that has repeatedly intrigued Simon: the use of a particular ethnic style as the basis for a song. Of course, many songwriters, especially those with some folk-music inclinations, have pursued this kind of approach to some degree. But for Simon it has included an unusual combination of dimensions. Few have explored such a wide range of styles—Simon's interests have encompassed gospel, many flavors of jazz and blues, reggae, South African popular music, various Brazilian styles, doo-wop, Cajun, and assorted Latino traditions. Few, if any, have done so with such a high degree of popularity (notable hits have included "El Condor Pasa," "Mother and Child Reunion," and the whole *Graceland* album); in this way Simon is distinguished from, for example, Ry Cooder, who has probably actually explored more traditions in greater depth. Third, the roles that the other styles play in Simon's work vary interestingly—as will be seen, he might use a particular performer to add a distinctive flavor to a piece, or he might attempt to replicate a style throughout a piece, or, as in this case, he might use preexisting musical material in a particular style and add his own contribution.

In "El Condor Pasa," Simon draws his music from an arrangement by Jorge Milchberg for the Peruvian group Los Incas of a song of the same name; apparently the song originated from some combination of folk song and a composer named Daniel Robles. This material, the instrumental part of which is actually performed on this track by Los Incas, consists of two arch-shaped melodic phrases, followed by two phrases that remain in a high register before a final descent to the tonic note E. The harmonies vacillate in the first two phrases between E minor and G, and in the remainder of the piece they emphasize C and G before closing on E minor.

To the first section, Simon provides text that uses rural images to express a desire for empowerment. As new melodic territory is explored, and the first C chord opens new harmonic territory, at the beginning of the second section Simon uses the word "away" to begin to express a desire to be free to travel at will rather than be "tied...to the ground" as a peasant farmer. In the first part of the second—and last—verse, the singer prefers to be a forest, and to stand on the earth, rather than to be a street; the second part of this verse is rendered instrumentally without text.

Simon's compositional method in "El Condor Pasa," in addition to drawing on a particular authentic ethnic style, exemplifies a distinctive compositional technique that was to continue to interest him. This strategy consisted of composing or appropriating a passage of musical material and then writing lyrics to fit it, and Simon used it on the next song on *Bridge over Troubled Water,* "Cecilia," as well. Experimentation had resulted in a rhythm track that he liked, and so he began to improvise words against the track.

The accompaniment ultimately came to include a smorgasbord of sounds. Some of the percussion consists of Simon and Garfunkel rapidly dropping bunches of drumsticks on a parquet floor and picking them up again. Simon's brother Eddie added a guitar track, and Simon contributed a manic xylophone line. The melody and lyrics share the catch-as-catch-can spirit implied by this assembly of sounds—against simple tonic, dominant, and subdominant chords in the key of B, the thoroughly syncopated tune goes up and down, mostly between the B and E around middle C, sometimes reaching up to the high G♯ at the beginning of lines and descending to the lower F♯ at their ends. Throughout much of the song a harmony line lies close above this one; the vocal quality and the nature of the percussive accompaniment result in a south-of-the-border flavor.

Meanwhile, the lyrics in the verses address the title character, as the singer begs her to come home because she is breaking his heart. In the only full verse, he explains that Cecilia took someone else into his bed with her immediately after he left it. In the final chorus, however, he is ecstatic because she loves him again. The tune for the verse resembles that of the chorus, and the whole song rambles through these and various interludes, adding up more to an infectious (and, as it turned out, quite appealing) ditty than to a weighty aesthetic statement.

"Keep the Customer Satisfied" is similarly transparent. It, too, is dominated by close two-part harmonies, but this time the effect is a rockabilly sound quite reminiscent of Simon and Garfunkel's early influences, the Everly Brothers. In this way it forms a bridge to the only track on the album not written (or, in the case of "El Condor Pasa," cowritten) by Simon, a live recording of "Bye, Bye, Love," composed by Felice and Boudleaux Bryant, but first made famous by Don and Phil Everly.

Simon's song romps through the account of a traveler—apparently a traveling salesman—who is glad to be home because of the rigors of the road. After the first verse expresses this sentiment, the chorus complains that people he encounters unfairly speak ill of him as he frantically tries "to keep [his] customers satisfied." A hint of impropriety suggested by the "county line" in the chorus is reinforced by the second verse, in which the deputy sheriff advises the singer to move along quickly because of the trouble he's creating for himself. After the chorus returns, the place of the third verse is taken by some frantic "whoa"s, and the final chorus, with slightly altered words that emphasize how tired he is, brings the singer's lament to an end.

While the song is not one of his most profound achievements, Simon does interestingly use some rhythmic maneuvers to underscore the singer's disorientation and dismay. The rock-and-roll style is established in several ways, including bass and drums with a shuffle beat (and punctuation by an organ, later joined by a horn section, at opportune moments). The verse opens with a harmonic progression that follows the first half of the 12-bar-blues pattern common in early rock and roll, and the remainder of the song also uses harmonies typical of the style. All of this creates a sense of predictability, against which Simon relocates rhythmic events: first, the last line of the verse continues longer than expected, running right into the first line of the chorus ("It's the same old story"), which is "properly" located; and second, the second line of the chorus is shifted so that it is a measure "late."

A different aesthetic sensibility entirely is exhibited by the slow, Brazilian-flavored "So Long, Frank Lloyd Wright." The song is accompanied throughout by a classical guitar playing mostly seventh chords in a Latin jazz style. The tune, sung by Garfunkel, floats gracefully above this accompaniment with a wide variety of contours, rhythms, and syncopations.

The opening section bids farewell to the architect in two halves that are very similar to one another, although the second half introduces strings and a drum that continue to the end of the song and reaches a more conclusive resting point, with the melody on G♭, accompanied by a G♭ major triad, in the key of G♭. This is followed by a bridge section that comments on architects in general, and Frank Lloyd Wright in particular, before leading back to the opening material. This time, however, the key has been raised a half step to G major, and, rather than the original melody being sung, the original chord changes (in the new key) accompany a solo flute (appropriate in its airy sound to the Latin style) that plays a new melody. The bridge is repeated, this time with instruments replacing the singing of the material about Frank Lloyd Wright, and it leads once again to the opening section. The opening material again appears in the higher key of G, but the words (to the second half of the section) are sung this time, leading to a lengthy fadeout of the words "so long" (to which Simon can eventually be heard yelling "So long, already, Artie" in the background).

In addition to displaying Simon's increased harmonic sophistication in this jazz idiom, this song is, as Simon has said, a farewell to Art Garfunkel (who had at one time studied architecture).[9] In the first section, the singer refers to "Frank Lloyd Wright" 's "song," says that he (the singer) "barely learned the tune," and describes the two of them "harmoniz[ing] 'til dawn." In the bridge, the singer says that most architects "never change [one's] point of view," but that he stops to think of his favorite architect when he needs inspiration. This reference to the creative process is, of course, a favorite Simon theme; also typical is his playing with the phrase "so long," which closes the verse on the end of the line "I never laughed so long," and is then repeated in the "farewell" sense.

As popular as "Bridge over Troubled Water" was, it has a strong rival in another track on this album, "The Boxer" (which was actually written and released as a single about a year before the album was released). Both songs are very effectively arranged, but "The Boxer," rather than drawing musically on the gospel tradition, is solidly located in Simon's folk-based style. Apart from the sophisticated arrangement, the song is very simply conceived with a basic folk-guitar accompaniment. It is played in the key of C (apparently tuned low to sound in B), and all of the harmonies are diatonic in that key. (Almost all the major and minor chords in the key are used—C, E minor, F, G, and A minor, omitting only D minor.) Furthermore, the song follows a very regular formal scheme—a verse-verse-refrain sequence repeats throughout, with very few, and very minor, variations.

Several ingredients build on these quite simple premises to contribute to the success of the song. Of course, one of these, as was the case with many of the duo's recordings (and especially some of the most simply conceived ones) is the sheer attractiveness of the musical texture—the sweetly harmonized voices and the rich propulsion of the fingerpicked guitar, combined in this case with various warm instrumental additions. More specific to this instance, though, are three other elements: the appeal of the persona projected by the song, the compelling marriage of melodic and harmonic structure with text in each verse and chorus, and the way that the arrangement shapes the whole piece.

The text tells the story of the boxer, who has been victimized by unscrupulous promoters and now is at the mercy of the mean streets of the city. In these circumstances he is made particularly attractive by various character traits that he reveals: he takes some responsibility for having been deceived; he admits to loneliness and even fear, and even to seeking solace with prostitutes; he is willing to work hard to earn an honest paycheck; and finally, he refuses to be vanquished by the odds that are arrayed against him.

Each verse is cast firmly in C major, and each "lie-la-lie" wordless refrain dips into the relative key, A minor, before ending again in C. It is the harmonic structure of the verses, combined with their text, that is particularly effective. Against a regular pattern of five four-measure groups, the harmonies take three trips away from and back to the tonic C harmony. In the first trip, they dwell on this harmony before moving through A minor to rest for four measures on dominant G harmonies, which return strongly, as is common with dominant harmonies, to the tonic C chord.

The second trip begins in the same way; the music again dwells on C and moves through A minor to G. This time, however, the G lasts for only one measure before slipping down to the subdominant F harmony for two measures before returning to C. The final trip condenses this same motion, with one measure apiece on G and F before returning again to C.

The result of these progressions is that, while the first trip moves rather straightforwardly from tonic to dominant and then back again, the second conveys a sense of poignancy when the dominant chord falls to the subdominant (rather than moving "forward," in classical terms, to the tonic), and this sense is echoed when the third motion from tonic does the same thing. These nuances directly support the text, because in each verse the first textual thought tends to be a fairly straightforward description of some aspect of the boxer's situation, matching the spirit of the direct harmonic motion. While this thought is often unpleasant, the second thought tends to reveal a more personal and/or poignant insight into the situation just described, and the falling-away motion to the subdominant underscores this.

Rather than employing a straightforward small-to-large dramatic-wedge strategy, as was the case with "Bridge over Troubled Water," the arrangement of "The Boxer" changes pace throughout, using distinctive instrumental colors to lend definition to the large-scale shape. After the memorable cascading acoustic-guitar introduction leads to a fingerpicked vamp, the first verse, in which the boxer introduces himself, features the duo accompanied by guitar.[10] A fairly subtle drumbeat that will be present for most of the rest of the song leads into the next verse; this verse's sense of starting the story from the beginning is underscored by the rhythmic chuffing of a bass harmonica.

The first refrain introduces one of the more famous sound effects in recorded music of the era, the huge crashes that respond to each of the duo's "lie-la-lie"s; according to Garfunkel, this effect (which appears in each refrain) was a concoction of Roy Halee's. It lends a sense of gravity to the refrain's wordless pauses for contemplation of the boxer's story. The next verse backs down to guitars (including a strong bass line) and drums as the boxer looks fruitlessly for a job, and the following verse features an *obbligato* synthesizer line—also a very memorable sound; the following refrain closely resembles the first one.

The last pair of verses somewhat echoes the first pair. As the boxer yearns to go home, the singers are accompanied only by guitars and drum; this verse actually takes a harmonic detour (in comparison with the other verses) as the boxer's thoughts turn away, and he is answered by a brief, sympathetic lead guitar line. The last verse changes to the third person, describing the damage that the boxer has sustained, although "the fighter still remains." The following refrain repeats several times, complete with crashes, but now strings are added, and they grow and swell along with obvious vocal overdubs. Finally, though, the texture backs down to the acoustic guitar, which plays one verse worth of accompaniment and concludes.

"Baby Driver" provides an immediate contrast in tone to "The Boxer." This rock and roll romp tosses metaphors around with a fair degree of abandon, but some of the main ones refer to the longstanding double-entendre tradition of blues and early rock. While the three verses of the song are mainly devoted to varied descriptions of the singer's parents' occupations and their effects on him, in the choruses he says that he is called "Baby Driver," he's "talking 'bout [his listener's] sex appeal," and he "wonder[s] how [her] engines feel." He concludes the third verse by inviting his listener to "come into [his] room and play."

Suitably, the song is accompanied by a rock band, led off by raucous slide-guitar work and propelled throughout by a four-to-the-bar bass line. The harmonic structure of the verse-and-chorus combination is blues-based, starting with the tonic chord but initially using the subdominant for contrast. In the middle of the chorus, the "engines" line is emphasized by an abrupt motion up to the supertonic chord (E minor in the key of D major); when this is repeated at the end of the chorus, the chord serves as the basis for a strong turnaround by leading through the dominant A7 chord back to the tonic.

The first chorus is followed by a brief interlude in which the singers sing "woo, woo" while the beginning tonic-to-subdominant motion returns. After the second chorus, though, the interlude is expanded to go through the changes for the entire verse and chorus: saxophones wail and honk rock and roll licks, the singers contribute a few Beach-Boys-style vocal maneuvers, and drag-strip engine-revving sound effects are included as well. Finally, after the third chorus, the singers provide more nonsense syllables, engine sounds push the music suddenly into a higher key and a faster tempo, and the song concludes with an announcer talking in the background about a world-champion driver.

As mentioned above, the text of "The Only Living Boy in New York" joins that of "So Long, Frank Lloyd Wright" in being directed at Art Garfunkel. The singer begins by addressing "Tom," Garfunkel's pseudonym from the duo's adolescent "Tom and Jerry" days, and wishes him well in catching his flight and acting (presumably referring to the Mexico filming of *Catch-22*). The remainder of the song describes the singer's solitude (as ironically expressed in the title line) as he casts about for ways to occupy his time, wishes "Tom" well in his pursuits, and encourages him to continue to "let [his] honesty shine."

Simon's musical choices support the dreamy, affectionate tone of the lyrics in several ways. One of these is the instrumental texture, which consists of ringing 12-string guitar sounds and sustained organ harmonies over a warmly loping, melodic bass line.[11] Against this background, Simon sings the first verse and refrain, accompanied by a 19-measure sequence of chord changes. These rock back and forth between the tonic B harmony and the gentle subdominant E chord before the bass walks down to the dominant to begin the refrain. Over this harmony Simon arpeggiates, singing gently syncopated nonsense syllables leading to the words "here I am" as the harmony drops back to the subdominant. Tonic and subdominant, again, conclude the refrain with the title line and lead into the second verse.

The second verse and refrain use the same set of changes, but Simon gives the music a free-form feeling by blurring the boundary between the verses.

He alters the melody of the second verse considerably, most significantly changing that of the first two lines so that they resemble that of the last line of the refrain. This, combined with the near-rhyme between these last lines' last word "report" and the refrain's closing "New York," as well as the continuous tonic-subdominant alternation across the boundary, makes it seem at first as though these beginning lines are an extension of the refrain.

After the second verse, a brief bridge uses the first-person plural to express uncertainty about where "we're gone," and, appropriately, Garfunkel joins Simon for this passage. It moves directly through a circle-of-fifths chord progression—G#7-C#m-F#7-B-E—to arrive back at the tonic-subdominant pair. At this point the verse-and-refrain changes appear again, but this time the vocals are ethereal, wordless choral "Ah"s, concluding by echoing, more slowly, the refrain's words "here I am." (This vocal effect, which Simon has described as "[his] favorite one on that whole album,"[12] was created by Simon and Garfunkel singing multiple overdubs very loudly in an echo chamber and then adding the result to the song very softly.[13])

Simon and Garfunkel return to sing the bridge again, and then Simon sings the third texted verse and refrain. A sense of conclusion is signaled as this verse begins with the opening text of the first verse; at this point, the melody, as well, is more like that of the first than that of the second. But this is not a complete return, for not only do later words and melodies in this verse vary from what has been heard before, but the singer's music is now overlaid with the choral material that was introduced between appearances of the bridge. And, indeed, after the singer concludes by repeating the last line of the refrain, the instruments kick up into a final pass through the bridge changes, and the choral material reappears—not once, but twice—leaving the listener with a sense of emotion that transcends the more rational thoughts of the singer.

"Why Don't You Write Me?" also deals with separation, but in a more lighthearted vein, and not explicitly connected with Simon and Garfunkel's relationship. The singer is in the jungle and asking someone—presumably his lover—the title question. He senses that something is wrong, but he is unable to return. He begs his listener to write and describes himself waiting for mail day after day until he kills himself, finally closing with repetitions of the title line.

Simon has described the music for this song as a bad attempt at a Jamaican style (especially in comparison with the hit "Mother and Child Reunion" that was soon to lead off his first solo album after the early *Paul Simon Songbook*).[14] The verses make heavy melodic use of a syncopated arpeggio figure; the changes proceed with little ceremony from the tonic E♭ harmony through an abruptly chromatic F7 to the dominant B♭7; this resolves deceptively to C minor before the E♭ returns and is decorated by A♭7. Three of these verses are mingled with three instrumental passages before a coda vacillates between various forms of E♭ and A♭ triads and seventh chords with blues flavorings.

While the syncopations may somewhat suggest Jamaican rhythms, the entire song is a stylistic pastiche. Comical-country licks in the instruments combine with vocal deployments and timbres reminiscent of several popular groups of the 1960s, and listeners may enjoy identifying their favorites among these.

The next song on the album is "Bye Bye Love"; over the applause that follows this performance are placed the opening notes of "Song for the Asking." This final song on this last studio album by the duo is in actuality a solo effort. Accompanied by solo guitar, with an orchestral arrangement in the background, the singer offers his song, asking the listener to accept his musical offering; he expresses some regrets and willingness to "change [his] ways," and offers to play "all the love that [he] hold[s] inside."

The accompaniment (apart from the orchestra) is very much in a simple fingerpicked folk vein. It is played in the key of C (tuned down to B) and relies mostly on diatonic harmonies. A distinctive flavor is achieved through some interesting rhythmic displacements and blues-tinged fills. There are two brief verses, followed by a bridge that starts on A minor in introducing the regrets but eventually provides a segue into the next verse; this in turn is followed by a final hummed verse.

Lasting only about a minute and 40 seconds, this song is, apart from the rhythmic details and perhaps the intrigue related to the singer's motivations in offering his song, his regrets, and his love, fairly straightforward. The soft tone of the text is clearly and simply supported by the character of the music. Simon does include one musically supporting detail that is a bit more subtle, however. While the melody in the first and last verses ends on the tonic note, the harmony at these points is the subdominant F chord, which then needs to proceed through G to C. This conveys a sense of the singer having said all he has to say, but with some uncertainty about how it will be received. And with this device, Simon brought the period of collaboration with Garfunkel to an end.

First Solo Albums after Simon and Garfunkel

Simon had written the vast majority of Simon and Garfunkel's original material from the beginning of the partnership. His creative role had, if anything, increased during the extensive process of producing *Bridge over Troubled Water*, especially under the circumstances of Garfunkel's extended absences as he pursued his acting interests. Simon was therefore entirely capable of independently continuing to develop material from the initial point of composition all the way to the finished recordings.

Garfunkel's absence, of course, posed a significant challenge. Whatever Simon did as a solo act would have to compete with the sound and image to which listeners had become accustomed, and in this case the standard was not only a known quantity, but by this time a fabulously successful one. While on the one hand this success gave Simon an abundance of name recognition from which to launch his solo career, on the other it had the potential to be quite daunting—it would be all but impossible for him to match the nearly unprecedented success of *Bridge over Troubled Water*, or even that of any of the three albums that had immediately preceded it.

PAUL SIMON

However imposing this problem might have seemed, the first fruits of Simon's solo work indicated that it had not prevented him from pursuing new compositional possibilities very effectively. He invested time in additional study of guitar and music theory. He also focused clearly on a few specific creative approaches. For one thing, he was interested in a leaner, more direct sound than had been evident on many of the last, heavily produced,

Simon and Garfunkel tracks, and in this he differed somewhat from a taste that Garfunkel (as well as Roy Halee) had developed for more lush styles and textures.[1]

This inclination on Simon's part fit well with a second impulse, his continuing interest in seeking out particular performers and styles that he could incorporate into his creative process. The simpler textures allowed these elements to be clearly evident in the final recordings, and this characteristic can be seen throughout *Paul Simon* (1972), the first solo album to follow *Bridge over Troubled Water*. (One indication of this element is the listing of musicians for each song, a practice followed on all the solo albums but none of the duo albums.)

Third, this approach to musical creation, in which Simon might appropriate a particular style to his own ends, and assemble its characteristic patterns along with other elements of a song, fit well with a textual style that he had also already found congenial. Specifically, many of his texts seem somewhat "assembled" from various kinds of purposes. Key phrases may seem to refer to a particular central theme, while others seem to manifest some combination of elliptical relation to the theme, allusion to some not-quite-fully-determined additional idea(s), and sonic or otherwise captivating interest in its own right. All three of these elements are evident throughout the album, and all three are present in the first, and most popular, track on the album, "Mother and Child Reunion."

This song emerged from some sessions that Simon did with a group of Jamaican studio musicians. His desire had been to experience their style personally so as to absorb it in a genuine way. (To that end, he had to make some arrangements with them that differed from the normal practice, because they were accustomed to being paid by the finished song, and the amount of time he wanted to spend with them in a kind of exploratory mode would have made this inequitable.)

Simon was pleased with the result of this process, and, similarly to the way he wrote "Cecilia," he recorded the instrumental tracks before writing the rest of the song. This final product is unlike "Cecilia," however, in the clarity of production—while some studio magic may have been performed at some level, each instrument can be heard distinctly in the final mix (which includes some non-Jamaican musicians, such as veteran studio pianist—mentioned above in connection with "Bridge over Troubled Water"—Larry Knechtel).

This final product is actually rather curious, especially for a song that has received as much airplay as this one has. This popularity is no doubt largely due to its overall infectious, upbeat sound, including the distinctive stuttering lead-guitar introduction, the decisive chord progressions in the chorus, and the female background singers who ease in after the first chorus and proceed to color the remainder of the song. Probably attractive as well was the way the title sounded simultaneously intriguing and comforting and, in fact, these features are developed in a text that is on the whole a bit more involved than the more accessible aspects of the musical surface might suggest.

Simon has said that the title is actually drawn from the name of a chicken-and-egg dish that he saw on the menu of a Chinese restaurant, and that he was led to address death in the text as a whole as a result of the death of his family's dog. In the first chorus, the singer predicts the imminence of the title event, without defining it further, in the face of a "strange and mournful day." This encouragement is begun in a high register, accompanied by a cycling subdominant-dominant-tonic (D-E-A) harmonic sequence in the key of A major, but at the end of the chorus the melody descends and a dominant E chord moves to an F♯ minor harmony. These two harmonies alternate to emphasize a minor sound while the first verse mourns the sad day. The verse in turn is concluded with a D-E sequence that reintroduces the chorus with its cycling pattern.

The second verse again describes the devastating effect of the unnamed tragedy. This is followed by the third appearance of the chorus, which is extended into a repeat-and-fade coda. The formal plan of the song is thus quite straightforward, and this transparency, along with that of the instrumentation and production, forms a contrast with the elliptical nature of the lyrics.

"Duncan" is similar in some respects to "Mother and Child Reunion": again Simon draws on an ethnically distinctive group of musicians and again he reportedly began with the music and added the words later.[2] In this case, though, the collaborators—Los Incas, with whom Simon had already worked on "El Condor Pasa"—are used to provide instrumental interludes, rather than establishing the main groove of the song, which is fundamentally an acoustic-guitar-driven ballad. Furthermore, the text in this case is a straightforward, albeit evocative, narrative along the lines of "The Boxer," rather than the more indirect expression exemplified by "Mother and Child Reunion."

The form of "Duncan" is extremely simple. Following a brief introduction, there are six verses, and every even-numbered verse is followed by an interlude. The song is in the key of E minor, and it uses typical folk-guitar chords—E minor, D, G, A, and C. The melody in each verse follows the same general outline, but Simon takes his customary liberties—not only are rhythms adjusted to accommodate syllables, emphases, and so on, but more significant options are explored as well (for just one example, in the second measure in each verse the tune sometimes rises to C and sometimes descends to F♯ or lower).

As in "The Boxer," the first verse of "Duncan" provides a setting and indicates in the first person that the singer is about to tell his story. In this case he then tells about his birth, leaving home and being destitute, and encountering a young female street preacher who ends his "long years of innocence." The text includes several memorable images—for example, Lincoln Duncan was "born in the boredom and the chowder," and later "just like a dog [he] was befriended."

Duncan's humble station is reflected by the simple structure of the song and by its limited harmonic vocabulary. At the same time, the harmonic structure of the song reflects his transient status by continually shifting emphasis within its narrow tonal range. The entire sequence of chords in each verse is Em-D-G-A-D-C-G-C-G-C-G-D-Em. The first D chord seems at first as though it could be a modal decoration of the E-minor harmony, but instead the following G-A-D progression shifts the focus toward D. Then the repeated C-G motions emphasize G; the following D sounds at first as though it could be a dominant in that key but instead finally moves modally back to E minor to bring the verse to completion. The finality of this arrival is underscored in most of the verses by the repetition of an emphasized text phrase and a melodic echo, as an A-F♯ motion is followed by B-G.

The instrumentation for "Everything Put Together Falls Apart" is very simple: Simon provides a jazz-style guitar accompaniment, and Knechtel adds fills on harmonium and electric piano. On the other hand, the harmonic language is considerably more complex than that in "Duncan." The song is based on a fairly elaborate series of changes, which appears two and a half times. The series suggests the key of C at its beginning and end, but E in the middle; since the song ends in the middle of the series, it begins in C and ends in E.

The melody sounds improvisational, with varied rhythms, steps, and leaps. It follows the same general path, although varied somewhat, with each appearance of the series of chords. However, there is not as much of a sense of verse structure as might be the case, because the melody and lyrics flow fairly smoothly across the boundaries between appearances of the series. The text rambles through the melody, sympathetically advising the listener about the dangers of a frenetic lifestyle and of trying to deny the unavoidable effects of painful situations and results. All in all, text and music in this song cooperate to produce a well-defined freeform, blues-flavored jazz style. In this song, as contrasted with "Mother and Child Reunion" and "Duncan," Simon does not draw on a specific, stylistically distinctive group of musicians. Rather, the focus here is on the exploration of guitar-playing and music-theoretic possibilities.

Some adventurous harmonic material is also present in "Run That Body Down," which continues the theme of acknowledging physical limitations. This song, though, moves forward more decisively than "Everything Put Together Falls Apart." While the texture is still quite transparent, a steady shuffle beat is now provided by bass, drums, and two guitars, with extra color added by vibraphone (adding a bit of jazz flavor).

Also clear is the song's verse-chorus structure. In each of the verses the singer is talking with someone—first his female doctor and then his wife (named "Peg," the name of Simon's wife at the time)—about an elusive ailment, and the chorus follows with the conclusion that one can't "run that body down" forever. While this structure is supported by a clear tonal focus on the key of D major, the harmonic progressions and occasional metrical shifts create something of a cycling, perpetual-motion effect that subtly supports the song's idea of continuous motion.

This begins at the outset of the song. The first chord is B minor, not a typical key-establishing harmony in the key of D. However, the chord immediately launches a circle-of-fifths progression that reaches D (Bm-Em-A-D). The remainder of the song rolls easily from one harmony to another, led by Ron Carter's loping bass line. Stable D harmonies turn to D7s, which resolve to B minor; F#+ chords that sound at first like dominants to B minor resolve instead to G chords.[3] At the end of the second verse, an F#+ harmony, instead of leading to the B minor that would move to D at the beginning of the third verse, shifts the tonal focus by moving to a relatively stable B major chord to kick off an interlude. However, just as easily, another F#+ chord then leads to B minor to accompany an electric-guitar solo while circling back to D. A third chorus follows, this time eventually repeating the question "who you foolin'?" and at last arriving on a dissonant B minor9 chord (one, that is, that adds C# to the stable B minor triad).

"Armistice Day" is an odd song. It opens with a free-form description of the observance of the holiday, combined with a reference to a woman who had willingly provided friendship for the singer. All of this is accompanied by two guitars, one with an altered tuning that drops the low E string to a D so that it can dwell on that tonic note. Much of the music played by the guitars sounds like material traditionally played by bluesmen playing with a bottleneck or similar hard tube slid along the strings (often called "slide" guitar), and many of the motives in the sung melody relate to these sounds. This section of the piece uses some changing meters, and the percussionist Airto Moreira supplies light touches throughout.

At the end of this section, the instruments vamp for several bars and lead into the second section, which consists of two verses in a straightforward 12-bar blues structure (with an extra 4-bar interlude between verses). The text here complains that the singer has been waiting fruitlessly to see his congressman in Washington, D.C., and asks a congresswoman to tell the congressman (presumably that the singer has been waiting). The text and melody are unusual in one respect: rather than following the most typical (for a 12-bar blues) AAB form in which the material of the first line in a verse repeats in the second line, followed by a contrasting line, this section places the contrasting line second, followed by a return to the first line, thus resulting in an ABA form.

By all accounts, "Me and Julio Down by the Schoolyard" epitomizes Simon's interest in the sonic value of texts, even to the exclusion of a clearly developed argument. The song's good-natured, rollicking tone was doubtless responsible for its receiving considerable airplay, and the meaning of the text was the subject of a great deal of speculation. Simon, however, has deflected such questions, describing the song as "pure confection" and indicating that he didn't have specific ideas in mind as the objects of some of the song's undefined references (most notably asserting that even he doesn't know "what the mama saw").[4]

All of this is most likely true, and examining the song with this assumption might be the most profitable approach even if it weren't. While the text is filled with unknown quantities, they are given a certain measure of coherence by being assembled into a logical-sounding narrative, mostly developed in the verses. The mama pajama sees something, and she and the papa pursue legal action against the singer; the singer is arrested, but a "radical priest" creates a media stir by getting him released. In the chorus, the singer gives some definition to the problem with the title line and refers to departing for an unknown destination, apparently leaving "Rosie, the queen of Corona" behind.

The music generally supports this distribution of information. As was the case in "Cecilia," the melody is thoroughly syncopated throughout, it uses plenty of skips, and it is accompanied in the verses by only tonic, subdominant, and dominant harmonies (although in the key of A here). This harmonic simplicity, along with a melodic range that is generally fairly limited, is consistent with the verses' dissemination of information. Things open up a bit to accommodate the choruses' more expansive commentary, however. While the key remains A major, a couple of chromatic harmonies, G and B, put some emphasis on D and E, respectively, and the melody ranges more widely. Finally, the generally lighthearted tone is reinforced by the syncopated strumming in the introduction, the whimsical percussion effects supplied by Moreira (the other instruments are two guitars and a bass), and a whistled chorus.

A spare accompaniment is about all that "Me and Julio" shares with "Peace Like a River." The latter song, supported by bass, drums, and Simon's acoustic guitar, is a haunting meditation on implicitly race-related urban strife. Here some of Simon's textual ambiguity serves him very effectively. The music follows an AABA format, with an instrumental interlude following the B section. The lyrics in the first A sections describe the pleasure of the singer's people when peace runs through a city late into the night and recall a former time of confusion and mistrust. The B section declares to oppressors that history will eventually conquer them, and the final A section describes the singer waking up early in the morning from his dreams and saying that because he's "reconciled" he's "gonna be up for awhile."

It seems that oppression has been lifted from this scene, and that the defiant B section is speaking from the past, but the reference to dreams implies that the pleasure and reconciliation of the outer sections may be expressions of internal conviction, rather than reactions to fully achieved realities. The musical setting helps to project this sense of a vividly perceived situation that may or may not be real in a number of ways. A pure richness is conveyed by the instrumental timbre: the guitar—the only source of melodic material that complements the singer—is played in the key of E minor, and the many open strings that this allows are further enhanced by the fact that the guitar is tuned down a whole step to sound in D minor.

The clear identity of the setting is emphasized by the fact that all the harmonies used—E minor, G, A minor, C, and D—are diatonic in E minor. The tonic E minor chord is consistently approached by either A minor or D, giving the song a diatonic Aeolian flavor rather than the classical minor aspect that would be lent by dominant B or B7 chords, with their nondiatonic D♯s. Within this pure context, though, subtle shifts of mood are created by regularly emphasizing the major G chord within sections before returning to the tonic E-minor chord.

These harmonic characteristics are aided by the integrity of the performance in establishing the song's vivid picture. This results partly from the effortless flourishes and blues-influenced licks in the guitar part. Moreover, though, while Simon's vocal work is not likely to be mistaken for that of the black man portrayed by the singer, it projects a solid persona in its own right, and the musical style of the song does not sound out of place with a white singer. And finally, Simon's falsetto at the end conveys a spaced-out ecstasy appropriate to the early-morning scene that has been described at that point in the song.

"Peace Like a River," "Papa Hobo," and "Paranoia Blues" form a trilogy that focuses on urban angst (with the brief instrumental "Hobo's Blues" serving as an interlude after "Papa Hobo"). "Papa Hobo" is a curious song in a number of ways. While the texts of the other two songs do not always explicitly state the menaces against which they are reacting, these can be readily, and fairly specifically, deduced. Furthermore, they are familiar: racial oppression in "Peace Like a River," and various interpersonal hazards—with associates, authorities, and hoodlums—that accompany the anonymity of a huge city in "Paranoia Blues."

In "Papa Hobo," however, while the singer is critical of the city, the targets are less clear and less familiar. The location is Detroit, which is said to seduce people somehow into "that automotive dream," and the singer bemoans the air pollution associated with the industry. While this is, and was at the time of the song's writing, a prominent concern, the singer does not seem primarily concerned with the issue in its own right, but merely as it contributes to his disaffection with this particular city. It is clear that he wants to leave, but his description of the city's attributes includes generally positive references to its basketball and hockey teams. Perhaps he is grudgingly acknowledging these positive assets, or he's listing them as means of seducing people to become residents, or they are put forth as second-class achievements in the absence of perennially powerful football or baseball teams.

Other information in the text, rather than clarifying these issues, simply adds details that seem not to relate to them and are puzzling in their own right. It is unclear why the singer is "dressed like a schoolboy, but [feels] like a clown," why he's making tips, how he's sweeping them up, what this has to do with Gatorade, why "Papa Hobo" has the wherewithal to "slip [him] a ride," how the weatherman lied, and why it makes a difference. In short, the song epitomizes Simon's inclination to make use of textual ideas that seem intriguing in their own right, regardless of the degree to which they can be synthesized into a coherent narrative or message. (And, indeed, in the case of popular songs, this lack of susceptibility to immediate comprehension may have been part of their appeal.)

Resistant though they may be to comprehensive interpretation, the images that Simon uses are relatively mundane. The harmonic structure of the song mirrors both halves of this situation in a striking way. The instrumental texture is dominated by Simon's acoustic guitar (with some body added by Knechtel's harmonium and a distinctive color, which connects to the folk "hobo" idea, provided by Charlie McCoy's bass harmonica). In the introduction the guitar sets forth the waltz meter with a simple boom-chick-chick texture on equally simple A and E chords, signaling a clear A-major tonality. And so the song begins, and the chords that it uses are usually either diatonic or ragtime-flavored secondary dominant chords. However, just as the text presents a series of simple images whose relationship to a larger picture is unclear, the tonality of the song slowly migrates around a circle of fifths. First it moves from A major to D major, which is followed in turn by G and C, and the song then ends in F major. This is quite unusual for a popular song. Occasionally two or even three keys will compete for precedence, and the key at the outset may not be the final key (as was the case with "Everything Put Together Falls Apart," although the way in which that song accomplishes this is also unusual). Nonetheless, a continuous evolution like this, especially one that does not follow a fixed pattern (such as a new key every verse) is very rare.

In addition to reflecting the meandering nature of the text's references, this process has the effect of setting up the next track, as the instrumental "Hobo's Blues" is in the key of F as well. This is a high-spirited duet between Simon and the veteran jazz violinist Stephane Grappelli, who initially achieved prominence in the middle of the century as a member of Django Reinhardt's legendary Quintet of the Hot Club of France, and compositional credit is given to both performers. In its 16-bar set of ragtime-flavored changes, major-minor seventh chords move by half steps and along circles of fifths.

After a four-bar introduction, the players go through the 16-bar sequence three times. Simon provides a rhythm-guitar accompaniment, against which Grappelli plays three varied melodies. One might speculate about the degree to which Grappelli's material was predetermined or improvised by the time of recording; in any event, it is likely that most or all of this material was created by Grappelli, while Simon may have been responsible for much or all of the harmonic basis of the track.

While the final member of the urban-angst set, "Paranoia Blues," is again a vocal piece, it also features a distinctive performer. Simon's singing here is complemented by a raw-sounding bottleneck guitar accompaniment played by Stefan Grossman, an expert on various folk-guitar styles. While drums and percussion provide a foreboding mood throughout, and a pair of horns fills out the chorus, Grossman's fills and harmonies constitute the prominent instrumental contribution. Furthermore, the sliding and arpeggiation of this style are echoed in the vocal line, in which many rapid skips convey the singer's distress.

The song includes three verses, with a single chorus following the second. Each verse is based on a 16-bar modification of a 12-bar blues progression—the first 8 bars proceed typically, with 4 on the tonic E chord, 2 on the sub-dominant A, and 2 back on tonic. However, rather than having a final four bars working their way from the dominant chord back to tonic, this song includes four extra measures of tonic and concludes with four that proceed A-E-F♯7-B7-E, so that the dominant B7 chord is finally used, but only briefly.

The chorus uses a slightly different pattern but resembles the verse in that most of it vacillates between subdominant and tonic harmonies with a quick A-B7-E cadence bringing closure and then repeating. These variations on blues progressions' moves among major chords are not particularly remarkable in themselves, but they do lend themselves to Grossman's technique, in which strings of the guitar to which the bottleneck or tube is applied, are tuned to a major chord (thus producing a major chord that is determined by the location along the strings at which the tube is placed). They also support the mood and pacing of the text well.

The text is purportedly inspired by an occasion on which Simon was detained by airport customs officials.[5] The second verse describes such an incident, while the first and third relate other hazards of life in New York City—betrayal by "so-called friends," and the disappearance of a meal at a Chinese restaurant, respectively. Each verse ends by demanding to know whose side the person that the singer is addressing is on. The chorus blames the city for the "Paranoia Blues," and echoes "Papa Hobo" in relating the singer's escape.

These ideas are reflected by the harmonic scheme, in that the singer's predicament as a victim is described at the beginning of verses and chorus, where the harmonies are similarly restricted, never able to move out of the tonic-subdominant oscillation. The more dynamic appearances of the dominant chord, in both verse and chorus, accompany points of decision, as the singer poses his question and describes his escape, respectively. Rather than using the four bars of tonic that are inserted into the verses to impart additional information, the singer takes this opportunity to moan "Oh, no, no" repeatedly. The third verse ends by repeating the "Whose side" question, and then the music almost stops, but the instruments resume with material from the chorus, suggesting that the "Paranoia Blues" remain to haunt the singer.

The final song on *Paul Simon*, "Congratulations," is a relatively straight-forward lament on romantic relationships. Cast in a soft, slow jazz style and accompanied by guitar, bass, drums, and keyboards, it follows a standard AABA form. In the first section, the title word is directed ironically at the singer's lover, who has apparently, in his view, caused extreme misery. The second section, perhaps somewhat improbably, builds on the notion of misery to describe people who seem to have lost their way in society and even the legal system. The bridge addresses the perils of love and its apparently inevitable destructive nature, and the final section pleads to know whether "a man and a woman" can "live together in peace."

This generally dismal perspective is supported by harmonies that methodically follow one another, often over bass lines that descend slowly by step. The melody in the A sections consists mostly of sighing descending phrases that roughly cover the territory between the high E and the A below it; these melodic shapes capture the text's sense of resignation. The bridge, as it makes assertions about love, turns things around with dotted rhythms that often skip upward, although the concluding phrases that return to the last A section also return to its melodic formula to tell the listener that "you won't stand a chance." After the last section ends, the music tails on behind it, cycling through chord patterns already presented and eventually moving to a conclusion with some rhythmic accelerations.

THERE GOES RHYMIN' SIMON

While writing his First Symphony, Johannes Brahms struggled mightily against the ghost of Beethoven, whose reputation as a composer of symphonies loomed large at that time over any aspirants such as Brahms. In these circumstances, the work took Brahms over 10 years to complete. By contrast, once this effort was brought to a conclusion, Brahms's Second Symphony came much more quickly and easily—a good deal of it, in fact, was written during a summer holiday. The tone of this composition is correspondingly different as well—whereas the First, in a minor key, is dark and intense, the Second is, in the words of many critics, full of the sunshine in which it was written.

Paul Simon had not struggled as much over his first fully produced solo studio album (*Paul Simon*) as Brahms had over his symphonic debut. But the contrast in tone between the first album and the second, *There Goes Rhymin' Simon* (1973), resembles that between Brahms's works. Although many of the songs on *Paul Simon* employ some leavening textual humor (and many use quite cheerful music), all of their texts include some fundamentally somber content, and for most the overall balance tips in this direction as well. (Apart from the high-spirited instrumental "Hobo's Blues," "Me and Julio" is probably the most light-hearted song, with "Armistice Day" or "Papa Hobo" running a distant second.) Indeed, the album has been complimented for the way it manifests an interest of Simon's, a dynamic contrast between the tone of the music and the tone of the text.[6]

On the other hand, the prevailing mood of *There Goes Rhymin' Simon* is decidedly positive. The most striking exception is "American Tune" with its *Weltschmerz*-laden outlook on America, and "Tenderness" and "Learn How to Fall" adopt rather jaundiced perspectives on love and life. Apart from these, though, "St. Judy's Comet" is an affectionate, playful lullaby for the singer's son, and "Something So Right" is a positive love song. The remaining five songs are all character pieces that, even if occasionally a bit cynical (as is the case with "Kodachrome"), seem clearly distanced from Simon's own persona.

Four of these songs, along with "St. Judy's Comet," resulted from a Simonesque collaboration, this time with members of the Muscle Shoals Rhythm Section. Simon initially worked with these musicians on "Take Me to the Mardi Gras," but the process went so well that the group went on to record the other four songs as well. "Kodachrome," probably the best-known of these, leads off the album.

As was the case with "I Am a Rock," the singer in "Kodachrome" projects a self-evidently untenable position, although, as had been the case with many of Simon's more recent songs, this position is not entirely clearly presented. The singer seems to acknowledge that his world is rather bleak, but rather than seeing it in realistic "black and white," he prefers to see it through the lens of his Nikon camera, and then translated into his private, full-color, "Kodachrome" version. The two verses describe two elements of his maturing years—his high school education and his dating life—neither of which was apparently very rewarding. The choruses extol the Kodachrome version, concluding with the plea, "So mama, don't take my Kodachrome away."

The musical mood is upbeat, with ample interest provided by the Muscle Shoals accompaniment, frequent skips in the melodic line, and occasional triple-meter bars thrown in. Both verse and chorus move forward harmonically in a decisive way—the majority of the chord progressions conform to principles of forward motion established in classical music, often moving through subdominant chords to dominant chords and then back to tonic, and sometimes using predictable patterns in which the roots of the chords move regularly by fifths (see Appendix for additional information about these norms). (The only exception is the motion from F♯ minor to A that, rather than seeming to move forward, conveys a sense of starting over as the coda repeats every four bars.) Finally, the key scheme supports the textual sense of the verse and chorus: the verses are in E, and the choruses are in A, which acts as a resolving tonic (with respect to which the verses' E acts like a dominant in need of resolution) and thus conveys the sense of security that the singer feels in his Kodachrome world.

For "Tenderness," Simon draws on another group of musicians, the black vocal group the Dixie Hummingbirds. Their rich, gospel-flavored background harmonies indelibly color the slow ballad, as the singer pleads with his lover to place a higher priority on tenderness than on the facts—truth, right and wrong, honesty. These sentiments are expressed in a straightforward AABA format, with each A section seeming to concede that she is correct about his faults, but asking for tenderness anyway, and the B section declaring that the two could work things out.

Much of the effect of the song results from its style and arrangement. The Hummingbirds' contributions are augmented by a standard instrumental ensemble of piano, bass, drums, and guitar, and the harmonies make good use of the singers by being colorful (with lots of sevenths and ninths) and interestingly varied. The tonal centers themselves are fairly clearly established, with C prevailing in the A sections (giving the Hummingbirds' bass the opportunity to finish on the very low C) and F♯ minor taking precedence in the B section (with perhaps some hints of its relative major, A).

During this B section, a big-band sound breaks out in the form of a blossoming horn arrangement. The net result is a foray into a slow jazz-gospel genre that Simon had not previously explored, and this kind of experimentation with genres in which he had not as yet recorded occurs several times on this album.

A good example is provided by the next song, "Take Me to the Mardi Gras." Simon and the Muscle Shoals musicians set a calypso tone in this easy-going rumination on life in New Orleans through the prevailing rhythms, Simon's vocal timbre, the syncopations in the melody, and the way that it is dominated by steps and repeated notes, with only occasional strategically placed skips.

The song is cast in an AABA form, and the A sections further convey the leisurely theme. The text urges the listener to take the singer to the Mardi Gras, and extols the freedoms that can be had there. The harmonic setting moves from the tonic A chord to the dominant E7 but then falls back through B minor to A, reversing the classically normative, forward-moving A-Bm-E7-A progression and thus reinforcing the sense of pleasant, leisurely motion.

To this consistent combination of musical and textual elements, Simon introduces three ingredients that, while not creating stark contrasts, add interesting dimensions. Two of these appear in the B section. It is sung not by Simon, but in falsetto voice by the Rev. Claude Jeter, a singer whose work had helped to inspire Simon to write "Bridge over Troubled Water."[7] Furthermore, the text in that section moves the idea of rest and leisure that the A sections advocate to a religious context, using Christian images of the afterlife such as laying one's burden down, resting one's head on "that shore," and wearing "that starry crown."

After the final A section returns to the New Orleans style of repose, an extended instrumental coda introduces the third addition. As the changes from the A section cycle repeatedly, an ascending trombone *glissando* ushers in a third collaborator, the Onward Brass Band. This group provides a full-blown Dixieland ride-out for the song, with the typical front-line instruments—clarinet, trumpet, and trombone—featured prominently.

"Something So Right," the love song that follows "Take Me to the Mardi Gras," is interesting in a number of respects. One of these is the availability of a previous version of the song, called "Let Me Live in Your City," that is essentially identical except for the chorus, which provides the title in each case. Even the two choruses are quite similar—much of the harmonic structure is the same, and the melodic content often only differs between the two songs about as much as sometimes occurs in other Simon songs from one verse to another in order to accommodate varying textual rhythms. These two versions, then, are much more closely related than are

"Wednesday Morning, 3 A.M." and "Somewhere They Can't Find Me" or "The Side of a Hill" and the "Canticle" component of "Scarborough Fair/ Canticle." (A recording of "Let Me Live in Your City" is included—identified as a "work-in-progress"—as a bonus track on the CD reissue of *There Goes Rhymin' Simon,* and the lead sheet music is included in the 2005 collection *The Definitive Paul Simon Songbook;* the two songs also differ, trivially, in that "Something So Right" is presented in the key of F while "Let Me Live in Your City" is in E.)

"Something So Right" uses a slightly more elaborate form than is the case with any of the other songs on this album except for "St. Judy's Comet." After an introduction, it proceeds verse-chorus-verse-chorus, but then a bridge appears before a final appearance of the chorus and an instrumental coda. The song also returns, to a degree, to the production values of the late Simon and Garfunkel days; while the beginning merely uses a somewhat full jazz-combo setup of two guitars, both electric and acoustic basses, drums, keyboard, piano, and vibes, the piece is later augmented by a string section arranged by Quincy Jones, and even some stray woodwinds toward the end.

The ballad comes across as being generally relaxed. It is tonally very stable, with verse and chorus solidly in F and a heavy emphasis on the relative minor key of D minor in the bridge (which has a text that is somewhat less relaxed than is that of the rest of the song). However, rather than being expressed principally by this stability, the leisurely tone is actually achieved more by harmonic, metric, and rhythmic irregularities that convey a sense of spontaneous freedom.

The verses are dominated by descending lines that tend to end on the tonic F note, supporting the singer's affirmation of his lover's ability to calm him down in the first verse and his acknowledgment of the difficulty of approaching him in the second. But the extent to which Simon varies these descents gives them both added interest and a sense of inevitability (because they can be heard to wind up in the same place even though they take different routes to get there).

In the chorus, when the singer explains that he "can't get used to something so right," a bit more steady motion helps to lend emphasis to his point. There is more upward motion and more reiteration of rhythmic patterns, and, although 2/4 and 4/4 meters mix freely, only one 3/4 measure is included, and it serves to help to punctuate the repetition of the concluding line. The bridge goes yet another step in this direction: it is briefer than the verse and chorus, it uses all diatonic chords until the turnaround to F at its conclusion, it uses 4/4 meter exclusively, and its melody presents a straightforward, parallel two-phrase structure. This regularity, along with the emphasis on the minor key, adds emphasis to its textual point that some people who have difficulty communicating their love still need to be told that they themselves are loved.

The regularity of this section, moving inexorably through the turnaround into the last chorus, sets up the culmination of the song. Here the strings reach their high point. The singer works through the last chorus, and then the instruments dwindle into a soft-jazz fadeout.

Simon returns to the Muscle Shoals group for the shuffle-blues number "One Man's Ceiling Is Another Man's Floor." It is begun and concluded with a distinctively foreboding sequence of downward-arpeggiated right-hand piano chords. These slowly work their way down the keyboard in the key of G minor before being punctuated by a brief left-hand riff. This intro and outro frame the main, vocal portion of the song, which is cast in an AABA form. Each of the first two sections discusses disruptions in an apartment house but concludes with a reference that admonishes the listener to remember the title phrase. The B section adds more sinister information, but the final A section, rather than adding more details, leads up to the refrain with an instrumental section featuring a bit of boogie-rock piano work.

The song's principal appeal lies on its surface with the catchy rhythms and timbres (Simon is joined not only by the instrumentalists, but also by some uncredited backup singers). But the words convey the ideas with a nice mix of directness and vivid images. Furthermore, Simon plays a tonal game that reflects the title.

The first A section turns the introduction's key of G minor into G major, and then moves to C, ending on an A-minor chord. The next section starts in C and moves the same distance, to F, ending on a D-minor chord. The B section digresses from the pattern by dwelling on D minor to underscore its sinister message, but the final A section picks up where the last left off, starting in F, moving to B♭, and ending on a G-minor chord, which then is continued in the outro.

The overall motion of the song, then, is reminiscent of that in "Papa Hobo." Each song moves among keys by a pattern of descending fifths— "Papa Hobo" using five major keys (A-D-G-C-F) and "One Man's Ceiling Is Another Man's Floor" using four (G-C-F-B♭). But the structure of "One Man's Ceiling" differs from that of "Papa Hobo" in two ways. First, rather than using a continuous evolution from key to key, the song employs a precise pattern in which each A section modulates in the same way from the ending key of the previous A section to the beginning key of the following A section, so that one section's ending is another section's beginning, just as "one man's ceiling is another man's floor." Furthermore, Simon embellishes this pattern with his use of minor chords in each key of arrival. This not only sets up the contrasting tone of the B section, but also provides an elegant means of returning to the framing sections' key of G minor.

This elaborate tonal architecture notwithstanding, "One Man's Ceiling Is Another Man's Floor" most obviously communicates on rather a light level. It has already been mentioned that the following song, "American Tune," is an exception to the predominantly positive tone of the album. More generally, though, this song simply operates on a more profound level than do the others. Although it has not received anything close to the amount of public attention given to "The Sound of Silence," "Bridge over Troubled Water," or "The

Boxer," anthems of the Simon and Garfunkel era, it belongs in their company and in fact was named Song of the Year by *Rolling Stone* magazine for 1973.

"American Tune" addresses the state of the nation in terms that are both discouraged and hopeful; Simon has said that it is a reaction against Richard Nixon.[8] It differs from most of his other work (and particularly the hugely popular songs just mentioned) in that it does not take American vernacular musical style as its point of departure. Instead, each A section of its AABA form is based on a chorale tune written by Hans Leo Hassler around the turn of the seventeenth century, and its harmonizations by J. S. Bach in the *St. Matthew Passion*. (One of these harmonizations appears in many American hymnals as "Oh Sacred Head, Now Wounded.")

In Simon's hands this music retains much of its original stateliness by virtue of the steady pace at which the harmonies change. Simon modifies the rhythm of the tune, mostly by repeating notes to accommodate extra syllables and adding syncopations. He occasionally varies the melody itself (most notably by rising to Es for emphasis where the original does not ascend so high) and harmonizes it in a way that differs slightly from any of the four that Bach uses (the music appears five times in the *Passion*, but two of these are harmonized identically, albeit in different keys). Toward the end of each section Simon adds some beats and increases the sense of conclusiveness by repeating the last line; whereas the original ends on E over the tonic C chord, Simon's version sets the E against an E chord, which leads through a diatonic circle of fifths (Am-Dm-(C/G)-G-C) as the last text line is repeated and ends on the tonic C note against the final C chord.

The overall structure of the chorale setting that Simon does retain serves his purposes well. Its four lines are rather simple, with a regular rhythmic pattern and a clear focus on the key of C major throughout, but each of the first three lines, after emphasizing a C chord halfway through, comes to a final cadence on an A minor or major chord. Only the last line (after an interior arrival on the dominant G harmony) concludes on the tonic C chord. Simon preserves this emphasis on A minor, and it supports the poignant tone of the text in the A sections.

In the first section, the singer describes his past failings and confusions and the hurt that he has suffered, but concludes that he's all right, merely understandably weary "so far away from home." The second section describes his acquaintances in similar terms, again adopting something of a philosophical attitude, but at the same time, apparently thinking that the direction they are traveling is a good one, "wonder[ing] what went wrong." The B section departs from the Bach material to describe a dream in which the singer dies and his soul rises and flies over him, "smil[ing] reassuringly" and watching the Statue of Liberty "sailing away to sea." The final A section returns to the theme of the first two, now placing the singer's uncertainties in the context of American exploration, ranging from the Mayflower to the moon. As he did when relating the earlier material, the singer indicates that one can't expect everything, but ends with a sense of his own fatigue.

Not surprisingly, the arrangement of "American Tune" supports its arc of textual development. The first section is heavily dominated by guitar and bass, with filling harmonies (perhaps from keyboard or strings) in the background. The bass occasionally steps in eighth notes in a way that mimics the original, typically pensive baroque chorale setting. The second section is set in essentially the same way, except that drums are added, creating textural expansion that supports the singer's expanded scope as he considers his fellow travelers. However, cymbals at the beginning of the B section signal its motion to a new textual plane, and this is then abundantly supported by a full orchestral string setting and some electric guitar work. This treatment recedes at the beginning of the last A section, leaving some more isolated orchestral touches, but the strings swell as the section proceeds, and they dominate the brief coda.

"Was a Sunny Day" returns to the transparent approach to production, limiting its obvious studio manipulation to some guitar overdubbing. For the choruses of this song Simon engages the assistance of yet another distinctive, but not widely popular, act, the folk-style singers Maggie and Terre Roche. They join him, Airto Moreira playing percussion, and Bob Cranshaw on bass to render a calypso tune that is pure whimsy. As the harmonies bounce around in the key of G major, the melody is typically syncopated, with occasional skips and downward-trailing phrase endings.

The song proceeds chorus-verse-chorus-verse-chorus. The first two choruses, led off by the title line and accompanied by acoustic guitar, bass, and percussion, proclaim the total lack of negative circumstances. The verses are both sung by Simon alone, add a low-key electric-guitar part, and introduce two lovers. First their status in life is described—he is a sailor in Newport News and she is "a high-school queen with nothing really left to lose"—and then their names are given—hers is "Lorelei," and his, obviously echoing the well-known 1955 song by the Cadillacs, "Mr. Earl," although she calls him "Speedoo." We learn nothing more about the story; the electric guitar lingers into the third chorus and then comes to the forefront in the lengthy coda.

Simon returns to the AABA form in "Learn How to Fall," combining it with a recurring riff to create an opposition of moods that shapes the song. The song begins with this riff, played three times as an introduction. It features a guitar arpeggiating a series of three chords—Bm-A-E in the key of E—that set a driving rock tone with their instrumentation (guitars, bass, and drums are prominent), a dominant-subdominant-tonic progression typical of blues-rock, and a modal flavor created by the use of a B minor, rather than major, chord (with the decisive D♮ leading to E exposed at the top of the guitar's line).

When the voice begins the first A section, the mood changes abruptly to a softer jazz sound. The music still moves forward decisively, but its gently funky tone supports that of the lyrics, which encourage the listener to learn how to fall before she learns to fly. At first the bass jauntily walks up from E to a bright subdominant A chord. Then the almost carefree tone is maintained as the harmonies work their way around a circle of fifths—G#m-C#9-F#7-B9-E7—but vary the specific quality of each chord as well as the length of time it occupies (even to the point of assigning C#9 to a half-length measure). When the E7 chord is reached, the bass starts its ascent again, but this time instead of reaching A, it "falls" back to F#, over which F#7 and F#m7 chords prepare to fall further down to E to conclude the section.

At this point the riff returns as an interlude, now played four times and prominently adding a pulsing organ line. The second A section echoes the music and theme of the first, but now with a sailing metaphor emphasized, and the organ remaining in the background. When it is followed by the interlude, an electric-guitar line is added to the pulsing organ. The three-chord pattern only appears twice in this interlude but then continues into the B section, in which Simon sings against six more iterations, fleshed out now with a horn section. Here the harder mood supports the text as it generalizes about the human tendency to strive for glory without thinking through the consequences.

After Simon finishes singing, the instrumental version of the interlude returns, now with a different electric-guitar line. The final A section returns to the gentle tone with the general musical sound of the first one, and mostly to the falling-flying theme as well (with the addition of a reference to "the tank towns"). The riff returns one last time and repeats to a fadeout, with the horns returning as it approaches inaudibility.

The importance of contrasting moods in "Learn How to Fall" is not replicated in "St. Judy's Comet." This lullaby is set in a low-key jazz style throughout. While the overall mood is quite mellow, the rhythms of the voice and instruments provide plenty of forward motion. The homogeneous mood makes sense for a lullaby, and Simon builds on it by mixing various kinds of harmonic and formal repetition with subtle variations.

After an introductory vamp that is spiced with atmospheric guitar effects, the first verse tells the boy that it's time to go to sleep. The same changes, and a similar melody, then invite the boy to see "St. Judy's Comet" in his sleep so that the singer can see it "sparkle in [his] eyes when [he] awake[s]." A third section introduces different music as the boy is once again entreated to lie down and close his eyes.

After a couple of measures of guitar effects, this entire pattern is repeated: the second verse expresses the singer's determination to succeed in singing the boy to sleep because if he can't, "it makes your famous daddy look so dumb," and then the second and third sections reappear. Finally, the first verse returns, and more guitar music goes to fadeout.

The overall formal structure is thus A (verse 1)-A ("St. Judy's Comet")-B-A (verse 2)-A ("St. Judy's Comet")-B-A (verse 1). The net effect is that the A material is used a great deal throughout the song. This material has an interesting arch-shaped harmonic structure. Three measures on a tonic E9 chord are relieved by a single measure of Amaj7. The harmonic rhythm—the pace at which chords change—continues to accelerate, with two chords occupying the next measure, and four the following one, before a measure of an A major chord leads back to the E9 chord again. Although the multiple appearances of this pattern are relieved a bit by some varied melodies, the melodies are always restricted to the territory between E and the B above it, with occasional C♯s neighboring the B. Furthermore, the melodic phrases tend to descend from the B to the E, conveying a recurring sense of resolution to the boy.

The B section introduces some new elements but relates in interesting ways to the A sections' structure. It opens up the melodic space to the E above the B, although descents, eventually all the way back to the lower E, continue to urge the boy to settle down himself. Its first seven measures also use harmonies from the A section, but they are refreshed by being placed in different positions within four-measure groupings, in each case changing between strong odd measures and weak even ones. The Amaj7 chord is now on the first measures of two groups, rather than the last of a group as it was in the A sections; an Am6-E/G♯ pair is on second measures rather than first; and the arrival on E9 comes on third measures rather than fourth.

"Loves Me Like a Rock," the final song on the album, is probably the second-best-known (behind the opening "Kodachrome"). As is the case with several of the other tracks, this song has plenty of appeal on its surface. The easily digested gospel-rock style with a shuffle beat; the straightforward verse-refrain structure; the fresh, but still familiar, call-and-response patterns; and the vocal work of Simon's collaborators (the Dixie Hummingbirds again) are all attractive elements that work together toward this end.

After the song is set up by a rich Hummingbird-hummed chord and the establishment of the shuffle beat by the instruments, Simon launches into the first of four verse-chorus pairs. In each of these, the verses use the call-and-response pattern, with the Hummingbirds echoing Simon's lines. On the choruses, the Hummingbirds harmonize along with Simon.

Musically, the three verses and choruses are very similar, with only minor melodic variation among them. In the first verse the singer tells about resisting the devil as a little boy; in the second he describes the same situation occurring when he was a grown man; and in the third he says that if he were the president he would similarly resist Congress. Each chorus claims that his mama loves him like a rock, presumably because of his virtue.

The song is shot through with gospel elements, from the use of the backup singers who confirm the lead singer's comments, to the overtly religious descriptions of resisting temptation, to the repositioned use of the phrase "rock of ages." (The degree to which it is repositioned—shifted from its original reference to Jesus Christ—depends on whether it refers to the singer or to his mama in the phrase "she rocks me like the rock of ages.") Each verse concentrates on tonic chords, relieved by motion to subdominant C and C7 harmonies, while the melody concentrates on chord tones. The choruses are a bit more adventurous, moving at least every measure among diatonic G, D, Em, and C chords, and even neighboring the C chord with an F harmony, before settling down to the G chord as the chorus concludes. After the third chorus, an extended emphasis on the G harmony, as the text "she love me" is repeated, allows the singers to continue improvising as the song and the album fade to an end.

STILL CRAZY AFTER ALL THESE YEARS

Simon's next album, *Still Crazy after All These Years,* was released in 1975, two years after the release of *There Goes Rhymin' Simon.* It was notable in a number of ways. It received widespread critical and popular acclaim and won the Grammy award. It includes a number of very rarely heard songs, such as "Night Game" and "Silent Eyes" (although some of the music for the latter was featured as background music in the movie *Shampoo*), but also five that received a great deal of airplay: the title track, "50 Ways to Leave Your Lover," "My Little Town," "Gone at Last," and "Have a Good Time." Furthermore, one of these songs, "My Little Town," was the first studio duet with Garfunkel to be released since *Bridge over Troubled Water* (this song was also included on Garfunkel's solo album *Breakaway,* released in the same year).

During the creation of the album, Simon continued and apparently intensified his study of music theory; this is reflected by a comment in the liner notes that reads, "I would like to express my gratitude to both Chuck Israels and David Sorin Collyer who helped me greatly with my music this past year." This study no doubt affected the writing of the individual songs, and it may have also affected some aspects of the structure of the album as a whole, that is, the ways that various songs related to one another.

Some of these kinds of relationships have already been noted between pairs of consecutive songs, for example, those between "Anji" and "Somewhere They Can't Find Me"; "The 59th Street Bridge Song" and "The Dangling Conversation"; and "Papa Hobo" and "Hobo's Blues." The first two of these involve the sharing of a musical structure, and the third involves a process of modulation through the first song that brings it to the key of the second. A larger, and commonly acknowledged, pattern governs the first side of the *Bookends* record album (LP); here the development of a textual theme, that of different stages of life, ties the songs together.

On a more general level, it is known that Simon developed a concern for the sequence of songs on an album with respect to musical characteristics beyond, say, a simple desire to provide contrast in mood. For example, in a 1990 *SongTalk* interview with Paul Zollo (conducted during the production of *The Rhythm of the Saints*), he discussed such issues as key relationships, tempo, overall length of songs, and length of time between songs, even describing beginning the composition process of a song with the key, tempo, and duration it needed to fit between two others that had already been written.[9]

The music theorist Peter Kaminsky has examined relationships among songs throughout *Still Crazy after All These Years* and has concluded that they are such as to make the entire album constitute a song cycle, rather than a mere collection of songs.[10] In order for this to be the case, the songs would need in some ways to refer to one another—for example, cooperating in presenting some narrative; cooperating in completing some musical process; sharing musical or textual ideas, and so on. In this case, for example, Kaminsky identifies the way that several of the songs on each side correspond to different stages of the singer's life and romantic relationships, respectively, and the way that each side emphasizes a particular style (harmonically complex jazz ballad and harmonically simple rock/gospel/blues, respectively) and closes with a "non-narrative" song.[11] He also shows how a circle-of-fifths E-A-D-G pattern in the introduction of "Still Crazy after All These Years" at the beginning of side 1 is echoed in the other songs on the side.[12] Side 2 then starts in C, the next fifth down, on "Gone at Last," proceeds down by step through B♭ and A to G♯ at the beginning of "Silent Eyes," the last song, and then works back up through A and B♭ to end on C.[13] Kaminsky concludes by comparing the album to two well-known nineteenth-century song cycles, Robert Schumann's *Dichterliebe* and Gustav Mahler's *Lieder eines fahrenden Gesellen,* and suggesting some similarities in the ways that the various works create coherence.[14]

"Still Crazy after All These Years" does indeed set the jazz tone for side 1. The foundation for its accompaniment is provided by an electric piano, the harmonic structure includes some fairly complex chords and progressions, and a saxophone solo is featured in a central interlude. In addition, the vocal line includes some jazz-like characteristics: at some points it swoops quickly up or down, and at others it comes out in sporadic bursts.

The song is cast in AABA form, as has been seen in many other Simon compositions. In the first A section the singer describes himself as antisocial and not very romantic, and in the B section he expresses feelings of disillusionment—while he's "longing [his] life away," he nevertheless feels that "it's all gonna fade" anyway. (Simon has said that the song is in some ways actually about himself.[15]) The final section hints that his frustration might result in violence, but that this would be excusable; this thought concludes, as do those of the other A sections, with the title line.

This textual progression is carried along, as Kaminsky has noted, by an avoidance of solid conclusions at the end of sections.[16] This device has the effect of repeatedly indicating that there is more to the story, and this sense is supported and embellished by the instrumental arrangement. First, the electric piano plays a brief introduction that melodically foreshadows the B section, and then the first A section's rather lighthearted anecdote is accompanied by just the electric piano and a subtle cymbal. The title line is sung twice at the end of each A section; here it first comes to rest on the tonic G note against a normal deceptive cadence on an E-minor chord.

This arrival heightens expectation that the second utterance of the title line will be accompanied by a tonic G chord, but instead it uses an unusually placed minor subdominant, C minor, and only after the vocal line ends do the harmonies move to tonic. As Kaminsky has pointed out, this minor arrival undercuts the positive, carefree kind of "crazy"ness claimed by the singer at this point.[17] It is just at the C minor chord that the bass enters, along with a string line, further indicating a deeper level of discourse than might at first have been imagined.

The strings drop out as the second A section begins, but the bass remains, pushing forward and thus implying that the listener's knowledge will similarly advance. This section again comes first to a G over E minor, but this time the second concluding line reaches a very unusually placed F/G harmony. This never resolves to tonic but instead lifts into the tonal meanderings of the B section. The harmonic contrast here is underscored by a swelling of strings and occasional winds.

Following the singer's conclusion that "it's all gonna fade," the music appropriately dissolves into an instrumental interlude, featuring strings and winds, that becomes progressively fragmented and rhythmically angular. This in turn resolves into a fairly standard, but attractive, saxophone solo (played by Michael Brecker) that is at first somewhat yearning, and eventually increasingly assured—thus leading naturally to the stable appearance of the final A section, but perhaps somewhat curious in the context of the overall textual motion toward discontent.

The final A section returns to the key of G and the electric-piano-bass-percussion trio accompaniment. Midway through, however, the music modulates up to A major, giving a faint sense of slightly demented triumph to the singer's declaration that he wouldn't be held responsible for his potential mayhem.[18] The orchestra reenters here as well. Once again, the first concluding line ends on a deceptive cadence (now on the new tonic note A over an F♯ minor chord), but this time the second one, although extended, does finally conclude on a tonic note *and* chord, as the strings drop out for the very last utterance of the title line.

The band for each of the first two songs on *Still Crazy after All These Years* is mainly drawn from the Muscle Shoals Rhythm Section, the group that had set the tone for much of *There Goes Rhymin' Simon*. This might seem counterintuitive, because while the songs they accompanied on the earlier album—"Kodachrome," "Take Me to the Mardi Gras," "One Man's Ceiling Is Another Man's Floor," "St. Judy's Comet," and "Loves Me Like a Rock"—tend to be relatively lighthearted, each of these two songs has a bit more of a serious tone (as does *Still Crazy after All These Years* as a whole). The frustration and disillusionment of the singer of the title track has already been described; "My Little Town" has a slightly different flavor.

Simon has said that he initially intended for the song to be a solo piece for Garfunkel, and that he designed it as a nasty antidote to the sweet songs that Garfunkel tended to favor.[19] "My Little Town" includes many devices—starting with the title—that signal a sentimental, nostalgic depiction of the singer's hometown, but this image is systematically undercut by a regular succession of blunt condemnations. The negative side of this combination is initiated immediately with an ominous bass-note piano introduction that emphasizes C# shortly after E, so as to imply a minor harmony. The first verse then begins with major chords; gentle, lyrical singing; and a mellow accompaniment supplied by piano, strummed guitar, bass, and drums.

While the song has a simple basic structure—verse-chorus-verse-chorus—it navigates between the sweet and sour with a variety of textual ingredients, harmonic and metrical manipulations, and stylistic references. After the first few sweet bars describe the singer's simple childhood faith, a left turn is signaled by an abrupt emphasis on F and C chords (after an opening focus on sharp-related harmonies) and an octave leap in the melody; this underscores the first cynical line of text, in which God leans upon the singer as he "pledge[s] allegiance to the wall."

As the singer continues to reminisce, the conversational nature of his thoughts is conveyed by irregular rhythms and meters (which make the lines sound relatively more like spontaneously delivered comments and relatively less like evenly measured song). A hint of bleakness arrives with a reference to the "factories," and then is confirmed when the singer's mother hangs the laundry "in the dirty breeze." The musical arrangement here continues to be sweet, with typical Simon and Garfunkel vocal harmonies, treating the cynicism ironically as the text goes on to describe the colors in the rainbow as being black because they lack imagination. This borrows an idea (but little more), from an image in lines by Ted Hughes that are quoted epigrammatically in the liner notes. Simon also syncopates the word "back" prominently, so as to emphasize its rhyme with "black" and "lack," adding to the ironic approach with a hint of poetic whimsy.

At this point the singing gives way to an instrumental interlude that seems more than anything to be pleasantly marking time—perhaps this is intended as an insertion of banality—before the chorus delivers a fully orchestrated, unequivocal verdict that the little town contains "nothing but the dead and dying," on each repetition starting on a bright D major harmony but ending on B minor.

The second verse is much briefer than the first and moves more quickly to the negative side. The singer was meaningless; he saved and dreamed of the future, but his eagerness is ultimately described in terms of latent violence. This time, the verse leads straight to the chorus, which is repeated several times, with the same major-to-minor path it traversed on its first appearance, until it fades out.

"I Do It for Your Love" is similar to the first two songs on the album in that it combines elements that convey positive ideas with a negative undertone. In this case, though, the latter is poignant and resigned rather than alienated or "nasty," as was the case with "Still Crazy after All These Years" and "My Little Town," respectively. Simon has said that "I Do It for Your Love" is about his marriage to Peggy Harper; it combines compelling musical devices with wistful lyrics.

The song takes an AABA form as its point of departure but elaborates on this slightly by making the last A section instrumental, and then returning to the B section before ending with a texted A: AABA(inst)BA [with "A(inst)" indicating the instrumental A section]. Each A section concludes with the title line, which thus acts as a refrain throughout the song's description of a couple's wedding, the early months of their marriage, and their differences. While it may have been inspired by, and capture some of the essence of, Simon's marriage, the song includes details that indicate a young couple of more typically modest means. The actual wedding is described in the first A section in rather bleak terms—the rainy day made the sky yellow and the grass gray, and the terse description of completing paperwork and driving away suggests a justice-of-the-peace situation rather than a more elaborate celebration—and the second A section goes on to describe the couple persevering through a winter-long shared cold in an old, musty apartment or house.

Throughout all of the texted portions of the song, the accompanying ensemble remains roughly the same—guitars, bass, drums, electric piano, and percussion combine with occasional string touches to create an attractive mellow jazz-flavored backdrop to Simon's gentle singing. In these first two sections, the key of G major is implied, but the tonic G chord is never reached. At the end of the first section, an A♯ diminished 7 chord resolves to Am7; when this in turn moves to D9, the D9 sounds like a dominant chord at a half cadence, suggesting that the next section may conclude on a G chord. The second section follows the same harmonic sequence, but this time Simon takes advantage of the symmetrical structure of the A♯ chord (perhaps as a result of his music theory study); as this passage shows, such a diminished seventh chord can be resolved in similar ways to widely diverging keys. In this case, rather than going through Am7 and D9 to reach the expected G major chord, the song goes through E♭7 and A♭ to the far distant key of D♭ minor to begin the B section.

Here the singer relates another poignant anecdote: he purchased an old rug in order to please his wife, but the colors ran before he could get it home. This leads back to the A section, in which the original chord changes are used, but they now serve as a backdrop for an instrumental solo by the accordionist Sivuca. The effect is a hint of a carnival flavor, underscoring the sense of whimsy often associated with the marriages of young couples who have little besides each other.

This A section concludes, as did the second, with the pivot to D♭ so as to lead into the B section. After an essentially verbatim recapitulation of this material, the final, texted A section appears. At this point the balance between good intentions and disaffection tips in favor of the latter, as the spouses' differences are elegantly assessed as "the sting of reason, the splash of tears / the Northern and the Southern hemispheres," leading gracefully to a rhyme as love "disappears." These developments cast the singer's recitation of the title line in a clearly ironic light; the irony is further emphasized by an extension in which the line is repeated while the harmonies push past the D9 chord that concluded the first section, at last reaching resolution on the tonic G harmony at the point of the relationship's dissolution.

Some of the text in "50 Ways to Leave Your Lover" originated in a name-rhyming game that Simon played with his young son Harper.[20] In this song, the idea is placed in the context of an adult situation, as a female confidante (who, as the song develops, clearly demonstrates the potential for filling a less disinterested role) encourages the singer to leave his lover. The song received a lot of airplay, and has one of the best-known drum hooks in the history of popular music (played by Steve Gadd, who became a frequent Simon collaborator), but beyond the slight slyness with which the confidante's ulterior motives are reflected, the song does not strive for much subtlety, ultimately retaining a large measure of the surface-level whimsy of its source.

The two verses are cast in E minor and use jazz harmonic progressions against a steady, marching meter that is set up by the opening drum riff. Each verse includes two essentially identical halves; the first of these concludes with a reference to the 50 ways, and the second concludes with this reference stated twice. In the first verse, the confidante is quoted as encouraging the singer to take advantage of these options. Then the chorus kicks in with a light rock style to recite some of the ways, each of which rhymes with a man's name. The key here is E minor's relative major, G; each chord lasts longer than was the case in the verses, and the chords relate to one another much more simply; and Simon is joined here by a trio of female singers.

The chorus is repeated once; this choice, as is the case with the near-repetition of musical material in the verse, serves to emphasize the simplicity of the song. In the second verse, the confidante expresses her desire to make the singer happy, and he requests another explanation of the 50 ways. Instead of providing this, though, she suggests that if they both sleep on it, he'll see things her way, punctuating this prediction with a kiss that helps him to believe that she may be right. The chorus then follows, once again with a repetition, and the drum lick leads the song to a fadeout.

As was mentioned earlier, the last song on side 1 of *Still Crazy after All These Years*, "Night Game," is not very well known. Kaminsky points out that this song and "Silent Eyes," the concluding song of side 2, were the only two songs that Simon did *not* perform while touring to promote the album, and he further observes that these songs are two of the three "non-narrative" songs on the album, and they are the only songs that are not fundamentally in the first person, thus supporting the idea that they fill specialized roles in the structure of the album at the ends of the respective sides.[21]

The entire song is accompanied simply by bass and Simon's gently picked electric guitar. It employs a slightly varied AABA form—each A differs at the end from the others, and the entire form is followed by an instrumental interlude and then a recapitulation of the last A section. The song is also characterized by a distinctive feature: most of its two-measure text phrases start with single 6/8 measures before reverting to the overall 4/4.

This regular alternation, shaped further by a small arch-shaped melodic motion, followed by a pause, for each phrase in the opening A sections, gives the song a resigned character that is appropriate to the text. The first two A sections tell matter-of-factly of a baseball game that is nearing its end (with "two men down...in the bottom of the eighth") when the pitcher dies. This account is accompanied by harmonies that stay close to the home key of D major. The B section broadens the sense of foreboding, describing the cold night and moon, the stars' bone-like whiteness, and the great age of the stadium, as angular melodies lead the music through emphases on various keys.

The final A section uses chord changes based on those in the earlier ones, but the melody now traces a different path. Instead of following a small arch in each phrase, it describes a larger, higher-reaching arch throughout the entire section in order to bring the story to a conclusion with "three men down" at the end of a lost season and the beginning of a desolate winter. The instrumental solo that follows is played by harmonica virtuoso Toots Thielemans, and is unusual in that, rather than using chord changes from one or more complete sections, it uses the chords from the second half of the second A section and then all those from the B section. The final A section, with its season-ending text, and a brief coda then conclude the song.

The despondent tone of "Night Game" is immediately relieved by the opening song of side 2. "Gone at Last," the straightforward gospel-flavored duet with Phoebe Snow, maintains its exuberant musical mood throughout. (Snow also appears, less prominently, as one of the singers on the chorus of "50 Ways to Leave Your Lover.") The lyrics of "Gone at Last" pose a problem in the first verse—the singer is enduring perilous times and has seen plenty of difficulties. But the main textual theme is his hope, expressed at the end of each verse and reiterated in each chorus, that his long string of bad luck is "gone at last."

The entire song is propelled by piano, bass, drums, and percussion, and the Jessy Dixon Singers provide backup. As Simon and Snow alternate singing duties, a simple plot unfolds around the male and female characters they portray. After Simon's first verse leads into the chorus, Snow sings the second verse, first observing "that boy" with sympathy, and then describing her own streak of bad luck. Simon and Snow share the third verse—Simon singing the first half and Snow the second—and they describe how the singers' relationship has given them new hope.

The song's rather simple textual premise is matched by its musical structure. Each verse is composed of two halves that are essentially identical musically, notwithstanding small melodic variations. Each ultimately traces the same path through the three basic chords of the key, first decorating the tonic C chord with the subdominant F, and then raising the level of tension with the dominant G7 harmony at the end. The chorus then more or less duplicates the second half of the verse.

The song's outstanding attribute, then, is not lyrical or music-structural subtlety, but rather a well-coordinated combination of attractive, listenable elements. Richard Tee's almost frenetic piano playing, along with the driving bass, generates a considerable level of excitement that is enhanced by the rather high range of the melody and the short bursts in which it emerges. (To be more precise, the melody is in Simon's high range, but Snow sings it at the same pitch level, with the result that she creates her own kind of *low-range* excitement.) The mixture of singers, and their natural proclivity for the gospel style (with the focus of its elation transposed here from spiritual to romantic salvation), further contribute to the mix of this well-executed, radio-friendly pop song.

As Kaminsky notes, " 'Some Folks' Lives Roll Easy,' an odd mixture of pop ballad (replete with lush strings), country ballad and jazz progression...looks back to Part I [as he has identified side 1] in its slow groove, chromatic complexity, and introspective mood."[22] The form of the song is superficially like that of "I Do It for Your Love"; two similar sections are followed by a contrasting section and an instrumental passage based on the first to create an AABA form, and then the contrasting section returns, followed by a concluding, texted A section: AABA(inst)BA. In the first section the singer describes the fortunate people of the title, but in the second, he comments that "most folks' lives" are not fulfilled. In the B section he calls on the Lord for help, in an unusually direct reference to such a divine relationship, and reveals that he includes himself in the second group. In the final section, he again describes the two categories of people.

Two elements of the song, though, make it somewhat unsettled. First, the status of the relationship with the Lord is somewhat uncertain. The singer confesses that he has no right to seek the Lord's aid, but at the same time the singer reminds God that God had promised he could be trusted in a time of need; ultimately, though, it seems that the singer has little confidence in this regard.

Second, the tonal structure of the song is a bit unusual. It is in the key of E major, but all of the A sections except the last one end with a strong emphasis on the key of A. This not only is an unusual role for the subdominant key to play, but also changes the character of the fundamental AABA form significantly. When neither of the A sections that precedes a B section ends with a strong conclusion on the tonic chord of the original key, the B section tends to take on more weight. Rather than seeming like a departure after a stable moment, it seems a bit more like a significant location in the midst of a journey (although in this instance, the harmonies of the B section itself are still typically mobile). This enhanced status, in turn, makes the text addressing the Lord seem less parenthetical than might otherwise be the case.

More straightforward is "Have a Good Time," by virtue of both its simple verse-chorus form and its consistent funky blues sound. Accompaniment is provided throughout by bass, drums, percussion, electric piano, and guitars, with a prominent slide guitar complementing Simon's vocal line. The funky quality of the verse is enhanced by one unusual metrical feature, as a regular alternation between 4/4 and 3/4 time kicks each line forward.

The lyrics have a familiarly Simonesque sensibility. With more than a hint of satire, the singer tells how he is having a good time despite many reasons he might have to fret. In the first verse, he says that his life is a mess, and that he's "exhausted from loving so well"; in the second he dismisses anxieties felt by people in the "heartland"; and in the third, the scope becomes even larger, as he advocates American materialism as over against the possibility that there is a dire "fate of mankind." Each chorus follows its verse by reiterating the title line.

The harmonic structure of each verse resembles the simple scheme seen in "Gone at Last," with similar halves that emphasize first the subdominant chord and then the dominant; the chorus is similarly uncomplicated. As was the case with that song, then, the premise of this one is fairly simple, and much of its appeal lies in its combination of this solid premise and skillful arranging. The saucy slide guitar catches the ear, and additional touches develop as the song progresses. A female background singer (Valerie Simpson, also heard earlier on "50 Ways to Leave Your Lover") echoes Simon in the first chorus, a horn section punches up the second half of the second verse and its chorus, and the two elements alternate and ultimately combine in the third. Finally, at the end of the song, a frenetic saxophone solo bursts out of nowhere, proceeding unaccompanied for quite some time, and thus underscoring the sense of irrationality that has permeated the singer's discourse.

This use of an instrumental passage to reinforce the subtext of a song was also seen in "My Little Town," and it is evident as well in "You're Kind," which follows "Have a Good Time" on the album. The text of this wry little ditty is cast in an AABA form. The first two A sections tell the singer's lover how kind and good she has been to him, improving his perspective on life and his social life significantly. The B section wonders at her treatment of him but then expands the singer's difficulty in absorbing her involvement in his life to a sense of agitation at the prospect of her permanent presence. This leads into the final A section, in which he tells her "goodbye" because he perceives that their incompatibility makes a long-term arrangement impossible.

The speed with which this relationship progresses from gratitude to dissolution conveys the notion that it is merely a token of the way things go, as opposed to dwelling on the poignancy of the situation. Several other elements reinforce this outlook, sometimes bordering on whimsy. One of these is in the realm of word choices—she improves his social life by "introduc[ing] him] to [her] neighborhood," a rather childlike way of conceptualizing social situations; she is compared to other "humans," not "people" (tending to move the singer toward a position of clinical observer, rather than one of active participant); and incompatibility is illustrated by the throwaway cliché of window-opening sleeping preferences.

The harmonic language supports a casual tone by being fundamentally simple, based on three chords within the key. A sense of whimsy is contributed by the addition of some superficial flavorings, including some added sevenths, ninths, and thirteenths, and a ♭VII chord—that is, a major chord that departs from the major key by being built on the lowered seventh scale step, A♮ rather than A♯ in the key of B. The entire second half of the AABA form is moved up a step to B major from the opening key of A, and it is followed by a passage of wordless, yodel-like vocalizations, a brief instrumental interjection, and a reprise of the final A section.

No less significant than these factors, however, is the larger context in which Simon places the song. The texted portion that has been described is preceded by a lengthy introduction consisting of an entire 12-bar blues form. This sets the tone for the whole song with its four-to-the-bar, repetitive bass pattern, its swing feel, and its mellow, rather than aggressive, electric-guitar lead line. These ingredients continue through the sung portion that has been described and are joined by a horn section that becomes fully present—but still in a low-key way—when the B section arrives. Finally, after the A section reprise, the music continues with another lengthy instrumental section, now with the horns in the foreground, that saunters along in a slightly different 12-bar pattern that nonetheless clearly presents a complete musical structure in itself. Upon arriving at the concluding tonic B chord, the music immediately walks up to the E that started the unit and begins again. The fadeout that ends the song leaves the impression that the music continues in this matter-of-fact way forever (even if we don't happen to be able to hear it) and thus reinforces the idea that the situation described by the text is simply a normal happenstance in the midst of everyday life.

The final song on *Still Crazy after All These Years,* "Silent Eyes," contrasts sharply with those that preceded it. The text describes the eyes of God watching Jerusalem, with an implied sense of judgment, as Jerusalem mourns and "we shall all be called as witnesses...to...speak what was done." The musical setting is ponderous and episodic, built around the slow flourishes of a piano with bass and drums throughout, and augmented by choral interjections. One might find it surprising that this rather distinctive texture is used, given the fact that much of the musical material was originally used in a minimalistic way, produced by just guitar and humming, in the soundtrack for the Warren Beatty movie *Shampoo.* However, this may seem less unusual if one recalls that "Bridge over Troubled Water," which now seems inextricably tied to its piano accompaniment, was originally written on guitar.

Peter Kaminsky argues that this very different song fits into his song-cycle interpretation of *Still Crazy after All These Years* by serving as an epilogue (a role similar to that played by "Night Game" with respect to side 1). He connects its text to the preceding songs with the notion that themes of hope and possible redemption address the singer's damaged situation after the various failed relationships that he has described.[23] (This is a conceptual premise that will be more explicitly explored within a single song, 10 years later, in "Graceland.") Kaminsky also feels that "Silent Eyes" sums things up by being "the only song [on the album] that truly combines harmonically complex and simple idioms," and by tracing a pattern from G♯ through A and B♭ to C, thereby bringing closure to the process traced by the earlier narrative songs on side 2, which began in the keys of C, B♭, and A, respectively. He buttresses this last point by noting that the *Shampoo* soundtrack version ends in F minor, but this version's ending brings it to the key of C that is necessary to complete the process he is describing.[24]

The song consists of two large sections with parallel beginnings—the first in G♯ minor and the second in A minor. The singer begins the first section by describing the eyes watching Jerusalem, to the accompaniment of a series of often-complex harmonies. He then sings a second passage that begins in a similar way but goes on to describe Jerusalem's sorrow and the way she calls him. At this point simpler harmonies are introduced, and the choir enters with comforting, wordless phrases, coming to rest in a warm A major.

The key darkens to A minor for the beginning of the second section. The music initially duplicates that of the first section (in the new key) but introduces new ideas (maintaining about the same level of harmonic complexity) to discuss the calling of witnesses. This passage concludes in F minor, and there then follows a coda shared by choir and instruments. Kaminsky interprets this as effecting the ultimate move to C, thus completing the pattern, and also delivering a final, negative verdict to the singer by ending in minor rather than major.[25] First the piano plays a four-measure phrase twice over an F-minor harmony, and then the choir enters for 12 measures that brighten to F major. The instruments respond with an alternation of D-minor and A-minor chords, which the choir echoes but brightens with C-G-C. But the choir then adds one more harmony, G minor rather than G major, and the instruments continue by alternating C minor and G minor chords, joined once again by the choir as they come to rest on a final C minor to close the album.

New Directions

Simon is not known as a particularly fast songwriter. Nonetheless, over the years leading up to *Still Crazy after All These Years,* he had produced a steady stream of work. When it was released in 1975, the album was the seventh full studio album that he had written since *Wednesday Morning, 3 A.M.* appeared in 1964. He became interested in writing for some genre other than a standard album—specifically, he wanted to explore the possibility of writing songs that would support the narrative structure of a movie, and he wanted to write the movie as well.

The result of this work was to be *One-Trick Pony,* a film about a B-level rock musician who is well into his thirties and has to come to terms with his career aspirations. But before Simon could pursue this endeavor single-mindedly, he had an obligation to fulfill: his contract with Columbia called for one more album. Apparently unenthusiastic about the writing work that would ordinarily be necessary for such a project, Simon entered into negotiations with Columbia. After a suggested album of songs written by other people was rejected, the decision was reached to release a *Greatest Hits, Etc.* album (1977). The "greatest hits" were 12 songs that had appeared on the three recent solo albums, and the "etc." consisted of two new songs, "Slip Slidin' Away" and "Stranded in a Limousine."

"Slip Slidin' Away," which received a great deal of airplay, is rather simple. Each of its four verses describes a scenario in which someone is unable to attain what he or she desires, and the refrain uses the title to express the inevitability of such situations. The refrain opens the song and appears after each verse, with an extra repetition at the end. The harmonies relate very simply to the home key of Ab—most belong in the key (Ab, Db, Eb, F minor) and a bit of flavor is added by a D♭7 chord in each verse and a couple of G♭ chords (major triads built on the lowered seventh scale step, G♭, rather than G♮, after refrains). The second half of each verse uses the same chord sequence that is used by the refrain, although the melody is somewhat different, and the melody at the beginning of the third verse varies slightly from that in the other verses.

The song is accompanied throughout by guitar, bass, drums, electric piano, and percussion. Simon mainly shapes the verse-refrain structure with his deployment of additional vocal lines, and to this end he resorts to his common practice of enlisting distinctive-sounding guest artists, in this case the Oak Ridge Boys. Their first contribution is to provide a wordless introduction that, while, brief, sets up the aspiration-quenched theme of the song effectively by moving twice from the A♭ major tonic chord to an F minor harmony; this motion will also characterize the beginning of the refrain and each half of the verses. (This is similar to the introduction to "My Little Town," which uses only a bass line, rather than full harmonies, but nonetheless implies first the tonic E chord and then the C♯ minor harmony a third below, and with analogous implications of disillusionment.)

Simon begins the song proper by singing alone through the refrain and the first verse, which tells of a man the singer knows who loves his lover so much that he fears he will disappear. (In a religious allusion, the man is said to have "wor[n] his passion for his woman like a thorny crown.") A harmony voice sings the next refrain with Simon while other voices decorate the background (all subsequent refrains are treated similarly). The second verse describes a wife who is depressed about what "might've been"; Simon starts this verse alone, but the harmony line is added for some of its second half. The third verse returns to a pure solo treatment; this and the melodic variation that takes it at the beginning to higher notes underscore its poignancy and its obvious autobiographical implications. It tells of a father who "came a long way" to explain to his son why he had done certain things, but winds up kissing him as he sleeps and returning to a home that is obviously not the same as his son's.

The final verse declares that, while people work through life and "believe [they're] gliding down the highway," God alone knows and plans their fates. This verse is colored by a detail at the beginning—when God is first mentioned, Simon is joined briefly by a bass voice in order to convey a traditional notion of God's character. Background voices join for part of the remainder of the verse. After the final refrain, Simon begins a coda alone by singing "mm"s that trail down from the high A♭ to end on C over the ubiquitous A♭-Fm motion. As he repeats this several times, the background voices join in once again, and his last phrase finally slips and slides away down to the low F.

More high-spirited, although comically dark in its own way, is "Stranded in a Limousine." The text of this song describes vivid details of an incident, while leaving enough elements undefined that it is not really possible for the listener to deduce a complete narrative. As was the case with "Gone at Last," the song is driven by the piano playing of Richard Tee; also present are bass, percussion, and guitar, with the assistance of a six-piece horn section featuring Michael and Randy Brecker and David Sanborn. After a pounding introduction that is embellished with flamboyant keyboard flourishes, the first verse tells of a "mean individual" whose car apparently stalls at a traffic light. The tongue-in-cheek lyrics are complemented by the ragtime-bluesy chord changes: the tonic E chord often includes its minor-seventh note D♮; early in the verse a similarly adorned subdominant A harmony (with its seventh G♮) appears; and at the end of the verse the A harmony ascends to kick off a quick circle of fifths to return with the title line to the tonic chord.

The second verse follows the same harmonic pattern, as the children in the neighborhood come running out to see the man. The melody uses the stock-sounding changes as an opportunity to vary significantly from the melody in the first verse, although it reproduces the first verse at the concluding circle of fifths.

The chorus uses different changes at its beginning (for instance, signaling that it is a different kind of section by starting immediately on the subdominant chord, and thus conveying a sense of excitement and instability). In its second half, though, it adopts the pattern of the end of the verse—tonic moving through subdominant and a circle of fifths back to tonic. Here it becomes clear that the limousine's occupant is at odds with the law, as a reward, a siren, and a flashing light are mentioned (and the siren is imitated—"wa-wa-wa..."—by the singer), but it also turns out that he has vanished.

The third verse describes the futile search for the man, who had "left that neighborhood just like a rattlesnake sheds his skin." The melody here differs again from those in the first two verses; although there are considerable overlaps among the devices used in the three, the specific melodic contour of each reflects the emphases indicated by its text. In the place of a fourth verse the horn section, which had already appeared in the chorus, comes to the fore. This is followed by a reprise of the chorus, with the closing line about the man's vanishing repeated twice; additional horn-dominated music accompanies sirens and the sound of police-radio communication as the music fades out. The various elements of this song—its harmonic language, instrumentation, sound effects, and offbeat lyrics (as well as occasional metrical variations that abruptly shift the rhythmic emphasis)—combine to create an overall effect of whimsy. In this respect the song resembles quite a few Simon works; just within the realm of songs that mention police, it is much more similar to "Me and Julio Down by the Schoolyard" than it is to "Save the Life of My Child."

ONE-TRICK PONY

As Simon apparently anticipated, and even desired, a project like *One-Trick Pony* (1980) naturally dictated different requirements for songs than would have been the case for songs that were to comprise a typical album. The songs play two kinds of roles in the film: some are songs that are actually performed by the character Simon plays, Jonah Levin, and/or his band in the movie, and others are heard as commentary during the action. As such, with respect to the degree to which a song's function is subordinated to the dramatic requirements of the movie, the two situations occupy intermediate positions between those of a song written by Simon apart from a movie, on the one hand, and typical background film music. While a regular "album song," notwithstanding other circumstances, could be viewed as a rather undiluted expression of the songwriter, the songs that are performed in this movie need to be songs that might be written and performed by the characters, rather than by Simon. Somewhat more bound by the movie's narrative purpose, at least in theory, would be the songs that comment on the action or themes, since the songs performed by the characters might be more free to address any topics, so long as the style of each song is appropriate to the character(s) performing it.

In turn, however, the "commenting" songs are not subordinated to the movie as much as would be the case with regular untexted background music, which is mainly intended to reinforce the narrative process without drawing attention to itself (and often without the viewer even being fully conscious of its presence). When a texted song is used, ordinarily there is no dialogue present in the film, and the viewer is intended to listen to the words of the song as they add insights to the action onscreen. The text can even comment in rather an elliptical way, in a case in which the song is explicitly addressing something other than the specific elements of the movie, and thus almost effects a momentary departure from the story that merely reflects a general mood—or even comments ironically by intentionally evoking a contrasting mood. The former situation, much more common, is often encountered in the innumerable instances in which songs that have been popular for years are incorporated into newly produced movies. A famous example of the latter is found in *Dr. Strangelove,* in which Vera Lynn's "We'll Meet Again" accompanies the triggering of a nuclear holocaust;[1] another that actually involves one of Simon's songs, although it is used in a television show rather than a feature film, is an appearance of "The 59th Street Bridge Song (Feelin' Groovy)," performed by Harper's Bizarre, on an episode of *Desperate Housewives* while one of the characters embodies the show's title as her rambunctious toddlers threaten to ruin her life.[2]

While these principles may seem reasonable in theory, the categories may be a bit more fluid in practice. For example, a song written and sung by a character might not only be an example of the kind of style he or she would favor, but also present textual ideas that reveal important information about him or her. Or a texted song that is not performed by a character might function more as background music, subconsciously reinforcing a mood, than as an important conveyor of textual ideas (in the narrated-voiceover mold described above). In view of all these considerations, the following discussion of the songs Simon wrote for *One-Trick Pony* will address the ways that each relates to the narrative.

The opening credits of the movie appear against a series of images in which the lights of an airplane approaching a runway for a landing alternate with scenes of Jonah Levin's musical experiences at various ages. First he is shown as a very young boy picking out notes on a toy piano; then with a group of junior-high peers, apparently performing *a cappella* doo-wop; and then as a bearded folksinger at a political rally for Eugene McCarthy. The plane lands and brings the audience to the present as a beardless, road-weary Jonah is shown walking through the airport with his bandmates on their way to yet another gig.

This sequence is accompanied by "Late in the Evening." (This song also happens to be the first track on the soundtrack album, although the album does not generally preserve the order of songs' appearance in the film.) The song very effectively supports the ideas that are presented visually. First, the airplane lights in the night sky (which may for some viewers not immediately be identifiable as such) are accompanied by the song's introduction. In this passage, a repeated guitar-and-percussion riff in an upbeat Latin rock style kicks off a 16-bar blues progression in F (the middle four bars of a 12-bar progression are repeated: FFFF B♭B♭FF B♭B♭FF CCFF). At the first move to the subdominant B♭ harmony, the instruments are joined by wordless voices that reinforce the disembodied, ethereal quality of the lights.

Following the introduction, the song proper consists of four verses, with additional instrumental passages preceding and following the fourth verse. Each verse is a 28-bar expansion of the introduction's last 12 measures (each B♭ passage now lasts for six bars, and each F and C passage for four). The fact that each verse thus begins on a nontonic chord—and one that is imminently expected to return to tonic—generates a sense of excitement (as is the case in the chorus of "Stranded in a Limousine"). This tone is reinforced by the way that the melody dwells for long periods of time on the high D and E♭, only dipping lower occasionally, particularly at points of arrival on the F harmony. (The climax of each verse consists of a slight inflection—E♮ rather than E♭ is sung on the first C chord to emphasize the concluding observation that it is or was "*late* in the evening.")

The text of the song coordinates with the images in the opening montage, corresponding very closely at first and somewhat more remotely toward the end. The first verse tells of the singer's earliest memory—at the age of one or two he heard music from the next room where his mother was enjoying the radio—and it accompanies the (slightly older) piano player. In the second verse the singer is experiencing the streets with his friends, and hearing the sound of *a cappella* singers. Again, the correspondence is not precise, as the image now shown is of the young Jonah as one of the singers.

In the third verse, the singer tells of learning to play electric lead guitar and overwhelming the audience in a bar. This accompanies the folksinger footage (involving an acoustic guitar). This scene continues into the instrumental break, in which horns take the fore against the material from the last 12 bars of the introduction, including the wordless voices. Finally, the fourth verse changes direction and tells a woman that the singer loves her as he has never loved anyone else. This is sung as the plane lands and the five members of the Jonah Levin Band walk through the airport. While there is no direct connection between lyrics and image at this point, viewers may get a subliminal sense that Jonah is doing what he is doing with the band because he loves it just as exclusively as the singer loves the woman. The album version of the song follows the fourth verse with four bars of percussion, horns over the entire 16 bars from the introduction, and then about 12 bars of vamping over a tonic chord to a fadeout. In the film, the 4 bars of percussion are followed by the last 12 of the introduction (with no horns) as the music fades out and a Hare Krishna approaches Jonah to initiate the first dialogue of the movie.

The musicians arrive at their hotel in what turns out to be Cleveland, where they are to perform at the Agora Ballroom. (While this is a high-prestige venue, it is eventually apparent that they are the warm-up band for the more current B-52s.) The second song in the film (it appears third on the album) is "One-Trick Pony," and it is heard in its entirety as the band performs it in concert. As one might guess from its title-track status, the song is more than just a sampling of the band's style; its text metaphorically sets forth the most essential ingredient of Jonah's persona, the fact that he can't conceive of life without his own "trick": making music on his own terms.

After an introductory instrumental vamp, the song begins with a 24-bar blues form in the key of A minor; the subdominant harmony is provided by a D7 chord, and the nontonic section during the third line (in the last eight bars) substitutes a relatively complex progression (G-D/F#-F-Bm7♭5-E7#9) for the customary dominant or dominant-subdominant option. The melody oscillates in a narrow range—mostly A to E—in a typical blues-chanting way. The text tells about the pony, who can only do one trick, but who thrives on the performance. The next section follows the same pattern and is similarly applicable to Jonah—the pony is naturally graceful and proud as he does his trick.

A chorus follows, beginning with harmonic motion that is less stable, and the melodic register moves up momentarily to touch the high A as the singer continues to describe the pony's God-given efficiency and grace. The range drops again as he compares these attributes with the awkward surfeit of maneuvers the singer needs "to get [him] through [his] working day." The clumsy, ill-at-ease observer for whom the singer speaks could simply be a vehicle for describing Jonah's competent musical activities. Slightly more subtly, though, this character could also represent Jonah's own incompetence while doing anything other than his music—his "working day" would thus embody his efforts to negotiate his marriage, the business and political aspects of his career, and so forth.

The text of the third verse sums up the pony's situation—he takes his shot (the line "gives his testimony" subtly refers to the black rhetorical strategy of "testifying" and thus inflects the circus metaphor with a taste of rock and roll) and lets the chips fall where they may; his only trick is all he needs. A guitar solo over the 24-bar blues pattern follows, providing a fourth verse, and then the chorus appears again, this time returning to the high register briefly to bring it to a conclusion. The title line is then repeated, with various instrumental licks, and the song is brought to a close. In addition to expressing important textual ideas, it has served the purpose of illustrating the band's synergy—the players' individual styles (both musical and visual) mix easily.

After the concert, Jonah spends the night with a waitress from the Agora. Their conversation reveals that he is separated from his wife and that he loves his son. It also reveals that much of the waitress's life—her childhood, her choice of job, and her current (but absent at the moment) boyfriend—revolves around her love for music, so that Jonah's appeal for her is partly based on his particular strong suit. (She is knowledgeable enough, incidentally, to have known immediately that one of the band members is joking when he says that Warner Bros. would pick up the band's drink tab, because they're not prominent enough to be signed with this company—which, in fact, was in real life producing the movie, and to which Simon had moved after fulfilling his obligation to Columbia.)

Jonah walks at dawn from the waitress's apartment to his hotel and calls his wife, Marion, telling her that he had been awakened early by a bad dream and thus had wanted to call her and hear her voice, and know that Matty (their son) is all right. Prevarication aside, his attachment to her is evident in the act of calling and in his tone as he speaks, and it is reinforced by "How the Heart Approaches What It Yearns" (the album's fourth song), the first two brief verses of which are heard as he walks and begins the conversation. The music has a country flavor, with just three chords—E(9), A, and B7 in the key of E—but it uses a very unusual 5/8 meter. The words refer to a situation similar to Jonah's, as the singer muses in the solitude of a hotel; he hears his lover's voice in a fever and drifts in and out of a dream. Each verse has three lines: the first, in a low register (E-B) sets up a situation; the second rises to B-E for an intensifying additional observation; and the third returns to the lower register to state the title line (presumably listeners excuse the poetic license of using "yearns" as a transitive verb!). On this occasion the title line is repeated at the end of the second verse, and then an instrumental passage fades out. This song will return later in the movie, but for now the dialogue takes over, as Jonah and Marion arrange for Matty to spend a couple of days with Jonah upon his return and manage to avoid a debate about a meeting that Marion has set up with their lawyers.

In the next sequence, the band is shown driving in a van later in the morning as "God Bless the Absentee" (ninth on the album) is heard. The musicians' dialogue occurs during instrumental portions of the song and combines with the lyrics to add insights into the band's perspective (mostly in the dialogue) and Jonah's state of mind (mostly in the lyrics). The introduction consists of a piano-driven vamp on three chords, during which the drummer, Danny Duggin (played by Steve Gadd—each of the band members is played by one of Simon's real-life collaborators), discovers a review of the concert in the local paper and is urged to read the part about "the veteran Jonah Levin Band." The first verse follows, and it speaks fairly directly for Jonah, describing the singer as a traveler with a five-piece band who has a wife and family whom he doesn't often see; it concludes with the title line.

During a brief instrumental interlude, Danny reads that the band was "highly regarded" during the 1960s and 1970s, but that, perhaps because it hadn't appeared in Cleveland for awhile, it had received a "muted reception." This draws indignation from the pianist, Clarence Franklin (played by Richard Tee), which, in turn, mildly amuses Jonah. The second verse then follows, in which the singer describes himself as a surgeon; his "knife," music, "cuts away [his] sorrow and purifies [his] life." In a bridge, he tells how he misses his woman and the refuge of his home; at this point, Jonah looks more solemn and pensive.

Danny continues reading; the review says that he, Franklin, and the bassist ("John DiBatista," played by Tony Levin) were competent, but it praises the guitarist ("Lee-Andrew Parker," played by Eric Gale). The music at this point, appropriately, consists of an instrumental verse featuring a guitar solo. The bridge returns, now describing the singer's son, and it is followed by a final verse that seems to depart from the main topic by describing the breakneck pace of change in society. The connection, though, is made clear as the opening vamp returns to repeat and fade, because Danny goes on to read the reviewer's thoughts about the band's—and Jonah's—present and past, noting that the band did not perform "Soft Parachutes," Jonah's "anti-war hit of the late sixties." The critic also opines that Jonah seems less ambitious, and Jonah's obvious displeasure is not ameliorated by the band's reflexive dismissal of the review.

"God Bless the Absentee" combines effectively and interestingly with the dialogue to convey information, but it goes beyond the pedestrian with some unexpected textual references—one line in each section, in fact, adds an extra dimension or captivating image. These include the apt "soft places" in the first bridge and the metaphor-extending "veins and arteries" and "highways [and] airports" in the second and third verses, respectively. These are complemented by the thought-provoking images of "the ace of spades" in the first verse and the "silver airplane" and "golden cross" of the second bridge.

Jonah returns to New York because some of the band's gigs have been canceled. He visits Marion, and they maneuver through some small talk and then squabble, making it clear that they care for each other, but that his inability to see himself doing anything else is incompatible with her feeling that rock and roll is juvenile, and her desire that he, at least when he's at home, be "really here." Then he plays ball with Matty, and it is obvious that they get along very well together. As they begin to return home, "Nobody" begins to play in the background.

This mellow ballad (seventh on the album) includes a simple verbal trick. Each verse asks a series of questions about who the singer's intimate companion is, and ends with the answer "nobody." But the chorus makes it clear that this is not the complete answer—it extends the answer to "nobody *but you, girl.*" That thought is elaborated within this mostly diatonic song with an expansive reference to the "whole wide world" that accentuates its breadth with a small flurry of out-of-key chords.

As the first two verses are heard, Jonah and Matty are seen together, and it seems that the special bond described in the song is that between the two of them; furthermore, the apparent negative answer might be referring to difficulties resulting from Jonah's absences and separation from Marion. As the second verse ends, Matty runs a few steps ahead of Jonah to meet Marion at the door of her apartment, and she lets him in but simply waves to Jonah and shuts the door. He is obviously disappointed, and it is at this moment that the chorus begins, revealing that the song is really addressing his relationship with her, and implying that she is the one who plays this unique role in his life.

As the song proceeds, Jonah and Marion are shown separately dressing and traveling to meet with their lawyers to sign separation papers. The ambivalent message of the song complements the action: although they are following through with the dissolution process, their expressions are resigned and somber. In this context, the positive sense of the song is poignant—it continues with the third verse and a slightly extended chorus. Then the chord changes of the verse accompany some 1950s-style wordless singing—at this point we hear some dialogue, as one of the lawyers reads crucial text. Finally, a chorus accompanies the completion of the signing chores, and, as Jonah signs, some concluding repetitions of the word "nobody" almost seem, after all, to undercut the positive message.

Jonah returns to his apartment to find answering-machine messages from his band members urging him to rejoin them; Matty asking when he's to visit with Jonah; and his agent, Bernie, telling him about a meeting he has arranged with Walter Fox, an important record executive. Jonah meets with Fox, an unnamed assistant, and the self-important Cal Van Damp, who is introduced as having "uncanny AM ears," in Fox's apartment. Fox urges Jonah to start with his strongest material, because he would have to make a strong impression on fans who might need something novel-sounding to overcome their impression that Jonah is a known (and presumably passé) quantity.

Although Jonah is alone with his guitar, he introduces his song, "Ace in the Hole," (sixth on the album) by explaining that the second verse is ordinarily sung by Clarence, thus making it clear that the song is properly played by the whole band. He then launches into the song. The first verse, over an up-tempo alternation of A7 and Bm chords, says that some think that Jesus is the "ace in the hole," but the singer is rather flippantly skeptical. As Jonah begins the refrain, in which the singer imagines Jesus calling him on the phone, he is interrupted by the entrance of Walter's wife Lonnie. Walter introduces her and prevails upon her to stay and listen to this "exciting material." Undaunted, Jonah apologizes to Lonnie that "it's just a voice and a guitar," and continues with Clarence's verse, which suggests that a nest egg of 200 dollars, the "price on the street" of "some quality," might actually be the ace in the hole.

Now he is interrupted by the ringing of the telephone; Walter allows his assistant to override his objections and takes the call. He congratulates another musician on his phenomenal success and agrees to his demands for a billboard advertisement; Jonah attempts to look congenial as Lonnie watches him sympathetically. Walter ends the call and says that Jonah's song is "nice." Cal asks what else Jonah has, and he plays the first verse of a ballad, "Long, Long Day" (tenth on the album). Walter cuts him off and says that this song is nice also, but it "just misses." Cal then lectures Jonah on the need for attention-grabbing elements—"spectacle"—in successful AM music, and Jonah, to Lonnie's amusement (but not to Cal's), baits him by suggesting that Albert Schweitzer (with whom Cal is not familiar) must have been successful by combining organ-playing and the "spectacle" of disease.

The camera cuts to a scene showing the band, back on the road, playing "Ace in the Hole." At this point the players are in the middle of the song, beginning a slow central shuffle section that describes life on the road in melancholy tones. (In the album version, this section is preceded by a third verse that says that once the singer's knowledge that he was crazy was his ace in the hole.) The final verse follows, suggesting that music itself is the ace in the hole. After an energetic vamp, this verse is repeated *a cappella*, and the refrain is repeated several times, to the enthusiasm of the crowd. It is clear that Jonah's earlier implication is correct, that this is truly a "band song," and both the textual conclusion about music and the song's potential for a vigorous ending allow it to be a vehicle for the band to express itself; this will have important implications in the role the song plays in its final appearance near the end of the film.

The band is next shown in a van, playing a game that they made up, "Rock and Roll Deaths," in which the goal is to be the last person to name a rock and roll musician who is dead—reinforcing the idea that the passage of time has not treated the genre kindly. This is further emphasized by the following scene, in which the band is shown performing "Long, Long Day" in its entirety. While the first verse of this mellow waltz, which Jonah had played for Walter Fox, described the singer's general weariness and desire for a place to rest, the second verse makes it clear that he's a little-known rock musician on the road. Widely ranging melodic gestures at the beginning of each verse introduce its main idea, and then the melody settles down more gradually at its resigned conclusion.

Each of the first two verses also ends with a crooned "goodnight, good-night, my love," connecting with the road-vs.-lover theme. After a bridge in which killing time on the road is suggested by a reference to "slow motion...jukebox in the corner," the third verse adds to this theme by saying that the singer "could use a friend." The intimacy of the song is emphasized by the fact that it is played in a small club, rather than the larger halls seen for "One-Trick Pony" and "Ace in the Hole."

The musicians travel to their hotel after this gig, accompanied by a couple of women and some weed. As they ride and then relax, the first verse of "Jonah" (eighth on the album) is heard on the soundtrack. This mellow ballad employs jazz changes and irregular rhythms and phrase lengths, first to relate details of road life (changing strings, checking out a venue, negotiating with "local girls"), and then, in the chorus, to say that, rather than being swallowed by a whale, Jonah was swallowed by a song. A second verse is played by a harmonica as the band rides again toward its next gig, telling stories about auditions and women as Jonah tells about the long history of the club where it is to take place.

They arrive at the club, only to discover that it has closed and the owner has left his wife and taken all the money from their joint account. The band is disheartened, and tension becomes apparent, as Clarence threatens to quit because he's not making enough money for his alimony and his dope bill. The band travels back home, first driving through the rain and then enduring airport delays, as the remainder of "How the Heart Approaches What It Yearns" is played. First, a bridge section describes rain on the night highway and a bone-weary traveler, and then a nylon-string guitar solo plays through the changes of one verse. The bridge returns, now describing a dream of making love, and Jonah is shown with Marion again, having sought her solace at this time of crisis. A final verse tells of the singer calling home from a phone booth as Jonah and Marion go to bed.

It is interesting to note that there is an alternate version of "How the Heart Approaches What It Yearns." Titled "Spiral Highway" and presumably written before "How the Heart Approaches What It Yearns," the song follows the same musical form, with the same harmonic structure throughout: two verses, bridge, verse, bridge, verse. The text, however, is only the same in one of these sections, the first bridge that tells of the bone-weary traveler on the night highway. The first two verses of "Spiral Highway," rather than referring to the lover, describe details of life on the road—hole-in-the-wall restaurants with jukeboxes, "pink motel[s]," and stress. The second bridge is instrumental, featuring a saxophone with prominent strings, rather than describing the impassioned dream, and the only text common to the two songs' last verses is "how the heart approaches what it yearns," which appears in the middle of the verse in "Spiral Highway," rather than being repeated at the end of the verse. The net effect of all these changes is that the singer's lover is mentioned much more throughout "How the Heart Approaches What It Yearns" than it is in "Spiral Highway," and this in turn allows the song to comment much more directly on Jonah's relationship with Marion in the film—both earlier in the movie when the first two verses are heard, and on this occasion of reunion.

The next song that appears in the film, "Oh, Marion," (fifth on the album) also has a fully formed alternate version, "All Because of You." (Recordings of both "Spiral Highway" and "All Because of You" are included as extras on the CD reissue of *One-Trick Pony*.) "Oh, Marion" is heard during a scene in which Jonah attends to various mundane chores in his neighborhood. The mindset that it illustrates is established by the preceding scene, in which Jonah and Marion rouse themselves shortly after making love and begin to squabble again. Marion says that she doesn't care about the band breaking up; she cares about their marriage breaking up and wants their family to be together. Matty wakes up, and Jonah and Marion put him back to bed together, but not before he, too, points out that Jonah isn't around enough.

At this point, then, Jonah is seen going about his business on the evidently cold streets of New York. First we see him digging in his pocket for change to buy a slice of pizza from a streetside vendor as the first verse of "Oh, Marion" is heard. The song starts in G♯ minor, and the bass line repeatedly descends from G♯ through F♯ and F to E, with drums shuffling along and punctuated guitar touches over a keyboard, as an introduction. This pattern continues with essentially the same understated instrumentation as the text enters to pose a problem: "The boy's got brains," but he doesn't use them. After this is repeated, the harmonies revolve into an emphasis on the relative major, B, and the melody reaches past its previous high point, C♯, to D♯ and E, to explain: the boy has learned that he laughs less when he thinks a lot. The final line reiterates the situation stated at the beginning, with a return to the C♯ peak and, through the first solid dominant chord since the singing began, a return to the G♯-E bass pattern.

By this point the scene has changed to one of Jonah entering a music store and buying some picks. During the instrumental vamp between verses, Jonah asks the clerk for specific items, and as their conversation comes to an end, the second verse begins. The same basic musical structure is followed, with some melodic variation; this time the boy's heart is on the wrong side, but it turns out that he moved it "for its safety's sake." As this verse proceeds, Jonah does laundry in a laundromat, and later walks down the street to his apartment. As he reaches the apartment, the expected last note of the verse is replaced by the first note of the chorus, which abruptly shifts to the first person and the major mode as the singer uses the title phrase to tell Marion that he is in trouble.

The melody leaps up here to B♯ (or C if reckoned in A♭ major rather than in G♯ major) instead of moving to the G♯ that would have logically concluded the verse. By doing so, it emphasizes the mode shift, since B-natural, rather than B♯, would have been heard in G♯ minor. The unexpected leap also accentuates the singer's sudden confession of his distress, and as the chorus continues, the melody ranges more widely, reaching up to the A♭, and some background voices appear, to help him explain that love is causing his distress. At the same time, sharp though the contrast is between the verse and the chorus, some continuity is maintained through the appearance of a similar descending bass line (now A♭-G-G♭-F) at the beginning of the chorus. This is reversed (E♭-F-F♯-G-A♭) to lead into the chorus's second half. At the end of the chorus, the minor vamp resumes as Jonah is shown being admitted to the office of his agent, Bernie Wepner.

In the film, "Oh, Marion" concludes at this point, having conveyed in third and first person the idea that Jonah is vulnerable, self-protective, and in need of Marion's help in the realm of love. The complete version of the song, as heard on the album, goes on to present a third verse in which "the boy's" voice and words "don't connect to his eyes." He explains that "when [he] sing[s] [he] can hear the truth auditioning." A fourth verse of scat-singing follows (with some elision like that at the end of the second verse), and then the chorus and a coda featuring a flugelhorn conclude the song.

The existence of an alternate version of the song provides an opportunity to see how Simon uses essentially the same form to develop a different topic. "All Because of You" differs somewhat from "Oh, Marion" in its melody (significantly so in the verses, which use some different contours, and in which Simon adopts a rougher, jazzier vocal style). The recorded version included on the *One-Trick Pony* CD reissue as a bonus track is listed as an "outtake," and in a couple of places the text sounds as though arbitrary words or syllables may be present in a work-in-progress.

Nonetheless, the form shapes this text as it does that of "Oh, Marion." At the beginning of the first verse the singer tells of seeking relief from his doctor for some ailment. The major section of the verse again provides an explanation: in this case the title line helps to tell the listener (presumably the singer's lover or ex-lover) that the problem results from her not saying "I do."

In the second verse, the singer seeks relief at the drugstore, with the same explanation that was given in the first verse. The chorus laments the fact that nobody loves him. The third verse describes his psychological disorientation, now concluding that it's because she wouldn't say "we're through" (this reversal either indicates that she is—at least in his perception—toying with him, or it results from the piece still being a work in progress, with promising phrases included regardless of strict sense at this point). The fourth verse tells of a visit to a gypsy, who offers no special solutions, except (now in the major section) the suggestion that the singer go away for a while. She wants to say "a week or two," but the last word is cut off by the beginning of the chorus, which eventually dissolves into some scat-singing and a lot of varied repetitions of the title line.

After "Oh, Marion" fades out in the film, Bernie tells Jonah about a "Salute to the Sixties Night" at a radio-and-record-industry convention in Chicago. Jonah has been asked to perform "Soft Parachutes," for which he would receive a good fee; moreover, Bernie points out, it would bring him good exposure with industry executives, including Walter Fox, who will be attending. Jonah objects because "Soft Parachutes" is passé in the absence of the war and he no longer performs it, and especially because the invitation is for him alone and not the band, but Bernie prevails. The next scene shows the event; the flavor of the evening is established as Sam and Dave and the Lovin' Spoonful are shown performing "Soul Man" and "Do You Believe in Magic," respectively, and Walter and Cal are shown in the audience. At the same time, Jonah's cynicism about the event is reinforced as he is shown backstage prompting an overweight Tiny Tim as he runs through "Tiptoe through the Tulips." Then Jonah is cued for his performance.

"Soft Parachutes" is very much a typical acoustic-guitar-based song of the urban folk tradition. (Jonah performs it alone, with his guitar, and it is presented in the same way as a bonus track on the CD reissue.) It is played in the key of G, which lends itself easily to the use of stock fingerpicking figures. The accompaniment for the chorus consists of a continuous stream of tenths that connect one harmony to the next (such as the opening E/C-D/B-C/A-B/G walkdown from a C harmony to the tonic G harmony). During the verse, the bass line steps down from G to F, and then from C to A in order to lead to the dominant D chord. This process occurs twice: the first half of the verse ends on the D, and the second half begins the process again, but this time the D is resolved to the tonic G.

The song is very brief in this performance: Jonah plays the accompaniment for the chorus as an introduction, then sings the chorus, a verse, and the chorus, and finally plays a bit on the guitar to provide a coda. The chorus juxtaposes attractive and unattractive images: "soft parachutes" and "Fourth of July" are followed by "villages burning," and it is revealed that it is bodies, presumably in body bags, that are like soft parachutes. The progression from one image to another aligns well with the progress from chord to chord described above, and the guitar also affects the vocal melody, as some melodic skips arise from figures that naturally fall under the fingers on the guitar.

The verse is more narrative, and this expansiveness is reflected by longer-maintained harmonies and longer, less mobile melodies. The singer briefly describes the preceding year, during which he was in high school and got high with his girlfriend; in the second half of the verse he describes a different kind of trip, as he is "flying down some Viet Nam highway" for reasons he can't explain. Although this is not exactly the kind of song Simon probably would have written in the 1960s, it exhibits typical reinforcement of textual content (or at least the text's style in terms of images vs. narrative) by musical characteristics.

At the party following the performance, Jonah insults Cal Van Damp, and Walter Fox instructs Lonnie to get Jonah out before he further damages himself and Walter. Lonnie tells Jonah of her mission, deciding at the same time to sweeten the deal by seducing him. In the following scene, however, Jonah is shown back in New York spending time with Matty as "That's Why God Made the Movies" (second on the album) is heard.

This song uses a jazz-blues style to spin a brief yarn that sheds additional light on Jonah's frame of mind. As heard in the film, it includes two verses and a chorus. An introduction sets up a slinky repeated-bass vamp, and the first verse quickly moves into jazz chords, accompanied by vibraphone licks and jazz-styled guitar and keyboard work. The vocal line similarly moves from blues hints in the first two lines (repeated notes and winding lines leading to downbeats) to jazz touches (irregular rhythms and leaps) later. These stylistic nuances coordinate with the text—at the beginning is the straightforward lament that the singer's mother died when he was born, but she tells him goodbye as the blues harmonies die away, and the jazz ideas take over as unexpected things begin to happen—the newborn has a conversation with his mother, who "leave[s] in style," and the verse concludes with the title line.

The second verse again begins with a somewhat traditional idea, albeit presented rather glibly: the singer "laid around in [his] swaddling clothes" (slightly reinforcing the religious reference of the title). The second line again includes a diminishing idea—the doctor turns out the light—as the blues ideas yield to jazz, and the unexpected occurs again, as the infant packs up and leaves with high hopes that God's cinematic provisions will bring about a good result.

The chorus shifts back to simpler harmonies, regular metrical patterns, and a simpler first- and second-person text, as the singer addresses a woman with somewhat maternal terms. He asks her to take him to her breast and "nourish" him with tenderness "the way the ladies sometimes do." These lines' maternal references include not only the image of a nursing mother, but also a recollection of the description of the mother in "Late in the Evening" laughing "the way some ladies do." The second half of the chorus places a clear emphasis on romantic love, as the singer asks to be told that the woman won't leave him for another man, but even this connects with the maternal notion, since it was his mother who left him earlier in the song.

The song stops playing in the film toward the end of the chorus, during a scene in which Jonah and Matty, having played some games and taken in a movie, are "shaving" together. In the album version, the remainder of the chorus further reinforces the romantic element by addressing the woman as "baby." It also adds a brief slide-guitar interlude and a fourth verse, the first half of which repeats the text from the first verse, and the remainder of which says that the singer had to make his own way after his abandonment, as would be the case for a child raised by wolves. While the film version lacks these sections, it still emphasizes Jonah's need for romantic love as connected with a need to be nurtured and comforted, and the parent-child scenes reinforce this sense as well.

In the following scene Jonah meets with Walter Fox, who tells him that he had been distracted when he had heard Jonah's music earlier, and that he agrees with his wife that the songs have potential. He wants Jonah to work with Steve Kunelian, a young producer,[3] who has a good sense of the Top 40 and "what's danceable." Potential problems immediately become apparent when Jonah has to insist on using his band rather than a rhythm section that Kunelian prefers; furthermore, after Kunelian leaves, Fox lets Jonah know that he suspects Jonah is having an affair with Lonnie by telling him that it would not be a good idea.

The fact that Jonah is indeed continuing his relationship with Lonnie is then made clear, as the next scene shows them talking as they get out of bed. She admits that she was somewhat influential in Fox's decision to record

Jonah but denies having told him to do so. She tells Jonah that he should be willing to accept her help, and that she is helping because she can tell that the music means a lot to him. (At the same time, she says that she has lost interest in the record business, unwittingly supporting Marion's position.)

The next sequence shows the recording process for "Ace in the Hole." Jonah and Clarence are shown joyfully laying down vocal tracks, but then Kunelian starts to discuss his ideas for adding to the track—he wants to put strings over Clarence's electric piano solo, which Jonah feels will make the record lush and not "ballsy," and he wants to dub a saxophone solo over a guitar solo that Lee plays. Jonah objects to this as well, but Kunelian thinks the additions will help in getting AM airplay. Three scenes then show the string track being recorded, a trio of women adding their vocals to the slow middle section, and the sax solo being added to the end of this section; as this music continues to be heard, the band, Kunelian, and Fox are seen listening to the playback of the AM-ified version of the song. Fox is enthusiastically moving to the beat, but he looks like a pretender among the members of the band, who are for the most part stoically silent.

After the playback, Fox proclaims that he thinks the record is very powerful. Jonah starts to point out that he'd been told that anything the band didn't like could be removed, but Fox cuts him off with a warning tone, citing the need for the record to be commercially viable. Later, the band tells Jonah that he should tell Fox that the recording needs to be changed, but his attempt is futile. (It is interesting to note that, in what may be a bit of self-parody, all three of the offensive added elements—strings, background women's vocals, and sax—had been used prominently in Simon's work as recently as his previous album, *Still Crazy after All These Years*—although not with the same homogenizing purpose to which they are put here.)

Jonah visits a bar and then is seen alone playing a bit of "Long, Long Day"; the music continues into the "Goodnight" section as he shows up at Marion's apartment. She receives him affectionately, and they talk a bit about Matty. Jonah asks for some Percodan, and she offers some aspirin, and then (after commenting that "I *am* Matty, just older") he starts to reveal that things are not going well. When she asks what is wrong, he can only reminisce about their earlier romance, and presumably they head to bed.

Jonah is then seen walking along the street at night with his guitar case. The second texted verse of "Jonah" is now heard; it describes the perseverance of aspiring musicians, who keep hoping that one more year will turn their dreams into gold. Midway through the chorus, Jonah enters the recording studio lobby and tells the receptionist that he thinks he left his glasses in the studio. When he has been admitted, he puts on his glasses (which he had actually brought with him) and puts the master tape of "Ace in the Hole" in the empty guitar case. The music continues into a new section; it begins as the verses did but quickly goes higher melodically and uses new harmonies, as the text toasts "the boys" "carrying soft guitars in cardboard cases" through the night. As Jonah leaves the studio onto a street momentarily devoid of other people, the lyrics ruminate on where the boys might have gone, and a mellow, jazzy instrumental coda fades out as he takes the tape out of its case. Jonah then grabs one end of the tape and throws the reel down the street, unwinding the tape so that it will be destroyed, and the movie abruptly ends. (The credits then roll against a blank screen as "One-Trick Pony" is heard in the background.)

One-Trick Pony shows how Simon was able to apply his songwriting art to a variety of narrative and dramatic functions within the context of a feature film. A song like "Ace in the Hole" serves primarily to shed light on the characters by illustrating how they would express themselves. While most of the other songs are *not* supposed to belong to the band's repertoire, though, they still include some element of commenting *for* characters, and not simply *about* them. All of these include at least some passages in the first person, and most of these express a point of view that is similar to Jonah's.

"Jonah" is the exception here, since it sets up the singer's subject as the most obvious parallel to Jonah. The other songs, though, range from those in which the first person could be Jonah (e.g., the first-person portions of "Oh, Marion") to those in which he is obviously somewhat elliptically related to the first person ("That's Why God Made the Movies"). Viewed in these terms, it is interesting that one of the other songs the band *does* perform, "One-Trick Pony," relates to Jonah in a complex way, as the singer and his subject could be seen to reflect different aspects of Jonah's character. All in all, this project offers a rich illustration of the variety of ways in which songs could relate to a narrative.

HEARTS AND BONES

Having tackled this challenge, Simon returned to the more standard approach of writing songs intended for consumption in the context of an album. Familiar as this premise might have been, the process was apparently not always easy. Simon suffered depression and writer's block during the period after *One-Trick Pony* and was only able to resume his work with the help of a Los Angeles psychiatrist named Rod Gorney.[4] One result of these experiences is that, as Simon has observed, several of the songs on the album, *Hearts and Bones* (1983), are more directly autobiographical than had been the case with earlier songs[5]—one might say that, in some ways, these songs relate to the narrative of Simon's life as the songs in *One-Trick Pony* relate to those of Jonah's life. To a degree, even the album cover reflects some of these concepts: Simon is shown out of focus in garish tones against an over-exposed backdrop that suggests a barrage of cultural stimuli—and this technological theme is reflected to some extent in the pervasive use on the album of such resources as synthesizers and Synclavier.

The first song on the album, "Allergies," exemplifies the autobiographical characteristic as well as the technological. The freely rhythmed and metered introduction is wreathed in synthesized sounds—even, at the beginning, modifying the vocal sound. The key of G is suggested, with some modal flavor lent by an F-major chord, as the singer briefly describes persistent allergies, ending with the complaint that they still remain. At the end of the introduction, though, a transition moves the music to A Aeolian and a steady rock beat, and the first verse becomes very regular—eight repetitions of a two-bar Am-F-D#-Em harmonic pattern make up the total 16 measures of the verse.

This regularity underscores the relentlessness of the allergies the singer is describing, and it is reinforced in several ways. The melody line continually retraces the space between C and A, creating in each half of the verse two two-bar phrases that are followed by a nonstop four-bar phrase. The text in the first half of the verse describes physical allergies, and the second half translates this to the emotional realm, saying that the singer's heart is allergic to the women he loves.

The verse then opens out onto the chorus, which returns to the general harmonic pattern of the introduction. Some of the introduction's melodic contours are reproduced here, but the steady rock beat persists from the verse as the singer complains about the allergies and pleads with a doctor to see him. However, while the verse's great regularity conveyed the allergies' power, the chorus helps to convey the singer's distress with some irregularities—in addition to avoiding strong closure in G and ending with a querulous melodic passage over the indecisive concluding harmonies (both of which occur in the introduction), it does not organize its harmonies into regular two- and four-measure groupings.

In its first half, the second verse uses the same music that the first verse did, and it also takes the tone of reciting unyielding facts. In a story surely derived from Simon's psychotherapeutic experience, the singer describes traveling to visit a famous doctor and staying in a hotel; the four-bar phrase observes that people like him never get well. The second half, though, digresses into some typical Simonesque whimsy, as the singer, having mentioned allergies repeatedly, wonders where they go to eat "after a show."

The chorus follows this verse, and it is followed by a variation of the introduction in which the original words are sung (so the allergies *still* remain); here, the intensity is increased with a regular meter and the raising of the music by a minor third. After this passage ends with a spoken "I...can't...breathe!" the third verse consists of a frenetic machine-gun guitar solo played by jazz guitarist Al DiMeola. The mechanical nature of this solo gives it a sense of intruding on the song, thus connecting with the persistent, invasive allergies as well as the alienating-technology theme. This, in turn, is followed by a last appearance of the chorus, and then a coda that combines DiMeola's stuttering guitar work with final repetitions of the title word.

"Allergies" is followed by the title track of *Hearts and Bones*. This song forms a pair with the seventh one on the album, "Train in the Distance," in several ways. Each is a mellow rumination on a romantic relationship (although each is undergirded by a fairly strong beat); each contains some fairly clear references to one of Simon's marriages; each draws a certain conclusion that is encapsulated in the title; and—unlike the other songs on the album—while each has plenty of interesting elements instrumentally, the emphasis of each on the relationship between two *people* is subtly reinforced by the absence of synthesizers and Synclavier on both.

The musical foundation of "Hearts and Bones" is provided by an acoustic-guitar figure that lopes through much of the song. The figure consists of syncopated parallel sixths, suggesting a Mexican flavor, that move over the bass notes of the three major chords in the key of E major. For example, at the beginning of the song E/G#-F#/A-G#/B are heard over E; later A/C#-B/D#-C#/E are heard over A; and at other times D#/F#-E/G#-F#/A are heard over B. These figures, first heard with some wordless vocals in a rather leisurely introduction, create a sense of motion that is realized by the text of the first vocal section. Here the relationship is described in terms of a journey that is both geographical and emotional: "one and one-half wandering Jews" are traveling in the Southwest, but also tracing "the arc of a love affair." (Both of Simon's parents were Jewish, as was one of Carrie Fisher's.)

The text develops a sense of almost aimless wandering, and several musical elements support this idea. The voice's opening melodic idea, descending from B to E, is repeated, and then is slightly condensed (losing a brief stop on A) for three more appearances, all over the tonic E harmony; the repetitive nature of the last two phrases is emphasized by the fact that the text in the last one is a translation of the Spanish "Sangre de Cristo" in the one that precedes it. The second part of the section contains a similar melodic device, as another descending melody is presented three times, each time a step lower than the preceding one, but each time avoiding a sense of arrival by concluding on a dissonant seventh chord. The section concludes by juxtaposing a geographical image of the inviting and the forbidding—mountain passes and stones—with the corresponding human image of the title.

The second section repeats the same music, but now the text describes the couple's wedding "the season before" (Simon's marriage to Fisher was very brief). This is followed by a contrasting section in which, at first, the couple debates an impromptu trip to Mexico. The harmonies alternate here between the tonic E and the subdominant A, and the instrumental motion is arrested at several points as the speakers express their ideas. But the conversation then turns to more personal questions, as the man acknowledges that he doesn't love her in the manner in which she desires to be loved, and some of the harmonies turn to minor during this passage.

Then the motion resumes with the guitar figure, and the text describes a different kind of return. The opening reference to the wandering Jews appears again, but it becomes clear that they are no longer together. They have returned not to their status at the beginning of the song, but to that of their lives before their marriage. The text concludes, though, by speculating about whether they will eventually recover apart, or "the arc of [the] love affair" will be restored; in support of the latter conclusion, the singer says that if one twirls two people's hearts and bones into one, "they won't come undone." The title line is repeated several times, and then the instruments repeat and fade.

To some degree the following song, "When Numbers Get Serious" exemplifies Simon's whimsical vein, but it also connects on the one hand with the theme of cultural angst, and on the other with the desire for fulfilling, romantic love. As the title suggests, the central image is numbers, and the text surveys the ways that they are evident throughout life. The song follows an ABABAC form, with a quasi-reggae sound established by rhythm and texture as well as vocal arrangement and style.

The first section adopts a somewhat gentle, conversational tone, as the singer describes the ubiquity and effortless activity of numbers in a series of brief, syncopated phrases. The melody freely combines leaps, steps, and repeated notes against a series of simple chords in a pure G major key. On the last line a harmony voice (also sung by Simon) tracks a third above the melody in a way that is typical of carefree reggae harmonizing, and the line runs on longer than the previous phrases to conclude, on a solid G harmony, that "when times are mysterious, serious numbers are eager to please."

An abrupt drop into an F#7 harmony wrenches the music into the distantly related key of B major for the B section. The main portion of this passage alternates between F#7 and B chords, as the contrabass guitar provides a walking bass line and the melody ranges more widely in order to express more personally engaged emotion on the part of the singer. He wants the listener to use the numbers to contact him via his address and phone but at the same time implores the listener not to give the information to "some madman." This leads to a realization that the numbers are out of control in life, and, with the help of an Em7 chord and some background vocals, the music subsides back into the key of G.

The second A section returns to the music and sound of the first, although the harmonizing voice enters earlier this time. While some of the text here is whimsical, stating that "two times two is twenty-two," and "four times four is forty-four," it suggests an almost sinister role for numbers, as they leave a mark on one's door and are associated with urgent telephones ringing. The concluding phrase is now altered to say that the numbers will always speak to us in these times.

The more cynical B section seizes immediately on this line of thought. The text here addresses the global situation, warning that numbers ("by the trillions") are everywhere, in the United States and overseas, and ending, as the background voices help to move back to G, by asking if the listener understands all this. The final A section responds to this information by turning away from the discussion of numbers for a moment and seeking solace in human love. The singer pledges his devotion and says he "will love innumerably" but ultimately concludes by returning to the importance of serious numbers in mysterious times. (Some of the lyrics here can be heard in another guise in the work-in-progress "Shelter of Your Arms," which is included as a bonus track on the 2004 re-release of the album; a snippet of lyrics from this song also shows up two albums later in "The Obvious Child.")

And now, instead of moving again to the B section, the music dissolves into a triple meter and the key of E♭ (a third-relation that is as far away from G on the "flat" side as B is on the "sharp"). In this new environment, the text seems to supersede the previous discussion by humanizing the numbers and bringing them within reach: when they "all come home," four becomes three, which becomes two, which becomes a One. While the meaning of this turn of events is not entirely clear, it seems to have removed the earlier suggestions of the numbers' alien, threatening nature.

Two of the songs on *Hearts and Bones* have the same name: "Think Too Much (a)" and "Think Too Much (b)." The latter is presumably given the "b" designation because it was written later (it bears a later copyright date in the liner notes, and Simon has confirmed this order of composition in discussing the songs).[6] However, it appears earlier on the album, immediately following "When Numbers Get Serious."

The musical structure of "Think Too Much (b)" is extremely simple. It is constructed entirely of a sequence of eight-measure units; in each of these a marimba riff establishes an A major harmony for four measures and then is essentially repeated a third lower to establish an F♯ minor harmony for four measures. After the first 3 of these create a 24-measure introduction, the next 10 accompany two 32-bar verses, alternating with two 8-bar refrains. The last 3 accompany a repetition of the refrain and provide a 16-bar instrumental coda against a wordless vocalization.

The texted portion of the song, then, consists of two verses, the first followed by a refrain, and the second followed by two refrains, all accompanied by the hypnotic alternation of A and F♯ minor segments. While the marimba is the most prominent instrument in the accompaniment, it is supported throughout by a bass line, and intermittent contributions are made throughout by various instruments as well as other sounds that resemble bleating animals and African vocalizing. Against all this, the singer uses a series of graceful, freely rhythmed melodic arcs to convey two related images in each verse.

In the first verse, he says that "the smartest people in the world" had attempted "to analyze our love affair." These people were in Los Angeles, which may mean that they are not a think tank oddly engaged with this topic, but rather sarcastically characterized entertainment-industry commentators. In either case, the juxtaposition of these sophisticates with the tribal setting suggested by the marimba and other rural sounds is a reflection of Simon's occasional penchant for unexpected music-text combinations. The verse goes on to say, in the first person, that the couple under examination looked at length at their "photographs" and eventually "compromised" as dawn arrived. The refrain follows, as the singer sings "Maybe I think too much" four times; the first two dwell on C♯ over the A harmony, and the third and fourth drop a third to dwell on A over the F♯ minor harmony.

The net effect of the repeated harmonies and the leisurely melodic arcs, supported by the rural third-world implications of some of the instrumentation, is a sense of responding to the oppressive glare of modern, high-tech public scrutiny (such as would have been applied to Simon's personal life, particularly his romance with Fisher) by withdrawing and ruminating. The desire for refuge is further developed in the second verse, in which the singer first says that the right side of the brain, dominated by the left, has to labor through the night, and then tells of his father comforting him and telling him that all he can do in the night is get some rest. The refrain then follows twice, and Simon's high vocalizations over the concluding instrumental measures reinforce the simple but wistful character that is evoked by this brief song.

"Think Too Much (b)" and "Think Too Much (a)" are separated on *Hearts and Bones* by "Song about the Moon." This song is similar to "Think Too Much (b)" in that its instrumental texture remains much the same throughout most of the song, with some contrast in the B section of its large-scale AABA format and some elaboration in its coda. While the two songs thus share a measure of textural consistency, however, their respective textures differ considerably from one another. "Song about the Moon" is accompanied throughout by a genially swinging rock ensemble composed of contrabass guitar, guitars, drums, and Fender Rhodes (a very common, industry-standard keyboard), along with the more esoteric Vocoder speech synthesizer and Synclavier synthesizer, both of which had been developed just during the preceding decade.

Not surprisingly in view of its title, the song uses the idea of a song throughout its three verses to propose a variety of possible connections between creative imagination and reality. Much of the text has a somewhat whimsical character, but at least some of it seems to aspire to making serious points as well. The first verse sets this tone, after a 16-measure introduction that consists of a repeated, low, bluesy hummed vamping line against mostly F harmonies, by purporting to give advice about how to write a song about the moon.

Against harmonies that lope along agreeably, the singer recommends that, if the listener wants to do this, he or she should experience the deep shadows and alien light of the afternoon "craters" (presumably among the buildings of a city), when "gravity leaps like a knife off the pavement." At the beginning of the verse's second half (as signaled by a slightly varied return of the opening harmonic sequence), the singer restates the listener's moon-song-writing goal. At this point, before ending the verse by declaring the song a success, he hints at its deeper value by referring to the song as "a spiritual tune."

The second verse develops this impulse by supposing that it is now a song about the heart (and the heart's desire for companionship) that is desired. The singer recommends that if the listener wants to write such a song, he or she should write a song about the moon. This is because the heart can act like other things that occur at night under the moon—a howling god, or an "explod[ing]" pistol.

At this point the texture yields to a more mellow, keyboard-oriented accompaniment for the brief B section. Here two descending phrases, each accompanied by a steady two-to-the-bar harmonic progression, describe a pair of images that contrasts with the preceding thoughts: a laughing boy and a laughing girl. Each of these is laughing very hard, the girl so much that tears are rolling down her face. This information comes with a C9 harmony that serves as a dominant to lead to the tonic F chord at the beginning of the final verse. At the same time, abrupt as the textual shift may have been *to* the boy and girl, the reference to her face leads directly into the text of the last verse, which now supposes that the desired song is about a face.

The musical entrance to this verse is somewhat blurred, as the premise is stated before the beginning of the harmonic sequence that had been established by the earlier versions. Now the singer recommends that the aspiring songwriter consider a vaguely remembered photograph and "wash your hands in dreams and lightning / cut off your hair and whatever is frightening." The second half of this verse connects the project of writing about a face to that of writing about the human race, and this, along with the references to a spiritual tune and a heart, seems inevitably to connect not only with Simon's occupation in general, but with his creative struggles at this time in particular. The song is rounded out with a return to the second half of the first verse, with variations in the vocal line that explore higher registers, and a coda—based on the introduction—that repeats and fades.

"Think Too Much (a)" uses a funky beat, with basic accompaniment provided by bass, electric guitar, and drums, and various vocal and instrumental (presumably Synclavier) effects added at strategic points. The instruments provide a rhythmically distinctive pattern alternating between A and D harmonies in the 16-bar introduction, and then continue as the singer starts the first verse. The text here essentially duplicates that found at the beginning of the second verse of "Think Too Much (b)," in which the sides of the brain are discussed, but the effect is glibber, as the rhythms are syncopated and the right side's nocturnal work is less sympathetically described.

The singer goes on, now against alternating minor chords (C♯ minor and F♯ minor), to consider whether he thinks too much, as some people say, or too little, as others do. As he describes his various advisors, the harmonic rhythm slows, eventually leading through B minor to an E chord. This serves to set up the second part of the first verse, still in A, which starts with a rapidly repeated low A on guitar. Against this, the singer describes his "mercifully brief" childhood, when he began to "think too much" with "girls from St. Augustine / up in the mezzanine / thinking about God, yeah." This leads to a refrain in which he speculates again, repeatedly, that he may think too much, over alternating E and F♯ minor harmonies as twittering noises are heard in the background.

The second verse speculates in whimsical terms about "a period of grace" when, instead of thinking too much, one's brain simply "takes a seat behind [one's] face." Everything goes well, with the world doing the Elephant

Dance (emphasized by heavy bass effects). Eventually, though, the second section of this verse, sung with a sweet high harmony, makes clear what this is all about: the girl whom the singer loves. He is always thinking of her, but he suspects that he may be overthinking this and should instead just act on instinct—hold her, not mold her, blindfold her, take her away. To underscore all of this somewhat irrational-sounding debate about rationality, as the closing E-F♯ minor refrain repeats and fades, it is overlaid with various effects, most noticeably the return of the text about the sides of the brain.

As "Hearts and Bones" referred, to a large degree, to Simon's relationship with Carrie Fisher, "Train in the Distance" addresses his first marriage, to Peggy Harper.[7] The central theme of this song (as it overtly explains at its conclusion) is the romantic belief that "life could be better"; this sense of yearning for something imagined but not actually possessed is embodied by the title image. The theme is proposed as a response to the story that the song tells about two lovers.

The song musically establishes the train idea with the introduction, which is based on four statements of a four-measure chord progression over an E♭ bass: E♭-D♭/E♭-A♭/E♭-E♭m7. The rich musical texture here prominently features the Fender Rhodes that provides the harmonic structure throughout the song, pulsing bass guitar and percussion, vibraphone, high and low wordless voices, and yet higher pulsing notes; the pulsing suggests the rhythm of train wheels, while some of the voices suggest a train whistle. At the end of the fourth statement of the progression, the title line is sung.

Each verse begins with a leaner accompaniment—mostly bass, electric piano, and drum set, to convey important information in a balanced pair of phrases. The verse then moves through a transition in which, as instruments and voices are added, the text adds a bit to the narrative. It then returns to the opening melodic material, which is now overlaid on two statements of the introduction's music, during each of which the singer concludes that "Everybody loves the sound of a train in the distance / Everybody thinks it's true."

The opening phrase pair effectively supports its straightforward narrative account in each verse by following a classically parallel pattern. Specifically, each phrase moves through the same harmonic progression until the end, where a slight variation allows the first phrase to conclude on the open-ended dominant B♭9 chord and the second to arrive on the stable tonic E♭ harmony. Furthermore, this progression follows a very rational pattern in each phrase, first moving over a descending chromatic bass line (E♭-B♭/D-D♭69-C7), and then leaving the C7 via strong fifth motion. (Simon adds one small wrinkle by extending the C7 harmony by a half measure in the first phrase.)

The first verse describes the man's attraction to the woman, who is married (as Peggy Harper was when her romance with Simon began) and compared to "Southern skies" (Harper was raised in Tennessee), and then his pursuit of her.[8] The second verse tells of their marriage and the arrival of a son (as occurred for the Simons), but then also the dissolution of their relationship.

At the conclusion of this verse, a contrasting passage appears; the texture here is again light, with the keyboard quite prominent.

This section is built on a long descending chromatic bass line from D♭ to F, which is finally broken by a B-A♭/B♭ move that leads to the beginning of the third verse. This music will appear again after the third verse. On each occasion its text provides a bit of detached commentary. In this first appearance, the singer refers to the man's and woman's disillusionment, indicating that they may have confused "negotiations and love songs."

The third verse tells of the couple's continuing contact, perhaps for the boy's sake, and mentions disagreements and also occasional pleasant times. When the contrasting section arrives to conclude the textual portion of the song, as indicated above, it explicitly asks what the point of the story is, and answers that it is that we all think that life could be better. This encapsulation is followed by a lengthy coda based on the introduction's four-measure phrase—first the phrase appears three times, with a couple of "train in the distance" lines sung, then five phrases accompany an alto saxophone solo, then a cello is prominently heard pulsing in four more before the voices and most of the other instruments drop out and the cello stutters to a stop.

The textual focus of "René and Georgette Magritte with Their Dog after the War" is unique on this album. The topic of the song, which is fairly faithfully indicated by its unusual (and unusually long) title, is esoteric. More to the point, it doesn't make a point, or at least no particular point stands out as clearly as is the case for the other songs. Its title is derived from the caption of a picture that Simon had seen (reportedly changing the phrase "during the war" to "after the war"), and the song describes imagined moments and impressions that the famous Belgian artist and his wife might have had in New York, but the most overt conclusion that is drawn in the song is that they somehow treasured the music of American doo-wop groups.

The entire song uses an AABA form, and the music is lent a simple elegance by its basis in clear harmonic and/or bass motion in the context of four-bar phrases. This is easily seen in the structure of the A section verses, each of which consists of four four-bar phrases with an insertion between the third and fourth. In each verse the first and last phrases have as their text the title of the song, further contributing to the sense of simplicity and symmetry.

This text line is the beginning of a sentence when it appears in the first phrase of each verse, but it is given something of a self-contained, caption-like quality by its musical setting. The melody descends from the dominant note to the tonic, B to E in the key of E major, and it is accompanied by a descending series of bass notes that move from tonic to tonic—E-D-B-A-E—the last one of which supports a tonic chord. The second phrase develops this matter-of-fact beginning, as the text describes something the couple did, the melody traces the same B-to-E path, and the bass line includes a new note that results in the loss of the last one—now E-D#-D-B-A—so that the new concluding note supports an open-ended A major 7 chord rather than the earlier, stable tonic E major harmony.

This development opens things up to a contrasting third phrase. The text here adds information that is less matter-of-fact than the actions described in the second phrases of the verses, and melodic and harmonic direction changes. The melody ascends from F♯ to B and then returns to F♯, and a similar bass line—F♯-G♯-A—supports the harmonies.

If there were no insertion after the last phrase, the most straightforward harmonic procedure would probably have been for this last chord to have its root, B, rather than A, in the bass (thus creating a simple B harmony rather than B/A). The last phrase would then have recapitulated the self-contained melody and bass line that accompanied the same text in the first phrase. However, the presence of the insertion and the nature of its text change the situation. In each verse, after an eight-eighth-note extension, eight measures respond to the preceding text by referring to the doo-wop groups. The first four recite their names (the Penguins, the Moonglows, the Orioles, and the Five Satins), and the last four describe their effect on the couple.

The chord progressions here are derived from typical doo-wop patterns (and stylistically typical background falsetto voices and repeated piano chords reinforce this idea). In the first phrase, each group name is sung to the same B-G♯-F♯-E melodic line against one of the chords in a E/G♯-C♯m7-Amaj9-B9 progression [these chords are slightly embellished versions of perhaps the most stereotypical doo-wop progression—tonic (E)-submediant (C♯m)-subdominant (A)-dominant (B)]. The second phrase then uses a different melody over a variation of the same chord progression—inserted chords smooth the bass line, and the final B9 harmony is omitted. These doo-wop-inspired progressions affect the harmonic structure of the third and fourth phrases: First, Simon smooths the entrance into the insertion with the dissonant bass A that precedes it (in the B/A chord) and resolves to the G♯ of the insertion's opening E/G♯ chord. Then, the concluding A major 7 harmony of the insertion leads to F♯m6 at the beginning of the fourth phrase, echoing the same kind of joint between the second and third phrases. Also as in the third phrase, the melody of the fourth phrase begins on F♯, but it otherwise duplicates the melody that accompanied the same titular text in the opening phrase. The harmonies, though, move here by simple fifth motion from F♯m6 to B9 to E.

In the first two A verses, the Magrittes are described as dancing intimately in their hotel suite to the music of the Penguins, and so on, and then being emotionally overcome by the style in which some mannequins are dressed.[9] The B section introduces new music (with background strings) to describe their falling asleep, only to wake up and find that "all their personal belongings have intertwined." A childlike innocence is suggested by simple, discrete four-measure phrases, and the harmonies often move deliberately by fifth motion or stepwise bass motion. Simon nicely conveys the timeless sense of sleeping with the line "decades gliding by like Indians, time is cheap," in which the series of long "I" sounds in "gliding by like" glides by in a rapid melodic descent that cuts across the established eighth-note metrical subdivisions.

The last verse is as cryptic as the last line of the B section had been. Here the couple is "dining with the power elite" when they see the doo-wop groups "in their bedroom drawer," "the cabinet cold of their heart." To add effect to this discovery, Simon sings freely, out of tempo, and uses some rich chords to harmonize the insertion. The verse's final tonic chord is replaced with an eight-bar coda in which harmonies progress twice from A6 to E, as the strings and falsetto harmony voices resume in the background.

"Cars Are Cars" is an odd little song that combines verses telling about how all cars are essentially the same with two interludes that take different tangents from this basic premise. The verses use brief, one-measure phrases with funky, punctuating accompaniment in simple triadic harmonies. The interludes complement the verses by using a variety of sustained seventh chords to develop more continuous thoughts, with four-bar phrases and legato articulation.

Each verse begins by repeating the assertion that "cars are cars all over the world" and then setting out four brief lines that rhyme neatly in naming attributes that all cars share. All of this is accompanied by a steady alternation of D and G chords in the key of G; this pattern is first established in the introduction. The verses then conclude by reiterating the opening line various numbers of times—once in the first verse, twice in the second, and three times in the third. In the second and third verses these reassertions very slightly expand the harmonic vocabulary by adding C chords to the D and G harmonies.

The first and second verses are separated by a brief, palate-clearing F/G harmony. After the second verse, the first interlude introduces the idea that people consider themselves to be different from one another around the globe. As the harmonies wander a bit from G major, but then return, the singer implies that this conceit is vain, likening it to "shoot[ing] at the moon." After the third verse, the second interlude uses the same music to describe a very comfortable, homey car that the singer once owned, and goes on to observe that he probably wouldn't have traveled as much if his homes had been more like this car.

After this interlude, the song is concluded by a coda in which the opening line is stated five more times. The melody here slowly rises from G to G during the first four statements, and descends back to the lower G in the fourth and fifth. This summary is given additional emphasis by an increasingly adventurous harmony voice. Finally, the instruments repeat the alternating D and G chords until they fade.

The final song on *Hearts and Bones*, "The Late Great Johnny Ace," follows on the end of "Cars Are Cars" without the customary pause. This sharply focuses attention on the somber mood of the sustained instrumental vamp that opens "The Late Great Johnny Ace," especially because of the contrast between this music and the punctuated, happy-go-lucky sounds that immediately preceded it in the coda of "Cars Are Cars." The contrast is further underscored by the fact that the introduction to "The Late Great Johnny

Ace" invites comparison to the introduction and coda of "Cars Are Cars" by virtue of alternating between two chords, just as those sections do, so that the consonant D and G chords of "Cars Are Cars" throw into relief the dissonance of the Abmaj7#11 and D7 harmonies of "The Late Great Johnny Ace."

This song uses three verses and a contrasting section in an AABA form to ruminate on the death of John Lennon. The first two verses set the stage by describing the singer's reaction, as an aspiring musician, upon hearing of the death of Johnny Ace in 1954. Each verse consists of two halves. In the first half, the singer describes what he is doing, accompanied by the Abmaj7#11 vamp (and continuing a melodic idea from the introduction), which eventually opens out to a G major chord. Just as this is seeming like a resolution to a tonic harmony, a seventh is added to the chord so as to lead to an emphasis on C, rather than G, for the second half of the verse, which uses a variety of harmonies and introduces new melodic ideas to describe how others communicated with the singer about Johnny Ace.

The singer says that he "really wasn't such a Johnny Ace fan." The B section of the song, however, indicates that he felt more of a connection with John Lennon. It breaks into a shuffle rhythm, and he describes living a bohemian life in London in 1964, highly aware of the Beatles and the Rolling Stones. Many of the harmonies are typical of a boogie-shuffle style, but they occasionally dissolve into some jazzier, more chromatic progressions to emphasize emotionally meaningful details, such as the girl with whom he was living, the irregular hours, and especially—at the end of the section—the music that was "flowing…and blowing [the singer's] way."

This last chromatic section leads back to the dissonant vamp of the introduction, and the third verse begins. Here the first half describes a stranger on the street telling the singer about Lennon's death, and the second half tells of their spending the rest of the evening at a bar, playing songs "for the Late Great Johnny Ace." As did the previous verses, this one comes to rest on a G major chord that sounds like a dominant harmony in the key of C. After the first verse this harmony led deceptively to the Abmaj7#11 chord that began the second verse, and after the second verse it led in a straightforward way to the tonic C chord of the B section. Now, at the end of the third verse, a cello sustains a low G, which leads to a coda written by the classical minimalist composer Philip Glass. In this passage, a violin and a viola create a typical (for the time) Glass texture by oscillating between chord tones. The mood of the song is sustained as the instrumental ensemble alternates between an A minor harmony and a Bb minor harmony while melodic fragments emerge from cello and bass clarinet. Eventually, a flute plays a simple, slow series of pitches ascending and descending, and the music stops.

World Music

GRACELAND

While the completion of *Hearts and Bones* may have been a significant achievement for Simon in light of the personal and creative difficulties that he had faced early in its creation, its public reception, as reflected by sales, was disappointing. This result from an album into which he had invested so much (including, as has been noted, unusually specific—at least for him—autobiographical elements) left Simon at a creative impasse. Where was he to go now for material that engaged him artistically and at the same time could communicate with a wide range of listeners? The answer came in the form of a cassette tape of South African "township jive," called *Gumboots: Accordion Jive Hits, Volume II,* that was given to him by guitarist Heidi Berg.

As he had so often done in the past, Simon used this distinctive musical style as a springboard for his own personal explorations. The album that emerged (released in 1986) was to be named after Elvis Presley's famous Memphis mansion, Graceland. It resulted in two Grammy awards, a transglobal political controversy, a significant contribution to interest in world music, and a decisive reversal of the decline in popularity that was suggested by the response to *Hearts and Bones.* It also constitutes an uncommon aesthetic achievement that richly interweaves multiple musical styles, innovative arrangements, an intricate network of textual themes, and attractive melodies.

In order to achieve this integration of disparate elements, Simon collaborated with several different groups of musicians. This creative strategy has already been observed numerous times in earlier albums. Most often, Simon worked with American artists with very distinctive talents, such as the Roche sisters, the Onward Brass Band, the Dixie Hummingbirds, the little-known roots guitar expert Stefan Grossman, and the uniquely mellow-voiced Phoebe Snow. Never before, though, had Simon used the approach in such a thoroughgoing manner throughout an entire album. Eight of the 11 songs use musicians drawn from four South African bands—Tao Ea Matsekha, General M. D. Shirinda and the Gaza Sisters, the Boyoyo Boys Band, and Stimela. Two songs, including one of these eight, use the South African *a cappella* church group Ladysmith Black Mambazo, and the final two songs feature the Louisiana Zydeco band Good Rockin' Dopsie and the Twisters and the East Los Angeles Latino band Los Lobos, respectively. (As Simon explains in the liner notes, these bands resemble several of the South African groups by virtue of their use of saxophones and accordion.[1]) Simon characteristically used these various sounds as building blocks in constructing songs, sometimes starting with a rhythm track produced by one of the groups and developing a textual idea on top of it, and sometimes cowriting with the other musicians in a more traditional way. In most cases, tracks were recorded in both Africa and the United States, and Simon added some of his customary American studio collaborators to the mix of many of the songs. Finally, the album includes two guest vocal appearances by iconic American pop artists, the Everly Brothers and Linda Ronstadt.

To the accompaniment of Tao Ea Matsekha, "The Boy in the Bubble," with music by Simon and Forere Motloheloa and text by Simon, introduces the album's textual complexity through a traditional verse-chorus division of labor: initially, verses narrate, while choruses comment. Thus, after the characteristic wheeze of the accordion sets a tempo, soon ratified by explosive drum strokes and then a driving bass line, the first verse presents a stark description of an urban terrorist incident. The mood is partly established by pitch structure, as the singer chants on only four relentless pitches—G, A, C, and D—that are harmonized in Dorian mode on A with a repeated four-measure pattern of A5, C, and D chords. Initially, the text is marked off in short phrases, as they describe "a slow day," but then the explosion brings with it a flurry of words that effectively convey not only the action itself, but also the rush of comprehension that an onlooker might experience in the process of realizing that an innocent-appearing baby carriage had actually contained a bomb.

This horrifying scenario is relieved by the chorus, though, as the key drops a step into a warm major tonality (G major, using the same pitches as A Dorian); only one melody pitch is added, but it, the B that fills the earlier gap between A and C, also reinforces the major quality of the scale. A very unusual feature here, perhaps based on the use of the accordion patterns, is the retention of the chord progression from the verse in the chorus with the single, but totally transforming, change whereby all the A5 chords are replaced with G harmonies. At this point the text retreats into a slightly more detached commentary on modern life. The melody takes on a folk-like quality, emphasizing the B and adding a voice (overdubbed by Simon) that tracks above the lead vocal in sweet consonant harmonies, and high synthesized sounds suggest gentle choral sighs. But the commentary here presents the listener with a kaleidoscopic swirl of images that reflect the mixture of social commentary, intimate revelation, and exuberance that will ebb and flow throughout the remainder of the album. Here these "days of miracles and wonder" are characterized by a wide variety of phenomena, all connected to technological sharing of information, and ranging from the familiar "long-distance call" all the way to a dying, far-away constellation. The parental, omniscient voice acknowledges that these images can produce anxiety, but concludes with comfort, urging "baby" not to cry.

Having established the roles of the verse and chorus, the song can then build on them to rhetorical advantage. The pattern is repeated for another round: the Dorian setting again conveys the tension of a stark scene, this time alluding to death at the hands of nature. And, again, this verse is chanted with accelerating syllables until the chorus settles into the comforting major key to repeat its initial text. Before the third round, though, the shriek of a synthesized horn section pushes the verse and chorus to new levels of intensity. Now, instead of increasing throughout, the verse begins with a rush of syllables, and instead of presenting a third narrative, it further develops the chorus's commentary on technology and commercialism. And, conversely, the chorus that follows hard on its heels, while continuing the commentary perspective ("And I believe..."), is endowed with new lyrics that borrow from the verses. Not only does it contain some hints of violence, but it also extends the rush of syllables, in "A loose affiliation of millionaires / And billionaires."

But this new text turns out to be an embellishment, not a total transformation, as it continues with a full presentation of the original chorus. Thus returned to this commentary, the song concludes with a search for resolution as it fades out with the repeated text "don't cry."

Three of the South African performers of this song also appear on the second song, the title track. They are joined by guitarist Chikapa "Ray" Phiri of Stimela and (overdubbed some months later) pedal steel guitarist Demola Adepoju from Nigeria. As Simon observes in the liner notes, the result "almost has the feel of American country music," and this flavor will be seen to be reinforced by several additional musical and textual elements.

Instrumental and stylistic differences notwithstanding, the song continues the search begun in "The Boy in the Bubble," but in a rather more personal way. The desire for comfort and reassurance in the face of senseless violence and the overwhelming profusion of modern technology is now turned inward into a search for personal redemption. Inspired by a trip that Simon had taken with his son Harper, the song tells the story of a pilgrimage, presumably from New York City, to Memphis. Over a constantly flowing, conversational groove, the lyrics unfold the narrator's ruminations on past failures and his desire for redemption.

As in "The Boy in the Bubble," verses and choruses fundamentally take on the traditional roles of narrative and commentary, respectively. The first verse tells of the journey, and the second flashes back to the point at which a relationship—perhaps the "first marriage"—broke down. (Simon has said that "'Graceland' is the continuation of the same story" begun by "Hearts and Bones."[2]) Each chorus begins by reiterating in some way that "I'm going to Graceland," and concluding with an echo of the "belief" in "The Boy in the Bubble," in this case that Graceland will receive us all. However, through the course of the song, these roles are blurred: the choruses contain a significant amount of expository information, and the third verse, especially, provides more commentary than one might ordinarily expect.

This evolution of rhetorical function is one of several means by which Simon uses the structure of the song to reflect the desire for transformation that is expressed in the lyrics. Others are more specifically musical. Most striking among these is Simon's treatment of the melody, which varies in some interesting ways from chorus to chorus, but to a remarkable degree among the three verses. These variations tend to respond to specific ideas in the text, especially in the emotion-laden recounting of the breakup in the beginning of the second verse, and they result in a sense of freedom that underscores the narrator's pilgrimage of liberation.[3]

"Graceland" is, of course, an appropriate name for a place where redemption is sought. Simon expands his focus on this iconic Southern mansion with several other references to Southern culture. Some of these are found in the lyrics of the first verse: "the Mississippi Delta," the "National guitar" (a steel-bodied variety, often played with a bottleneck in a blues setting), and "the cradle of the civil war" (whose lack of capitalization in the lyrics provided in the liner notes reflects its possible application to domestic strife as well).

Others, though, are conveyed in musical ways. The bottleneck style of playing a National guitar connects with the pedal steel guitar that is actually used in the recording, and Simon remarks in the liner notes on the connection of the latter instrument to American country music. Perhaps even more specific is Simon's use of the Everly Brothers, with their rockabilly associations, as backup singers. They ease into the song by evoking the wind at the end of the second verse, and their presence alludes to personal redemption not only as Southern references, but also in their personal significance as crucial early influences on Simon and Garfunkel.

Having conveyed a search for deliverance from both external and internal demons, the album broadens its exploration into connections in life, fraught with absurdities, poignancies, exhilarations, and heartbreaks. In many of the remaining seven African-based songs, Simon apparently used extensive passages of music that had already been composed by the African musicians and added some elements, particularly lyrical and melodic, to them. This approach is similar to one that he had already used many times in constructing his songs, in which he started with a rhythm track that he liked and wrote a song over it; the only difference is that in most of those cases he was solely or at least largely responsible for the creation of the basic track.

Most of the songs that result from this approach on this album thus automatically contain typical elements of the South African "township jive," since in many cases the foundation of a song is provided by the actual musicians playing music that they wrote. Moreover, many of them share a distinctive, significant characteristic: the harmonic structure of much or all of a particular song consists of a brief sequence of chords, repeated many times as an *ostinato*. "I Know What I Know" provides a clear example of both of these features.

This account of some flirtatious sparring that occasionally borders on the surreal is based on a song performed by General M.D. Shirinda and the Gaza Sisters (and, while the words are simply credited to Simon, the music is attributed to Simon and General M.D. Shirinda). The harmonic structure for the entire song consists of a single two-measure series—three beats on a G chord, one on F, two on C, and two on F—that occurs 10 times in each of the three verse-refrain sequences in addition to running through the instrumental introduction and the instrumental/vocal coda. This is established by guitars playing in a distinctive style, drums, and bass throughout the song.

Over this accompaniment, Simon sings the verses, in each of which a heavy dose of repeated notes accommodates a lot of syllables in two couplets. In the refrain, the singer declares the title line, as the Gaza Sisters sing and whoop exuberantly in the background. The singer goes on to insist that he will "sing what [he] said" about the way things work.

In the first verse, the singer tells of meeting a woman who asks if she met him "at the cinematographer's party"; he responds, "who am I to blow against the wind." In the second verse, he tries to figure out what she means when she says that he "reminds [her] of money," and in response *she* delivers the line about the wind. The third verse conveys a sense of return to the first verse, as the singer speaks positively of the woman; she repeats the line about the cinematographer's party, and again it is he who asks about the wind. (Moreover, the rhymes in the first couplet of the third verse match those in the first couplet of the first verse.) In sum, Simon uses the distinctive instrumental texture, the wordplay, and the uninhibited vocal style of the Gaza Sisters to support an overall lightheartedly satirical tone in the song. While to some degree the text suggests alienation and an inability to communicate in meaningful ways, the subject matter lacks the global or personal gravity, respectively, exhibited by the previous two songs.

A very similar mood, although perhaps slightly more serious from the singer's perspective, is conveyed by the following song, "Gumboots." Here the chord progression again spans two 4/4 measures. In the key of D, one measure of D is followed by two beats apiece of G and A, and this pattern repeats throughout the entire song.[4] The basic track is provided by the Boyoyo Boys, and two of them, Jonhjon Mkhalali and Lulu Masilda, share musical composition credit with Simon.

Simon, however, receives sole credit for the words. After an instrumental introduction, these are presented in three verse-refrain pairs. In each verse, the singer describes a situation in two lines that descend from D to D, but incorporate many rapidly repeated notes along the way. He then gives his response, starting, "I said 'hey' "; one line here stays between the Ds and the second again retraces the D-to-D descent. All of this occupies 12 bars (six iterations of the D-G-A pattern), and then one or more statements of the plaintive refrain, "You don't feel you could love me but I feel you could," are presented, with a summing-up flavor created by starting on the high F♯ and thus superseding the Ds that have started three of the lines in each verse.

The stories that are told are fairly accessible, but they are somewhat unusual, especially with regard to their juxtaposition with one another. In the first verse the singer describes a difficult discussion in a taxi with a friend "who had a little bit of a breakdown." The arrival of the refrain indicates that this friend may in fact be a potential lover, and some of the text in the verse indicates that the singer was doing some verbal maneuvering and glibly minimizing the friend's situation. In the next verse, now (and until the end of the song) supported by female backup singers, the singer describes "[falling] into a phone call." The following lines suggest that the conversation didn't go well, despite his cockiness, and he contemplates giving up on the relationship; this is followed by two statements of the refrain (each echoed by the backup singers).

At this point an instrumental interlude is inserted in which saxophones— "added...to the original track" by Simon, aware of their common use in " 'township jive' music"[5]—respond, almost jeeringly, to what has preceded it. First a single sax lays out an eight-bar descending melody that ends on the dominant note A, and then this phrase is repeated by three saxes in harmony, now ending on a tonic harmony. The third verse then begins.

Here the singer describes a flirtatious encounter on the street with a "Señorita" that seems to show promise; this (again characterized by the singer's brashness) is concluded by two statements of the refrain, and it is unclear whether this is a new romantic prospect or the same woman whom the singer has been addressing earlier in the song. While the order of the verses seems to suggest the former interpretation, the latter is reinforced by the fact that, following an eight-bar interlude in which the saxes play their harmonized melody, the first verse starts over and fades out. This may indicate that the "Señorita" verse is something of a flashback, or that the new relationship is inevitably destined to follow essentially the same path that had been followed by the old one (or even that incidents like the Señorita situation lead to the kind of difficult discussions that the first verse describes with the original woman).

Romantic difficulties are also discussed in the next song, "Diamonds on the Soles of Her Shoes," but in this case much of the story is told in the third person, and it differs further from "I Know What I Know" and "Gumboots" in that it touches on class issues and is characterized by poignancy rather than selfish superficiality. Here Simon combines an introduction set against *a cappella* African sounds, a rhythmic and harmonic groove similar to that of "Gumboots" for the main portion of the song, and the striking image of the title to paint a distinctive picture of a relationship. Furthermore, as is often the case with such portraits, the song includes enigmatic elements, along with its suggestive references to the couple's social situation.

In the introduction, cowritten by Simon and Joseph Shabalala, the leader of the South African *a cappella* group Ladysmith Black Mambazo, the group sings African words to create a syncopated shuffle-rhythm background in E major. Eventually Simon sings against them, introducing the characters of his story: a rich girl with diamonds on the soles of her shoes and a poor boy who is "empty as a pocket"—at this point the other singers join his English text. In a refrain-like passage, Simon and the other singers alternate between E and A and B chords to reiterate the title line a few times.

The music comes to a halt, and then a bright electric-guitar line helps to lift the song into an F major groove, presented by guitars, drums, and a distinctively growling fretless bass. At this point the chord progression that ran through all of "Gumboots" begins to do the same thing in this song—now transposed to F, it presents one measure of F, followed by two beats apiece of B♭ and C. Against this groove, Simon sings the first of two verses with a highly syncopated melodic line supported by periodic gentle background-vocal pulses. The first section of the verse says that people say that the girl is crazy, but wearing the diamonds helps her "to lose these walking blues." In the second section, the singer says that "she slipped into [his] pocket"; she feels that she's been taken for granted. The singer here adopts the first person, as if he were the poor boy, but this identification seems debatable because the singer mentions his car keys, which one might expect that the poor boy wouldn't have. The third section is a refrain, with falsetto singing and bass work, that dwells again on the image of the diamond-studded soles, "as if everybody knows what [the singer is] talking about."

Following an interlude characterized first by a brass section and then by more falsetto singing, background-vocal pulses, and nimble bass runs, the second verse follows the same three-section pattern as that of the first. In the first section, the two lovers communicate cryptically with one another and the boy compensates for his non-diamonded shoes with the application of after-shave. In the second section the girl asks to go dancing, but the couple instead falls asleep in a doorway "on Upper Broadway"; without further elaboration, they are now described as having "diamonds on the soles of *their* shoes." Apparently the boy has somehow gained these, because after the refrain and another brass-dominated interlude, a coda presents the opening lines of the first verse again, but now they describe the singer, who has already taken on the role of the boy earlier in the verse. The song closes with a lengthy coda in which at first all singers reiterate syllables from the refrain of the introduction. Eventually a falsetto voice enters above this ostinato; here the falsetto idea has evolved into an *obbligato* style typical of American doo-wop of the 1950s. Finally, though, all instruments and voices besides Ladysmith Black Mambazo and African drums drop out, and these remaining performers repeat to a fade.

"You Can Call Me Al," the most widely broadcast song on the album, thanks in part to its portrayal in a popular and strikingly low-key music video featuring Simon and Chevy Chase, also paints a portrait, but in this case its subject is an individual man who is extremely ill at ease with his place in the world. The refrain proposes that the listener be his "bodyguard," but it seems that he needs emotional protection as much as any other kind, because the listener is apparently a woman with whom he would like to be on personal terms, calling her "Betty" while she calls him "Al." The refrain is cast in the first person, and most of the first two verses also quote Al.

The form of the song as a whole consists of four verses with refrains (the third is a pennywhistle solo), along with an introduction and coda. As is seen in most of the songs on the album, the harmonic structure here consists of repeated two-bar chord patterns, although the pattern varies slightly from verse to refrain: both are a bit more complicated than some of the other songs, but the most important chords are F-Gm-C in the verse and F-B♭-C in the refrain. This regularity allows the main interest of the song to be found in the textual arena, as the man's haplessness is portrayed by a torrent of verbal devices that range from cross-references of sense or sound within the song to a scattergun array of references to phenomena outside the song, sprinkled liberally with so many clichés that they make things that are not clichés sound like clichés (e.g., "incidents and accidents").

After a brass section provides the distinctively syncopated hook of the introduction, the first verse starts, as will each of the succeeding verses, with a line that sets the humorous tone by sounding like the present-tense beginning of a joke: "A man walks down the street..." The man bemoans his paunch and his difficult life, and wants a "photo opportunity" or "a shot at redemption" (offering a humorous perspective on the theme of "Graceland"); he doesn't want to be a cartoon, although the listener can tell that he already is one. In the second section other voices join him in a repetitive revving effect as he mentions additional threats to his well-being, and he conveys a sense of superiority by saying that he doesn't find it all amusing. In the refrain, which is set against the music first presented in the introduction, the singer is joined by an additional voice, sounding hollow at the octave below.

The second verse conveys more angst; the man's attention is short and his nights are long. Furthermore, he feels that he has lost his "role model," who has gone into the alley "with some roly-poly little bat-faced girl." This phrase not only connects sonically with the word "role," but also relates this second section to each of the others, as each refers somehow to animals. After the instrumental third verse, which connects with the common use of the pennywhistle in some South African popular music, most of the final verse eschews quotation of Al in order to comment directly on how he might relate to larger issues. Perhaps his alienation comes from the fact that he's in the Third World, or he's foreign, but finally there seems to be some awareness of transcendent elements as "he sees angels in the architecture" (the first two syllables of this word rhyming with an earlier, Third-World, reference to the "marketplace").

The coda begins with a fifth trip through the chord changes of the verse and refrain. Simon sings "na, na, na" during the verse part, using pitches drawn from the earlier melody, and a two-bar bass lick is inserted before the refrain, which has no singing. Finally, the refrain continues to repeat to a fade as some of its phrases are reiterated.

The duet with Linda Ronstadt, "Under African Skies," resembles other songs on the album by repeating a single two-bar chord progression—E♭-A♭-E♭/B♭-B♭ in the key of E♭—throughout. Furthermore, the song uses bass, drums, percussion, and guitars to provide a fairly strong shuffle beat throughout (Simon says in the liner notes that "Hilton Rosenthal describes [this] as a Zulu walking rhythm"[6]). However, the general tone of the song, as established both by the vocals' slow pace during the verses and by the subject matter, is considerably gentler than is the case for songs such as "I Know What I Know" and "Gumboots."

The harmonic structure and formal units constructed from regular four-bar phrases create a simple setting for an attractive and elegant song. First, a two-bar guitar riff repeats for 12 measures as other instruments accumulate in the introduction. This texture continues as Simon sings the first verse with Ronstadt providing harmonies; its 16 bars describe Joseph, whose life reflects the night, moonlight, and stars of his African skies.

Against a more vigorous accompaniment, Simon then sings the chorus alone. In its 16 bars, he uses a more highly syncopated melody, with more leaps and skips, as the singer declares that this is about memory, indwelling love, dreams of identity, and "the roots of rhythm." After the guitar riff provides an eight-bar interlude, Simon and Ronstadt sing the second verse, which fills out these themes by introducing a second character, a woman, speaking in first person, who grew up hearing "mission music" in Tucson. Apparently referring to herself, she prays for "the wings to fly through harmony."

After this verse, the two singers repeat the phrase "Ka-oombah oombah oombah oh" through an exuberant 16-bar bridge. This leads into a recapitulation of the first verse, after which the guitar riff is absorbed into atmospheric sustained sounds to conclude the song. The song thus addresses the general themes of alienation and cultural angst that pervade the album by implying that the two characters have found each other through a deeply ingrained connection with a musical impulse that transcends cultural and geographical boundaries.

These same themes are addressed in different ways in "Homeless," whose text expresses unease, but whose structure reflects a fruitful collaboration between Simon and Joseph Shabalala and Ladysmith Black Mambazo. This entire song is performed *a cappella*, using various textures, with some African vocal effects and antiphonal singing. English and Zulu texts alternate in the song, and this results in large measure from the compositional process, which

Simon describes in the liner notes.[7] The overall form is a kind of block structure, in which loosely related texts follow one another.

The entire song is based on an F♯ major scale, and lines tend to gravitate toward important notes in that scale, especially F♯ and C♯. The introduction, written by the group, uses a harmonized traditional Zulu wedding melody with Zulu words that describe people living in deprivation in caves. This leads to the title section, originally written by Simon, and modified and extended in Zulu by Shabalala, that uses descending phrases to develop Simon's textual idea, "we are homeless, homeless / moonlight sleeping on a midnight lake."

The next section is an antiphonal passage that Simon wrote to provide a transition to musical material from a preexistent Ladysmith Black Mambazo song. After that is sung, Simon's transition appears again. This time it is followed by another preexisting element, a declaration that the group is the best at singing in this style, and this concludes the song.

Simon has said that the latter part of the title of "Crazy Love, Vol. II" was intended to distinguish the song from Van Morrison's similarly titled song, as well as to relate to an idea that love had started and stopped twice.[8] But it might also highlight for the listener the fact that the song develops a character similar to the one depicted in "You Can Call Me Al." In this case, the story of "Fat Charlie the Archangel" is told in three verses, each followed by a chorus in which Charlie declares repeatedly that "I don't want no part of your crazy love." As was the case for other songs on the album, simple and repetitive chord changes lend a sense of simplicity to this vignette. But it is made arresting by a profusion of captivating textual images and a continuously evolving tapestry of attractive accompanimental effects. This latter attribute, combined with the jaded subject matter, exemplifies Simon's penchant for mixing unlike features within a single song, as has been mentioned in connection with the album *Paul Simon;* in fact, Simon had noted with reference to "Peace Like a River" in his 1972 *Rolling Stone* interview with Jon Landau that "That's just a thing with me, to do something that sounds pretty or light to have a nastiness in it. That's just a style; I don't do it consciously, it just comes out naturally with me."[9]

The song resembles "Under African Skies" in that it begins with a 12-bar introduction based on a 2-bar guitar riff as other instruments join in. (This riff includes two guitars, but both songs feature the performer Chikapa "Ray" Phiri, who is credited with co-arranging both songs, as well as "You Can Call Me Al.") The chord progression for these two bars is G-Am7-G(or G/D)-D in the key of G, again reminiscent of the tonic-predominant-dominant motion of "Under African Skies," "Gumboots," the main section of "Diamonds on the Soles of Her Shoes," and the general motion of both sections of "You Can Call Me Al." This two-bar sequence continues into the verse, which consists of four four-bar phrases, but it is replaced at the end of the first and third of these by Em-D-C-D sequences. The deceptively approached E-minor chord in each of these accompanies the last word of a line of text and colors it with a sense of dismay (a bright splash of guitar notes each time notwithstanding); in the first verse, these include the striking images of Fat Charlie "slop[ing] into the room" and being compared to a "lonely little wrinkled balloon." Although Fat Charlie claims to have no opinions, he can perceive that he is unhappy.

The verse ends on a dominant D chord, but rather than beginning with the G that would resolve it, the chorus drops suddenly into F, and Charlie's dismissals of "this crazy love" come out in four four-bar phrases. Each of them begins with a simple F-B♭-C-F cycle; the first three end by moving through B♭ to the dominant C, but the last one resolves the C to F before the G major riff begins to set up the second verse. The chorus is propelled by heavy drums on the weak beats. At the same time, though, the texture is sweetened by some swirling guitars and a high harmony voice.

The riff before the second verse is similarly sweetened by wordless vocalizing and Synclavier piping. These sounds and sustained harmonies continue into the second verse, in which Charlie has no opinion about verbal sparring with his wife, and imagines that the evening news could be reporting that his life is on fire. The second chorus follows, although its second half is now replaced by "oohs" rather than text. In the following riff, a soprano saxophone subtly joins the texture and continues along with the Synclavier to warm up the third verse. Now Charlie files for divorce and regrets the time that this will cost him and the weight that he will have to lose; he now expresses his lack of opinion in the second half of the verse rather than the first. The sax also appears in the final chorus, in which Fat Charlie's exasperation and vehemence is emphasized by Simon's melody reaching up into a falsetto range, and the sax leads the way into a brief instrumental repeat-and-fade.

The final two songs on *Graceland* are collaborations similar to those of the first nine, but each of them uses an American band. Simon says in the liner notes that he chose two bands and styles that used saxophone and accordion so as to have a "musical connection to home" from the sax-and-accordion-heavy South African music.[10] The first of these was the Cajun Zydeco band Good Rockin' Dopsie and the Twisters, with whom Simon created "That Was Your Mother."

This song is a celebration of "*le bon temps*" musically and, as it turns out, textually as well. Only two chords are used, F and C in the key of F, and the entire song is based on eight-bar units: four of F, two of C, and two of F. These provide the backdrop for the band's jamming and for the singer's syncopated tale, which employs a lot of skips among chord tones in the 16-bar narrative verses and additional rapid repeated notes in the choruses (also 16 bars) that describe the joys of partying in Cajun country.

After the song is kicked off by an eight-bar accordion solo with a four-bar extension, the singer, accompanied by the band with prominent accordion, bass, drums, and washboard, begins to tell the listener a story that took place "before you was born, dude." In the story, the singer was a traveling salesman, always on the move. The chorus finds him standing on a city corner looking for a place to have a good time, and then the sax provides an interlude with three eight-bar solo passes.

In the second verse the singer tells of encountering a pretty girl, and the chorus is altered to describe him wondering how he can pick her up. The accordion provides an eight-bar interlude this time. In the third verse, the title line reveals that the singer is addressing his son, and the punchline is that, although the singer loves him, he wants to make clear that the son is the "burden of [the singer's] generation," and it was before the son was born that "life was great." Following a last take on the chorus and an eight-bar drum solo, the accordion leads the instruments on a final eight-bar rideout.

Simon created the final song on *Graceland*, "All Around the World or The Myth of Fingerprints," with Los Lobos, an East-Los Angeles-based Latino rock band. The lyrics of this song are as elusive as those of any track on the album, as they connect rather elliptically both within the song and with the themes developed in the other songs. These lyrics are distributed among verses and choruses, all of which connect with other songs by using only three chords, in this case G, C, and D in the key of G. The verses are accompanied by an acoustic-guitar-dominated texture, while the accompaniment for the choruses focuses on accordion and saxophone; as was the case in "You Can Call Me Al," this accompaniment is first heard in an instrumental introduction.

The first verse, with a syncopated, folk-like melody, tells of a reclusive, famous "former talk-show host." He declares that "it was the myth of fingerprints" (although the identity of "it" is left unspecified), and that "they're all the same." The sense of *Weltschmerz* suggested here is developed a bit in the chorus, which uses a more propulsive melody to describe the routine of a weary sun setting and a "black pit town" being lit up at night, and ends with the first part of the title, by way of suggesting that the mundane passage of time is universally inescapable.

In the second line two of the band members add vocal harmonies to Simon's melody. This verse talks about the Indian Ocean, thus reinforcing the idea—first conveyed by the "black pit town"—that the story is located in South Africa. The verse describes an army post that is "abandoned ... just like the war." This, too, is somehow attributed to the myth of fingerprints, and the following chorus varies slightly from the first one by changing the weary sun to a "bloody" one. The last verse, again with three singers, recapitulates the first one, except that a small reordering in a line at the halfway point sets up the last line to rhyme by saying that "we must learn to live alone" rather than the earlier "they're all the same." This is the closing thought of the song, although it is echoed by a repeated vocal coda that is mostly textless but includes the words "live on, live on, live on" as it fades out. On this note, then, that is somewhat whimsical because of the loosely connected images, but ultimately pessimistic with respect to themes of alienation in an industrial, technological culture, *Graceland* ends.

On a purely artistic level, the *Graceland* project proved congenial for Simon for a number of reasons. Throughout his career as a songwriter, he had demonstrated a penchant for finding new musical materials and incorporating them into his music or, more radically, using them as bases for his music. The latter approach worked better for him than it might have for some other writers, because, while many might routinely begin with text and melodic ideas, Simon often started with a swatch of musical material, as it were, and created textual and melodic ideas against it. Furthermore, not only did this inclination facilitate his appropriation of various elements of South African music as starting points for the songs on the album, but these materials themselves were very attractive. In addition to the fact that their relative simplicity probably enhanced their flexibility, their combination of familiar, consonant harmonies with novel rhythms and textures was naturally appealing to listeners.

THE RHYTHM OF THE SAINTS

The success of *Graceland* surely encouraged Simon to pursue a similar process on his next album, *The Rhythm of the Saints* (1990). This project shifted the geographical focus to Brazil, the appeal of which was surely partly related to Simon's long-time interest in the music of Brazilian composer Antonio Carlos Jobim.[11] It reflects an even more consistent process of composing—or one might even say "assembling"—the songs. While various songs on *Graceland* were recorded in various places or combinations of places, and they range from sounding almost purely African (as in "Homeless") to partaking entirely of another tradition (as in "That Was Your Mother" and "All Around the World or The Myth of Fingerprints"), portions of each of the 10 songs on *The Rhythm of the Saints* were recorded in both Brazil and New York (although in two cases, "Proof" and "Born at the Right Time," additional portions were recorded in Paris as well). Furthermore, as with most of the songs on *Graceland*, it is clear that these portions generally do not follow one another within a song, but rather are layered on top of one another, and that usually the Brazilian portion tends to be the basic rhythm track upon which Simon layers vocals as well as additional instruments.

Such a process could theoretically be very simple, with a clear division of labor: Simon might simply locate an existing Brazilian texture, appropriate it wholesale, and then add other elements. It is likely that the reality was usually more complex. On the one hand, in many cases Simon probably rather actively influenced the basic track or tracks in terms of modifying their original makeup and/or deploying them throughout a song. On the other, while the liner credits make it clear that he drew upon a wide range of American and African musicians for the "added" elements, the Brazilian style, too, is evident beyond the basic rhythm track. In any event, though, the way that the songs are assembled points to two particular areas of compositional interest (in addition to common concerns such as textual content and melodic structure): the nature of the instrumental and vocal materials in a song, and the ways that the song's form is articulated (especially in relation to the deployment of a basic rhythm track or tracks).

In "The Obvious Child," the rhythm track consists of an unpitched drum pattern, performed by Grupo Cultural OLODUM. At first an introduction is provided by gradually evolving rhythms. Then a continuous pattern sets in, with only slight variations for most of the song. There are two exceptions: (1) about three-quarters of the way through the main, texted section of the song, a series of rolled embellishments is added; and (2) after this section, the continuous pattern is broken by more intermittent, evolving rhythms, which lead to a wordless falsetto coda that again incorporates the continuous pattern.

Against this rhythm track Simon sings the song, accompanied also by strummed acoustic guitar, using diatonic and modally flavored major chords, and occasional harmonica, Akai EWI Synthesizer, and background vocals. (The EWI is an Electric Wind Instrument, played very similarly to the way a saxophone is played, in this case by Michael Brecker.) Somewhat consistently with the guitar style, the vocal style is generally reminiscent of an assertive, 1960s-era folk anthem. It presents the text in an evolving musical form that draws on the familiar AABA format that Simon has so often used (in the following discussion their labels will appear in quotation marks to indicate that, because of this evolving process, "A" sections are not as thoroughly similar to one another as is ordinarily the case).

The text is not entirely transparent, but seems to be presenting the thoughts of an older adult who is coming to terms with his humanity. In the first "A" section, he expresses a preference for a somewhat peaceful existence, while at the same time acknowledging that things won't be perfect, and that there's no point in "deny[ing] the obvious child." The gradual exposition of his thoughts is supported by an evolutionary melodic structure, as each melodic phrase builds on elements of the previous one, until the last three break free of this process. The second "A" section starts in a similar way melodically, but breaks into new ideas at the end. Its text recalls an idealistic time of youth with a girl. A contrasting section describes the birth of a son named "Sonny" and his own marriage, parenthood, and increasing responsibilities. A third "A" section then follows, in which the singer describes his ruminations at dawn—again, the section begins with the same melodic material as that of the first two sections, but concludes with yet additional ideas.

At this point, as the rolled embellishments are introduced in the drum track, the melody takes on a tone that is quite different from what has gone on before—slower, more even rhythms poignantly describe Sonny in the midst of a mid-life depression. This is followed by a recapitulation of the very first "A" section: most of the text is the same, but some melodic elements are drawn from the other "A" sections. Finally, after the drum pattern is broken, the falsetto of the coda has a 1950s doo-wop flavor that, like the folk sounds earlier, reinforces the sense of the passage of time conveyed by the text.

Because the continuous rhythm track for "The Obvious Child" was unpitched, Simon could articulate the form of the song with harmonies that he added, and he did indeed do this—for example, although the "A" sections differ from one another melodically, each has essentially the same harmonic structure, and this helps to determine their identity within the form. A different premise in the next song, "Can't Run But," however, yields a very different formal result. Here the basic rhythm track is provided by *pitched* percussion, and this consists of a repeating pattern that exhibits very little harmonic motion: 11 measures of A-minor harmonies with various added notes are followed by a single measure that walks up in octaves from E—E-F#-G-G#—to an A to begin the pattern again.

Because this pattern continues through the entire song, there is never a sense of harmonic closure, since each iteration simply dwells on A minor before leading to the next, and the form cannot therefore be shaped further by harmonic structure. In fact, to a large degree the overall effect is somewhat hypnotic, as the vast majority of the melody emphasizes a very narrow range between A and C, with occasional forays above or below, and this tends to support the repeated text of the refrain "I can't run, but I can walk much faster than this..." At the same time, though, Simon does establish a kind of verse-refrain alternation, as the verses differ from the refrain textually, as well as using slightly different—if strongly related—musical material.

Furthermore, the verses and the refrains are interestingly deployed against the repeating 12-bar harmonic pattern. After a single mallet instrument plays a repeated pattern for 4 bars, instruments are gradually added to the texture during two 12-bar groups. A third group begins with 4 instrumental bars and ends with the 8-measure refrain. Then the first verse lasts for *16* measures, thus occupying one entire 12-bar group and 4 bars of the next, leaving 8 bars to be filled by the refrain.

The first verse refers to environmental issues in vaguely ominous terms. After a 12-bar interlude in which 4 measures of vocalizing are followed by 8 instrumental measures, a second 16-plus-8-bar verse-refrain pair occupies two more 12-bar groups. This verse moves to personal concerns, as the singer describes (again in vague terms) a dream about the listener (presumably his lover) and him, concluding with an image of another couple dancing and "rubbing against us."

After the refrain, a third verse follows immediately. In one sense, it brings some resolution to the preceding verses, as it combines nature images with personal ones ("A winding river gets wound around a heart"), but it ends by moving to a new realm, the current state of the music industry. The piece ends in a way that is consistent with its hypnotic nature throughout: this thought is left hanging and undeveloped as the earlier interlude begins again and the music fades out.

"The Coast" includes a larger complement of instrumental forces, with various vocals (including contributions by Ladysmith Black Mambazo), percussion instruments, a brass section, and the EWI synthesizer (again played by Brecker). Perhaps most distinctively, though, it introduces to the album the guitar playing of Vincent Nguini, who shares music-writing credit for this song with Simon, receives credit for the guitar arrangement on this song and "Spirit Voices," and shares this credit on three others. The song is introduced by an accumulation of percussion instruments that provide a rhythm background throughout, and then a buoyant guitar line sets up a simple four-bar, three-chord pattern (B♭, E♭, and F in the key of B♭) that is repeated once.

There are three verses in this song, and the last is bracketed by two slightly varied versions of a chorus. The chorus declares the singer's love for the listener, and refers impressionistically to summer skies and stars "all along the injured coast"; it uses syncopated bursts of melody, supported by backup singers, brass punctuations, and the same three-chord harmonic palette to make its case. The verses generally paint a picture of life on this coast. Each consists of three sections—one that describes specific details with a melody that runs in counterpoint against the initial guitar line and harmonic pattern; a second that adds some C-minor harmonies and comments on the loneliness and sorrow of this life; and a third that adds a D♭ harmony (hinting at the key of B♭ minor) to help support a low, funky refrain that cynically mentions monetary value.

The only formal component that presents significantly different text upon its reappearance is the first section of the verses. The three of these do develop a general train of thought, although this hardly constitutes a coherent narrative. In the first verse they describe a musical family that finds lodging in a harbor church. The second verse views the local market in the context of the whole world, and mentions the scarcity of food for some. After the first chorus, a drum interlude and a return of the introductory guitar line set off the last verse. This verse returns to the church of the first verse but implies that this can be the setting for more transcendent insights; this transformed perspective is supported by the addition of synthesized reedy chords that suggest a church organ. The final reiteration of the chorus, though, implies that this transcendence is somehow mixed with the brokenness that can be found in the world, and the song fades to an end.

The form of "Proof" is very similar to that of "The Coast"—three verses are complemented by a chorus that is sung before and after the third. The chorus, which is actually presented twice on its first occurrence with a brief interlude intervening, uses long bursts of repeated melodic notes, brass punctuations, bass licks reminiscent of *Graceland,* and three chords (G, C, and D in the key of G), to describe people's unreliability and declare that proof, not faith, "is the bottom line for everyone." The interlude, presented less assertively but still with the same three chords, expresses the singer's insecurity about features—his face, race, sex, and financial status—that he feels should vouch for his identity. This is sung against a repetitive chant sung by women.

The verses present more of a consistent "ethnic" flavor than is the case in many passages in the earlier songs. The accompaniment is dominated by steel-drum sounds, which form the basis for the "rhythm track" in this song, although their pattern changes from section to section. Furthermore, the singer uses a flexible, syncopated melody, against continual background vocals and the same three chords occasionally colored with a modal-sounding Dm7, to speak directly to his lover. In the first verse he speaks hopefully of their ability to make their fortunes and "leave this loathsome little town"; he imagines her dressed richly for their wedding. An interlude then introduces the brass that will play an important role in the chorus.

In the second verse the singer comments on the inevitable effect of time on the relationship, suggesting gently that the lovers' focus will wander and blur. This is followed by a second interlude that features piping sounds reminiscent of Crosby, Stills, and Nash's "Marrakesh Express," and then by the doubly presented chorus. In the aftermath of this endorsement of the provable, the third verse poetically urges the singer's beloved to persevere. The chorus returns, however, and its last line, "Proof is the bottom line for everyone," repeats and fades against the women's chant to end the song.

Although most of the sections of "Proof" are very similar to one another with respect to harmonic structure and basic rhythm track, instrumentation and melodic style effect a fair amount of contrast so as to distinguish verse from chorus, and both from interludes. Much less contrast is present in "Further to Fly." Tuned drums dwell throughout on a low, repeated A♭-A♭-E♭ pattern with E♭, the tonic note of the song, falling on the downbeat of the 3/4 measures. At cadence points the E♭ moves briefly to D, and the harmonics change throughout the song, including a variety of jazz chords in the key of E♭ minor. The way that these elements strain against the E♭, combined with melodies that dwell extensively on particular notes and the Latin-jazz style of singing that Simon adopts, sets the tone for a mystically passionate, yearning text. These features also make it possible to emphasize particular textual ideas, as, at certain points, the harmonies move strongly against or into alignment with the E♭, or an emphasized pitch provides a point of reference for a local descent or a long-term descent.

The first verse consists of three sections. In the first, an E♭m11 harmony and a melodic B♭ are featured as the text says that the listener may experience exhaustion, but the section concludes by repeating the title phrase. The second section changes the musical background by emphasizing a B double-flat (B♭♭) in the melody. This note changes the underlying harmony—its technical name is now E♭m7♭5, but the important effect is simply that it has changed, and that this change is heard in the alteration of the melodic B♭ to B♭♭. The change conveys a need to return, as the singer describes a mysterious lover in the listener's life. The melody does indeed slide back up from B♭♭ to B♭ at the end of the section as the title appears again. Now the E♭ harmony takes on a third structure—it becomes E♭7, acting as a dominant chord leading to the A♭m chord that prevails over the third section (enhanced with chiming guitars) as the exotic flirtation and desire is described. The melody here dwells at first on C, but ranges more widely than it did in the earlier sections, as more dynamic harmonic motion suggests the passion that is described.

The same sectional structure is found in the second verse. In the first section, the singer questions his sanity. In the second, while the harmonies remain as they were in the first verse, the melody ranges higher, conveying desperation as familiar things vanish. This leads to the third section in which the singer predicts that he may lose the listener; as melodic notes continue to fly higher than they did in the first verse, he continues to describe the nature of desire.

An instrumental interlude maintains the mood while providing a brief respite from the text. The third verse is abbreviated, essentially omitting the second section. Its text continues to develop ideas of unreliable perceptions, the elusiveness of love, and the power of desire, including a reference to the "Rose of Jericho," which had made an earlier appearance in "The Coast." The song drifts off as the instrumental interlude reappears and fades out.

An elusive, powerful lover is also featured, combined with a complex Latin rhythm track that gradually coalesces in the introduction, in "She Moves On." While, as the title suggests, the singer is unable to keep the object of his desire, he is so exhilarated by the experience of having been with her that he claims to feel good anyway. The bright tone of the song is expressed textually by an eight-measure passage that appears at the beginning and end and describes the "fine day" as "the sun hits off the runway."

The first four-bar half of this passage starts with two measures on a B-minor harmony and ends with two on E minor; the second half reverses this process. Most of the rest of the song (including a wordless female vocalization that precedes this passage) consists of repetitions of this eight-measure pattern. While sections of verses are still distinguished from one another by melodic content, the simple recurrence of this (simple in itself) harmonic unit lends an additional breeziness to the telling of the story.

Each verse contains four eight-bar units. In the first section of the first verse, after a saxophone-dominated interlude, the singer conversationally describes, in a low melodic register, the way he feels "blessed," as his "heart . . . splashes inside [his] chest." As was the case with "Further to Fly," this section ends with the title phrase. The second section suddenly reaches up to a high F♯ to begin the description of a dramatic moment, but a verdict is again rendered by the title phrase. In the third section, female voices coo the woman's words as she tells the singer that he has "underestimated [her] power." The singer responds in bursts that repeatedly reach up melodically before falling back down as he expresses his fear that he will be abandoned and forsaken; this last eight-bar section expresses his emotional limbo not only with these melodic contours, but also by remaining throughout on a single (B minor) harmony.

The second verse is preceded by a guitar-dominated interlude. Then, in its first two sections, the singer accommodates the woman by taking a walk with her and then agreeing with her philosophical perspective on love (these sections are a bit more continuous than they were in the first verse, with the title phrase following only the second one). The last two sections more or less recapitulate those of the first verse; this time, in the last section, the singer feels that the woman has "captured the breath of [his] voice in a bottle." Nonetheless, after another guitar-dominated interlude, he finishes with the description of the "fine day" that opened the song, and then female voices return to the opening vocalization to fade out.

"Born at the Right Time" uses a substantial Latin percussion track, but as a whole it leans more toward a generic pop/rock style than is the case with "Further to Fly" and "She Moves On." A prominent guitar riff is repeated throughout over chord changes that recall the many three-chord songs of *Graceland* (although the typical F, Bb, and C [in F] are spiced up a bit with a chromatic G13). Simon also recalls *Graceland* by using an accordion, played by C. J. Chenier. The song juxtaposes depictions of infants who are innocent, but also, as the title suggests, potentially powerful in some mystical way, with images of people overwhelming the earth.

A 12-bar instrumental introduction starts with a 4-measure vamping three-chord unit, and then uses 8 measures to present a chord sequence (including the G13) that will form the basis for the verses of the song. This sequence is immediately repeated to accompany the first verse, which introduces the infant theme. Here a gentle melody slowly descends as references to Moses (a baby boy in "reeds and rushes") are parlayed into the suggestion of mystical power ("eyes as clear as centuries"). These ideas are then consolidated by the three-chord chorus, in which eight brief phrases in eight measures simply sum up the infant's charmed existence, concluding with the title phrase.

The second verse combines two of the initial eight-measure chord sequences. The first uses a new, syncopated melody as the singer brashly describes his and his cosmopolitan friends' self-indulgent tourism, but the second returns to the original, gentle tune as innocent, native infants are described gazing at him, "their uninvited guest." The fact that they share musical material with the first infant that was described suggests that these babies also share his mystical significance (and in this way, of course, they differ from the more powerful—in appearance—singer and his friends). This implication is reinforced by the immediate return of the chorus, which is followed by yet another reference to *Graceland,* a brief *vocalise* that is quite similar to the one at the end of that album, concluding "All Around the World, or The Myth of Fingerprints."

The third verse retraces the ideas found in the second. First, the new melodic material describes the effects of overpopulation, ultimately claiming that a strain is felt as a result of each single birth. However, then the gentle melody redeems one such birth, repeating the text from the first verse with two changes: the redemption of the previous text is signaled by the opening word "but," and this infant is a baby girl rather than a boy. The chorus makes a third appearance, along with the vocalise heard earlier, and then music from the opening four measures (which had also appeared as interludes between verses) fades to end the song.

"The Cool, Cool River" also depicts a societal struggle and uses musical contrast to represent competing interests, but it differs significantly from "Born at the Right Time" with respect to both the prevailing style and the degree of contrast, which is much sharper in "The Cool, Cool River." This song begins with a restless strummed vamp on an F#m11 chord[12] in the somewhat unusual meter of 9/8. The sound is consistent with a Latin jazz atmosphere, and Simon chants against it with flexible rhythms and a limited melodic range (E-A) to describe a mysterious, inexorable force.

The harmonic and melodic ranges open up a bit as the force is somewhat cryptically developed into the "cool, cool river." The harmonies trace a four-chord-per-measure F# Dorian pattern, F#m-G#m-A-G#m, which perpetuates the sense of restlessness and instability as it unevenly divides the nine eighth notes, and the melody reaches up to C#. The F#m11 and the A melodic ceiling return as ideas of government and class subjugation are introduced, and then harmonies and melody expand again to recall the river.

At this point the musical texture and style shift radically as the singer attempts a different perspective. A fingerpicked acoustic guitar dominates, and while the 9/8 meter is retained, each measure is clearly divided into three even beats, and there are four four-bar phrases. The key brightens from F# Dorian to A major, which results in typical open-string folk-guitar figures in G on the capoed guitar (most distinctively the G-C alternations in the third measure of each phrase). The singer begins, with a gentle melody and fairly simple rhythms, by imagining an untroubled future.[13] In the second half of this section, though, threatening images are described in less regular rhythms, and the singer acknowledges remaining hopes and fears.

The F# Dorian music returns, and the singer connects the river to anger as it relates to love, finally seeking refuge in prayers, "the memory of God." Once again the A major music brings hope of a future without suffering. The threatening images reemerge, but this time the music takes a new turn. As the streets "send their battered dreams to heaven," the section is extended, and a mysterious warrior responds. This development seems to transcend the formal expectations of the alternating sections, and his words are accompanied by regular brass punctuations at the beginning of each measure. But the end result is still equivocal, as some of his words are considerably more elusive than one might expect of a hero, and the song returns to the F#m11 vamp to fade out.

A percussive rhythm track runs throughout "Spirit Voices." The song's musical core, however, is provided by a charming, syncopated, 16-bar guitar line based by Nguini on a traditional Ghanaian song. Against this material the singer sings a gently syncopated melody that tells of a journey, always conscious of the prevailing spirit voices, to seek help from a *brujo*, or magical healer. The story is enhanced by additional sections based on other material and additional instrumental and vocal elements.

In the introduction percussion instruments enter first, setting up an intricate rhythmic pattern against which the guitar line is played. Then the singer sings against two presentations of the line, first telling of the journey and then commenting on the magic that prevailed. In a contrasting EWI-flavored section he describes his group's arrival at the *brujo*'s door, where various infirm people wait to be healed.

After a buoyant instrumental interlude featuring sliding bass licks, the same three musical sections return, and the singer describes details of his surroundings, calling on various kinds of water to "wrap this child" and heal her, and (in the contrasting section) becoming somewhat intoxicated with "herbal brew." At this point new music accompanies Portuguese lyrics, written and sung by Milton Nascimento, in which a different character (apparently the *brujo*) admonishes the singer, warning him that the passion and faith of his heart will determine the outcome. Falsetto background voices are featured here, and they continue as the guitar line returns. They drop out as, in one last 16-bar segment, the singer continues to observe magical phenomena and acknowledge the spirit voices; this last thought is reiterated as the voices return and the music fades.

While the last track of *Rhythm of the Saints* is the title track, it is also the only song on the album that does not include its own title. Although "rhythm" does not appear in the lyrics, however, it is not hard to find in the song. A constant percussion pattern begins at the very outset and continues throughout, setting the tone for a static, low-contrast process along the lines of "Can't Run But" and "Further to Fly." The "saints" connect with the singer's prayers, as the song relates his efforts to overcome hazards, in the course of which he invokes the Yoruban deities Olodumare and Babalu-aye.

This account is distributed through a simple verse-chorus scheme, all in C Mixolydian mode, with a very limited palette of C, B♭, and Am harmonies. In the introduction, 4 measures of percussion are followed by 12 of chanting background voices and a 2-measure vamp. In the first verse, the singer addresses possible weaknesses and hazards with a syncopated, undulating melody complemented by brief melodic guitar responses. A nice effect is created by reserving the oft-skipped B♭ until its arrival at the end of the first line, and this technique is expanded in the second half of the verse, when the singer's appeal to Olodumare is emphasized by the addition of a low E and F and a high E.

In the chorus, the chanting voices accompany the singer as he obsessively dwells on G, only rising briefly as high as B♭, to describe the "reach in the darkness" to survive. After a 12-bar percussion interlude during which the texture is very gradually varied, the second verse continues to describe treacherous people, this time addressing the less-than-sympathetic Babalu-aye. The already-repetitive chorus now appears not once but twice, and the song fades in an understated conclusion to the album.

"Thelma" was originally considered for incorporation into *The Rhythm of the Saints* but eventually excluded.[14] At the time of Simon's 1990 *SongTalk* interview with Paul Zollo, the song existed only as an instrumental track temporarily dubbed "the shuffle tune." Because of the placement that Simon envisioned for it on the album, the track was "light and easy" and in the key of F.[15] In its completed form the song retains this mood, as it rambles amiably against a funky, low-key rhythmic pattern.

The song is somewhat reminiscent of "Cecilia" in the way it addresses a woman to the accompaniment of light-hearted music, but the lyrics here are less madcap. The form is constructed from two basic harmonic patterns. Most phrases use a four-measure, self-enclosed F-Gm-F-C-F sequence, accompanied by a rhythmic guitar riff. Contrast is achieved by a somewhat more poignant eight-measure unit in the relative minor key (actually treated modally as D Aeolian)—Dm-C-Bb-C-Dm/Dm-C-Bb-C; this follows the first four F sections, then the next three, and then the last three, and its last chord leads to the beginning of each following F unit. The melodies for the three D sections are fairly similar to one another, but about six different melody types are used for the 10 F sections: one begins each of the first two series in F, and one, dwelling initially on a high Eb, serves as a kind of refrain in each of the three series in F, as the singer tells Thelma how he will need and treat her.

In the first series in F, he speaks of how life can be good, and then, in the D passage, describes missing her while traveling. The second F series warns her not to listen to what others say about him, followed by a D-passage account of a long-distance call that "fall[s] on [her] yesterday scars." In the final F series, the singer reiterates his devotion. The final D series introduces a new element at the eleventh hour, as he describes seeing her in a hospital bed with a baby, concluding that, as "winter sunlight hits the family tree . . . everything else becomes nothing at all." At this point the music returns to F, and the F riff repeats and fades.

Explorations

THE CAPEMAN

Paul Simon has completed three original projects (not including various compilations and live albums) in the years since the release of *The Rhythm of the Saints*. The first of these, the Broadway musical *The Capeman* (with lyrics cowritten by Derek Walcott), followed the longest gap between projects of Simon's career: the musical appeared in 1998, and the associated album in 1997. (It is not surprising that the previous longest gap preceded *One-Trick Pony*, Simon's other foray into a new genre; in each case, of course, much of the time involved surely was spent learning about a challenge that was both new to Simon and much more complex than the process of producing an album.)

The Capeman underwent a good deal of revision as it was being prepared for public presentation. Since the album was released before the musical's brief (as it turned out) run on Broadway, and since in any event the album does not contain all of the music heard in the musical, the album does not in itself present the complete narrative. Nonetheless, it is quite possible, and most informative, to consider each of the songs in the context of its place in the narrative. This is especially true because of one way in which this case differs from that of *One-Trick Pony*. The songs in *One-Trick Pony* included songs that the characters actually performed *as performances* in the movie (but usually did not communicate directly for the characters); songs heard in the background that clearly reflected Jonah's specific perspective; and other background songs that conveyed ideas consistent with those of the characters. In contrast, as is the case with most songs in musicals, all of the songs on the *Capeman* album would have been presented in the performance as musicalized dialogue—that is, direct expressions of what the characters are thinking as they are thinking, whether they are addressing other characters or thinking to themselves aloud for the benefit of the audience. In this situation, then, the persona for each song (identified for most songs discussed in this book as "the singer") is simply the character in *The Capeman* who is singing the song, and the song can be simply interpreted as an expression of this character's thoughts in a particular situation—enhanced, in fact, by what we learn about the character in the rest of the musical.

The Capeman is an account of the true story of Salvador Agron, a teenaged member of a Puerto Rican gang who was convicted of murdering two other young men in New York in 1959. Partly because of Agron's habit of wearing the flamboyant garment that gave him his nickname, the case became sensationalized, and in fact Simon remembered hearing about it as a teen himself at the time. In setting the story to music, Simon chose to use typical ethnic styles such as doo-wop, Puerto Rican flavors, and some country-western elements. In one way, as Simon mentions in the liner notes to the album, the emphasis on Latin styles was a natural development from some of the work that he had been doing with *The Rhythm of the Saints*.[1] On the other hand, the styles and forms that resulted tend to be much more familiar to American ears than are some of those found on *The Rhythm of the Saints*, because the model styles themselves are more Americanized.

After committing these murders, Agron spent 20 years in prison, during which time he apparently matured considerably, as well as learning to read and write and becoming educated in other ways. The musical is presented as him telling his story, and so at times not only is the young "Sal" seen as the story unfolds, but also the older "Salvador" appears, narrating or commenting on the action. He is the main singer in "Born in Puerto Rico," which uses a Puerto Rican style to present Sal's background and explains how he got involved with his gang, the Vampires.

After an acoustic-guitar-dominated introduction, the song begins with an AABA form. Each of the sections forms a complete musical phrase in D minor, ending with an A7-Dm cadence. In the first two, Salvador describes, in the first person, where he was born, how he got involved with the gang, and how his ethnic background identified him. The B section emphasizes F, the relative major key, as Salvador says, as if to Sal, that only he knows him, and he will tell his story. This section concludes in D minor, and the final A section is split between Sal and the Vampires singing of their heritage and Salvador recalling his family's arrival in the New York winter.

After a torrid trumpet interlude, the A and B sections are used throughout the remainder of the song. First Salvador uses an expanded B section to tell Sal how his family became established in the city and then to repeat his promise to tell Sal's story. Then an A section is again split between Sal and the Vampires describing Sal's arrival and Salvador describing how quickly he left the city (after his conviction). An expanded A section allows some of the gang members to introduce themselves (speaking, not singing), and Salvador to sing about the sensational publicity and recite a litany of the institutions in which Sal lived, ending with "Twenty years inside, today you're free."

Salvador follows this observation with a B section in which he sings sympathetically to Sal about his inability to "read [his] story" (whether because of illiteracy or prison restrictions). A chorus repeats "I was born in Puerto Rico" in F, against another trumpet break. The song then concludes with a return to acoustic-guitar riffs in D minor.

The next song on the album, "Satin Summer Nights," depicts a night in which Sal is first caught up in the romance of the city, and then told by Tony Hernandez (his eventual partner, the "Umbrella Man") that he must join the Vampires in order to survive. The song is cast in doo-wop style throughout, with generous doses of vocal harmonizing. It begins with two verses sung by Sal against a slightly modified blues structure provided by the background vocals. In each verse the stereotypical 12-bar pattern is doubled in length at first, so that the first 4-bar phrase on the tonic G harmony (slightly embellished) is 8 measures long instead, and the second 4-bar phrase—ordinarily two on C and two on G—also becomes 8 measures long (4 plus 4). However, the final 4-bar phrase remains 4 bars long in this song (two of D7 and two of G), so that the whole structure, rather than being a fully doubled 24 measures (8 plus 8 plus 8) is only 20 measures long (8 plus 8 plus 4).

These modifications do not constitute striking departures, and the overall effect reinforces the 1950s doo-wop sound, since the blues form is common for this style. While the doubling is not extremely remarkable, it conveys a certain sense of expansiveness, and this supports Sal's gently syncopated romantic soliloquy. In the first verse he describes the streets[2] and his desire for romance, and in the second he declares his faith in Saint Lazarus, acknowledges that his carefree days won't last long, and expresses his desire for romance once again.

After the second verse the background voices change their harmonic pattern. During an interlude in which a solo guitar makes an appearance, they establish an eight-bar (G-G-Em-Em-Am-Am-D7-D7) sequence, even more stereotypical for doo-wop than is the blues pattern, that repeats for the remainder of the song.[3] Against three of these cycles "Bernadette," aided by "Cookie," sings enticingly to Sal about the prospects for romance in the city. During the next seven, Tony makes his case, sometimes speaking and sometimes singing about how vulnerable unprotected Latinos are to the various gangs, but how powerful the Vampires are.

As he concludes by demanding an answer, saxophones enter to punctuate his repetition of Sal's name. They continue as Sal answers. Despite Tony's aggressive argument, in one final cycle of the 8-bar pattern, Sal reiterates his faith in Saint Lazarus and pleads for the preservation of "this satin summer night."

In "Bernadette," Sal sings of his love for the girl. After a bright guitar-vamp introduction, he sings a jaunty phrase in G that will serve (with different words each time) as the beginning of each of the song's four sections; while these could be called verses, each will develop in a unique way. The first continues, embellished with light bells and bass and a high Everly-Brothers-style vocal harmony, to tell Bernadette in simple G major terms that Sal is looking forward to seeing her tonight. Suddenly, though, more harmony voices are added briefly, and then Sal sings alone as the meter changes, a saxophone is added, and the harmonies get a bit more interesting. Here the text dissolves into a brief fantasy: Sal imagines their romance to be a movie, and himself to be Sal Mineo, before the original tempo and key return and the opening melody starts a new verse.

In this verse again Sal begins by telling Bernadette how much he admires her against a simple bass, guitar, and bell accompaniment (but no harmony vocal). Another dissolve takes place, this time more extensive and involving saxophone, falsetto background voices, and piano, and eventually a full doo-wop vocal section. A bluesy C minor (major7) chord accompanies a chromatically poetic reference to "the breeze that wraps around you," and "satin summer nights" are also recalled. The last word of this section, "forget," sets up a nice device in which the return of the opening melody (and the original tempo and mood) sounds like both an opening to a new section and a conclusion to this one, since this melody ends on the rhyming word "Bernadette" and (as it had not on its previous appearances) on the tonic note G.

After this line, the third section opens out into a full-blown up-tempo doo-wop sound, with full harmonies and nonsense syllables such as "dom," "doo," and "wop." As this moves forward, in a passage reminiscent of songs such as the Del-Vikings' "Come Go with Me," Sal invites Bernadette to join him in a special hiding place with the stars and lights of the city shining for her. This leads to the fourth verse, which more or less reprises the third, except that it ends abruptly before the "Come Go with Me" passage, as the syllable "wop" is repeated over an open-ended D harmony. As it turns out, this reveals the fragility of Sal's hopes to be left alone, because his use of this innocent, stereotypical *a cappella* singing syllable in the course of romancing Bernadette leads to a beating at the hands of an Italian gang.

As a result of this, Tony and the Vampires are enabled to make their case once again for Sal to join them. This is done in "The Vampires," a song influenced by the Afro-Cuban guajira-son style. This style typically exhibits a duple meter, moderate tempo, and a repeated pattern that emphasizes tonic, subdominant, and dominant harmonies, and all of these are present in "The Vampires"; in particular, the pattern is provided by a piano vamp that accompanies the entire song with a repeated two-bar, five-chord progression (Gm-Cm6-D7-Cm-D7). Against this, Tony sings in brief melodic phrases, interspersed with spoken comments and responses sung by the Vampires as a group. The stylized conversational tone is supported by the melodic shapes: while they vary considerably, most of the phrases take on a uniform chanting quality by virtue of emphasizing D near their beginning and falling to B♭ at their end.

After the piano, drums, and a trumpet establish the vamp in an intro-duction, Tony establishes his authority by demanding various privileges. He declares that strength is the basis for survival, and the Vampires sing in a refrain that "[they] stand for the neighborhood." Tony asks Sal if he wants to fight for his people, and then introduces him to the Vampires' lair; the terror the place holds for a "white man" is emphasized with the song's only high G and trumpet interjections. Tony shows Sal his lethal umbrella, and explains that the Vampires provide "dues," introducing a refrain that invites Sal to join "if you got the balls."

Tony then goes on, again aided by trumpet responses and some background vocals, to tell how an Irish gang beat up one of the Vampires, "Frenchy Cor-dero." This leads to repetitions of his refrain inviting Sal to join them, as the other Vampires respond with their refrain about standing for the neighbor-hood. As this ends, the harmonies change and the trumpet takes off on a jazzy solo, which is followed by a brief jazz piano break provided by Oscar Hernandez. The piano then winds back to this vamp, and brass punctuations bring the song to a conclusion.

Sal joins the gang, and "Shoplifting Clothes" depicts the gang's visit to a store to get clothes; it is here that Sal steals his trademark garment. The song is an up-tempo piano-driven boogie woogie built on a succession of 12-bar blues progressions in E♭. Piano, drums, guitar, and bass are heard through-out, and voices provide background harmonies—while a smooth salesman speaks—and duet choruses at other times.

The first 12-bar section (with a 2-bar alteration at the beginning) features the duet singing doo-wop syllables and the title. The second presents the first chorus, in which the duet moves to a slightly higher register to describe the time of year for clothes-shopping and mentions stretching one's "hard-earned money." The voices then vamp for 4 bars and fade to the background for two 12-bar verses while the salesman starts to make his pitch and then claims that wearing his store's clothes will make his customers irresistible to women. (In each verse, the salesman speaks three rhyming lines.)

The chorus and vamp return with saxophone fills, and then the salesman gets three more spoken verses—recommending various "looks," pushing a hat, and regretfully saying that the cape is not for sale. The chorus returns once again, followed by a 12-bar coda on "de-de-det"s that stays in the high register; the sax helps out on these and on a final chorus, which is concluded by a brief piano punctuation.

The same basic piano-bass-drums-guitar ensemble, and an analogous alter-nating form, undergirds "Quality." After four bars of background vocals, similar to those heard on the Cadillacs' "Speedoo," on the tonic B♭ chord, the introduction establishes the fundamental harmonic pattern. While fal-setto "ooh"s and a declaration that a girl's way of moving has the title trait are sung, the accompaniment presents two bars apiece of E♭ and B♭ harmo-nies, three of an F harmony, and two of B♭; the extra measure of F provides a dramatic pause before the payoff line, "it's got quality."

The singer uses this harmonic pattern twice in verses that, respectively, ask the girl to go downtown and urge her not to be shy, each time ending with the declaration about quality. Then the tempo drops to a slow shuffle beat, and the women respond in girl-group style (still with the men in the background). They use the same harmonic pattern—but without the extra measure of F—twice, to ask if the boy will be truly the girl's and if he will marry her.

The first tempo returns, and the singer again (with the nine-bar scheme) seeks the girl's attention and describes her quality. Two eight-bar (but still up-tempo) units accompany a 1950s-style sax solo, and then the singer tells how observers say that *he* has quality. The women recapitulate their passage and add eight bars that tell in Spanish of their desire to have (unavailable) assurances about the future. Finally, the song is rounded off by a return of the introduction, which ends by drifting off into falsetto.

The Vampires go to avenge Frenchy's beating. They find two boys, whom Sal stabs to death, although it turns out that they had not been involved with Frenchy. Sal is captured and seems defiant and unrepentant. The next song, "Can I Forgive Him," presents a conversation in which Sal's mother, Esmeralda, pleads with the mothers of the slain boys to forgive Sal.

The form of the song is most fundamentally determined by the alternation of the three women singing (a feature that is obscured by the fact that the song is performed on the album by Simon singing alone with his finger-picked guitar). The first section consists of Esmeralda's plea on Sal's behalf. She sings a melody against a specific chord progression twice, but this does not sound very much like two verses, because a clear verse structure would ordinarily be defined by strong arrivals at boundaries on the tonic harmony (D minor in this case), and these are not provided here.[4]

Instead, Esmeralda's faltering words are first presented with irregular rhythms, changing meters, and a variety of harmonies, as she describes the fragmentary impressions the women may have of her son. When she describes Sal's true nature as an infant, a weak cadence is reached on D minor, but this is further qualified by an entreating "Señora." The second verse uses the unstable harmonies to describe the fate of both one of the slain boys and Sal, and reaches the D minor cadence when she predicts that the state will seal Sal's fate; this phrase is repeated with a more conclusive cadence in the relative major key of F.

In the next section, one of the mothers responds by describing the injustice of the situation. Her answer is much less focused on a particular key, wandering from harmony to harmony as she uses repeated melody notes to criticize the violence of the "Spanish people" and the sensationalism that attends the crime and that she must face. The end of her section suggests C minor, and then emphasizes an E♭ that sounds as though it might be a dominant note in A♭, leading to that key. At this point the second mother begins with some obscure harmonies that will eventually focus on A♭ in the most stable verse structure to be found in the song.

Conceding that her religion indicates that she should forgive Sal, she sings brief phrases that descend from D♭ to B♭ before settling on A♭ over an A♭6 tonic chord; these gestures are repeated from the refrain that asks the title question and concludes that she cannot forgive Sal. The woman then sings another verse that traces a similar path. At this point, Esmeralda interjects in a brief passage—at first in G minor but ending on an E♭ harmony—that God, too, lost his Son, but the bereaved must still go on. This protest is in vain, though, as the E♭ leads back to the key of A♭, and both mothers sing another verse that describes the horror they are experiencing and concludes once again that they cannot forgive Sal.

"Adios Hermanos" depicts the point at which Sal is sentenced to death. As has been seen in several of the songs in *The Capeman*, it addresses dramatic concerns with an alternating structure, in this case A-B-A-B-A. During the A sections Sal, sometimes joined by Salvador, relates the details of the occasion with a chanting, recitative-like melody that uses many repeated notes and patterns to convey a lot of information. This is accompanied by an *a cappella* group that repeats a single, typical four-bar doo-wop chord progression throughout these passages. (The basic progression, D♭-B♭m-G♭-A♭-D♭ in D♭ major, is embellished by a couple of brief harmonies (shown here in italics): D♭-*A♭*-B♭m-G♭-A♭-*E♭m/D♭*-D♭.) The B sections focus on Sal's sister Aurea, who calls on the Angel of Mercy for help; she is accompanied by a female choir and an organ, and the theme of a religious sanctuary is further supported by an emphasis on the subdominant key of G♭ major. While these sections remain clearly distinct from one another, the characters increasingly mix in them as the song progresses.

In the first A section, Sal tells of leaving the house of detention for the courtroom; Salvador joins him to describe the threats that had been posed by the rival gangs. At the end of Aurea's first B section, Sal joins her to acknowledge that "sisters grieve." Then he recounts the sentencing in the second A section. Here Salvador joins him and describes the threats posed by the media.

Sal joins Aurea earlier in her next section: after she mourns the frequent deaths of "Spanish boy[s]," he bitterly says that when "a white boy die[s]...the world goes crazy for...Latin blood." In the final A section, Salvador joins Sal earlier to describe the way he was shackled after the sentence was pronounced. Sal then sings about his trip in chains with Tony through Spanish Harlem, and Aurea and Salvador join him to sing of prayers for him and to sing the title line.

After some time has passed, the news comes that Sal's death sentence has been commuted. Esmeralda and Aurea rejoice. However, Esmeralda's husband, a preacher who had beaten Sal, speaks cruelly about him, and Esmeralda leaves him. In "Sunday Afternoon" Esmeralda dictates a letter for Aurea to write and send to Sal; the letter speaks of her difficulties and her longing for him and for Puerto Rico.

The song is cast in a Latin folk style; although some background orchestral strings are used, the most prominent instruments are acoustic guitars, with additional contributions by a flute and stylistically typical percussion instruments. A simple ABA form is used in the key of A minor throughout. The A sections are graceful and simple, each consisting of two identical sections in which descending sequences of melodies, arriving at cadences on the dominant E chord, convey the sense of inevitability that Esmeralda expresses.

In the first A section she describes the declining afternoon sunlight and the tall buildings that shut her in. Then in the B section, which is characterized by faster dance rhythms, she tells of her longing for Puerto Rico. This section consists of three identical 16-bar subsections; each of these in turn includes 4 4-bar phrases. In the first subsection Esmeralda reminisces about Puerto Rico, in the second she rues her bad marriages, and in the last she describes her poor employment situation.

Returning to the A section, Esmeralda says that she is resigned to the fact that the *barrio* is now her and Aurea's "own little nation." She urges Sal to "keep [his] Bible near [him]," concluding (and finally reaching a cadence on the tonic A minor) with a line that will become the basis for the next song: "time is an ocean of endless tears." "Sunday Afternoon" begins with a guitar introduction based on chord changes from the B section, and it ends with a coda in which Esmeralda hums the A melody one more time.

"Time Is an Ocean" depicts Sal's process of transformation during his years in prison. It is cast as a duet sung by Sal and Salvador, with Sal speaking from his perspective in prison, but also calling out to Salvador, as his "savior." Salvador responds by offering the perspective and encouragement that Sal needs to benefit from his ocean of time. On the album, the parts of Sal and Salvador are sung by Marc Anthony and Ruben Blades, respectively, who played the roles in the musical, and the style and instrumentation is more along the lines of a contemporary pop song that Anthony might sing than is the case with many of the other songs on the album: it is piano-driven with a Latin beat and a full complement of additional instruments—guitars, percussion, winds, horns, and strings.

There are three verses, each with a refrain, although the verses are defined more by their chord changes than by their melodies, which share many features but also vary widely. The melody lines are rather free, and thoroughly syncopated in the verses, although less so in the more stable refrains, which also have more straightforward harmonic progressions than those in the verses. In the first verse, Sal seeks direction as he is no longer on death row, and Salvador speaks retrospectively of the length of time that it took him to start to move forward. In the refrain, the two repeat Esmeralda's closing line from "Sunday Afternoon," and Salvador tells of writing his story.

The next verse is begun by an instrumental passage, and then Sal acknowledges his mother's letter and says he will soon be transferred. Salvador begins the refrain, and then Sal encourages his mother to return to her beloved Puerto Rico. Salvador begins the final verse by decrying the politics of the system; when Sal chimes in about how "white" the prison is, Salvador urges him to write in order to keep his sanity. In the final refrain, rather than beginning with the title line, Salvador uses a different melody to continue to remind Sal about his tremendous disadvantages when he first arrived in prison, and Sal resolves to better himself. The refrain is extended as they bid one another goodbye, finally concluding with the title line.

Sal begins to learn to read and write, and some of his writing is seen by people outside his prison. One of these is a Native American woman named Wahzinak, who begins to write to him. He decides that he wants to pursue further studies, and "Killer Wants to Go to College" records a conversation between another inmate and Virgil, a prison guard, about Sal's ambitions.

The song uses a country-western shuffle style, accompanied by guitars, bass, piano, and drums, and follows a simple 32-bar AABA form. The A sections use a standard A-F#m-D-E-A progression in the key of A; this is also used in an 8-bar guitar introduction that focuses on a stereotypical alternation between the notes E and F#. In the first two sections, as the other instruments join the guitar lines, the inmate mocks Sal's aspirations to go to college and get paroled, and accuses him of wanting to be a celebrity. Much of the melodic line here is modeled on a typical arpeggiated boogie-woogie bass line, conveying a lack of imagination on the inmate's part (because a competent singer would sing a different, melodically interesting line above such a bass pattern) and/or a kind of sarcastic belittling of Sal's desires (because of the implication that these, like the melodic line, are just what one might expect).

The B section moves, again typically, to the subdominant D7 chord and eventually to a dominant E7 to set up the return of A. Here Virgil dramatically asks whether Sal is truly rehabilitated and cynically recalls his defiance when he was first arrested. A harmonica enters at this point; it, along with the different harmonies and Virgil's repeated melody notes, underscores the contrast in this section. The A section then returns, with all its musical characteristics, as the inmate concludes sarcastically that Sal would declare his harmlessness. Finally, the introduction returns, with harmonica added, as a coda to end this brief (one minute and 51 second) song.

Virgil presses his case further in "Virgil," a conversation between him and the prison warden. This song, also, is based on an AABA form. It begins with a 16-bar introduction that establishes its menacing tone with an electric-guitar solo in D minor that recalls the background music in spaghetti Westerns, thus invoking a sense of danger as well as one of cliché. The first half of this passage moves from a D minor chord to the dominant A, and the second retraces that path before falling desolately through G and F chords back to the tonic D-minor harmony.

This pattern is the basis for the A sections. In the first, Virgil complains about his own inability to pay for his children's education with his income, and in the second the warden responds that Sal has earned the right to go to school. The guitar then walks up from D by half-steps to the subdominant key of G for the B section, but this turns out to be G major rather than G minor. The bright, open country key supports Virgil's text here, as he has a comforting thought: he thinks about his deer rifle and the pleasure he has when hunting "when the air is free," and he imagines using his rifle to solve the present problem.

In the next A section, Virgil warns that a smart, quiet inmate like Sal is the type to start an Attica-style riot. The remainder of the song reuses the A and B sections: first an aggressive electric-guitar solo is set against the A changes, then Virgil swears in a B section that Sal won't graduate or go free, and finally the introduction returns as a coda.

"Killer Wants to Go to College II" uses essentially the same accompaniment (without the harmonica) and overall structure that was heard in "Killer Wants to Go to College." In the lyrics here, however, Sal is addressing Wahzinak. In the first two A sections he acknowledges her attempts to help him with things that she writes to him. The contrast of the B section brings him to describe his emotionally deprived youth, and he continues to describe the perils of those days in the concluding A section.

Throughout the song, Sal's melody differs for the most part from the melody sung by the inmate in the earlier version: it is higher and moves more smoothly (although one line in the B section very nearly duplicates Virgil's at the corresponding location—both lines refer to Sal's desperate situation in his youth). At the beginning of the coda, however, the inmate sings, with his original tune, "Killer wants to go on T.V." Then the supposed glamour of Sal's publicity is challenged as the coda goes on for a bit more than twice its original length while a 1975 interview with Sal is heard; here Sal tries honestly but, in the interviewer's opinion, unsatisfactorily to answer the question of what he would say to the parents of the boys that he killed.

Sal presses for permission to go to college, and also to be paroled. He is granted the permission and told that parole is still five months away. Tormented by Virgil, he decides that when he is allowed to leave the prison to attend classes, he will take a bus instead to Arizona to join Wahzinak. He is followed by St. Lazarus, and when he gets to the desert he is tormented by visions of his youth. Lazarus tells him that he must confess his sin and repent in order to find peace, and he decides to turn himself in. He is required to stay in prison for three more years, and his communication with Wahzinak is broken. Eventually, though, he is released to return, with the manuscript that he has written about his life, to his neighborhood. There he reunites with his friends and his sister, and finally with Esmeralda, who assures him that his repentance has saved him.

The final song on the album, "Trailways Bus," was cut from some of the performances of the musical, but it depicts Sal's trip as he escapes to the Southwest. Its story is narrated by Lazarus, but within the song Wahzinak, a border patrolman, and Sal also sing. Throughout the song a mellow, flowing folk-country style is established with the aid of a recurrent, gentle guitar riff.

The basic four-phrase structural unit of the song is presented after a strumming guitar, bass, and the guitar riff enter in six introductory bars. As these instruments continue, Lazarus uses a combination of graceful melodic curves and repeated notes to describe "a passenger" (Sal) riding the bus into rolling farmland in two simple, three-chord phrases in E. (Each phrase is four bars long, but three extra bars are inserted to enhance the leisurely pace of the song.) In the next phrase, an A-minor chord borrowed from the key of E minor is joined by some additional instruments to suggest some poignancy and then move toward the key of C as Lazarus describes a farm couple whom Sal curiously observes. In the fourth phrase, Lazarus summarizes by saying that the bus is entering Washington, D.C. as the key turns back to E.

The next section follows the same harmonic and melodic pattern (with minor variations) as Lazarus describes a family on the bus and Sal's emotions as he seeks freedom while riding past the Capitol building. He concludes with another summarizing statement about the bus: this time, as he says that the bus is turning west, the harmonies turn too, going from C to G rather than returning to E, and the word "west" is colored with the first appearance of a pedal steel guitar.

At this point, the new key and the pedal steel accompany Wahzinak as she tells Sal of her eagerness for his arrival. During this eight-bar passage the key changes to D, and then Lazarus resumes his narrative, using the music of the first two phrases, but now in the key of D rather than E. He recounts the arrival of the bus in Dallas, referring to Kennedy's assassination, and describes Sal hearing music and Spanish words after many years away from freedom. This experience is then depicted musically in an instrumental interlude, as first a guitar and then a trumpet play leisurely mariachi-flavored solos, with an accordion added to the background.

The key abruptly shifts back up to the original key of E, and the A section begins once again. In its first half Lazarus tells of a border patrolman boarding the bus, and then the officer asks if Sal is an alien. As the poignant second half begins, Sal replies flippantly that he is an alien—from outer space. He concludes hopelessly that officials will continue to hound him forever, and this sentiment is supported by the fact that the key has stayed this time in C and he twice stops singing on a D over the dominant harmony of G. Lazarus then reinforces the same idea by singing that Sal is still haunted by his fears and his actions; he concludes by repeating the phrase "phantom figures in the dust" with the same inconclusive music Sal has just used, thus communicating that Sal must still come to grips with his demons.

YOU'RE THE ONE

The cover and liner art of *You're the One,* released in 2000, depicts Simon in a baseball cap, a natural-wood electric guitar, and a hooded jacket woven into earth-tone stripes ranging from orange through reds and beiges to dark brown. The various-colored fabric of the jacket is used as a background for the pages of the lyric booklet. The songs on the album range in style and subject, but as a whole the tone is that of a village storyteller combining whimsy and fable to connect the commonplace with universal truth. This perspective is reinforced by the pictures of the casual Simon in his baseball cap and one in which he has donned the tribal-looking jacket and is half in shadow; it is also addressed by the first song, "That's Where I Belong."

The song opens with an exotic introduction that combines a droning vielle (a medieval fiddle) with bamboo flute lines. Then, accompanied by ethnic percussion, gentle electric-guitar chords, and cosmic-sounding sustained instrumental whistling, the singer introduces the verses that are to come. He describes the mysterious process of sound becoming a song and uses the title line to refer to his storytelling role; the entire introductory passage is solidly focused on the key of E♭ major, with a few chromatic touches.

The connection between the transcendent and the commonplace is sustained throughout the rest of the song. After the rather free delivery of the singer's preface, the three verses adopt a more regular tempo, and the singer is joined by (presumably) Vincent Nguini's melodic guitar lines as was the case in several of the songs on *The Rhythm of the Saints*. Each verse consists of a series of graceful descending melodies rocking back and forth among the three chords A♭, E♭, and B♭, with one long ascent, about three-quarters of the way through, arriving on a C minor harmony. In the first two verses, these features accompany winsomely affectionate lyrics as the singer tells the listener of his pleasure in her company (it seems to be a woman who has captivated him, but this is not explicitly clear), concluding with the title line. Even with this hint of romance, the storytelling idea is suggested as the singer says "every end a beginning," and the sustained whistling continues to suggest the notion of timelessness.

An instrumental interlude follows, with steel-drum-like sounds and sliding bass licks (played by Bakithi Kumalo, again reminiscent of some of his work on *Graceland* and *The Rhythm of the Saints*), and this enhances the gentle tropical-island atmosphere. The final verse takes this theme farther, describing an island man with a banjo and a radio. At the same time, the transcendent is suggested by his going "where the water meets the sky," and once again the singer identifies with these themes by singing the title line. The song concludes as a guitar plays a simple series of chords twice, each time ending inconclusively on C minor (A♭-B♭-Cm, A♭-B♭-Cm), and the whistling continues.

The storyteller begins with a lengthy (at least by popular-song standards) saga, "Darling Lorraine." This account of a New York couple's marriage lasts over six and a half minutes, and includes a variety of accompanimental devices, formal components, and emotional settings. With regard to this last feature, Simon's lyric writing ranges from cleverness to poignancy.

The pitched-percussion-pattern introduction suggests that the text of the song might be set in an exotic locale (as was the case in "Spirit Voices," for example), but instead just a guitar remnant of the pattern is distilled out to become part of the accompaniment as the singer, Frank, sets his tale in Middle America. In the first verse, his initial uncertainty upon meeting Lorraine is reflected by a sustained tonic D minor harmony, and his melody focuses on notes in that chord, actually conveying a D Aeolian setting. The harmonies then start to move, and the melody to dwell on other pitches, as Frank approaches Lorraine; Simon plays with the lyrics here as Frank introduces himself "with the part of me that talks," rhyming the last word of this offbeat expression with "New Yawk." The harmonies start to emphasize the relative key of F major as Frank describes Lorraine's attractiveness, but then slide back to D Aeolian as the title phrase concludes his confession of unworthy love.

The next verse explains that Frank and Lorraine got married, but trivializes this by correcting a halfhearted attempt to romanticize Frank's life, and by referring to "the usual marriage stuff." The verse continues by telling how Lorraine decided that she'd had enough. This leads into a bridge in which an indignant Frank tells Lorraine off; the key is unstable here, but B flats have been replaced with B naturals, and eventually Frank, with a suggestion of G Mixolydian, tells Lorraine that he doesn't need her. As he says her name, though, his tone softens and the key leans toward C major; he repeats her name, and instrumental passages featuring a cello lead him to confess his love again and slide back to D Aeolian.

This sets up the beginning of the third verse, in which Frank acknowledges that he feels like a failure in his career but says that he still feels good with Lorraine, who seems to be above these concerns. An interlude follows in which the mode shifts to a warm D major, and, as mellow horns join the texture, the singer adopts the role of narrator and recounts, in the third person, a vignette in which Frank and Lorraine enjoy a pancake- and *Wonderful Life*-enhanced Christmas day (the movie connects with Frank's fantasies in the preceding verse of how his life might have gone). The harmonies lead to tidy cadences.

All is not resolved, however, because the bridge returns, with slightly more acerbic comments. As was the case the first time, this bridge begins to soften as Frank says Lorraine's name. But this time things go in a different direction: Frank learns, again with the cello accompanying, that Lorraine is very ill. The D Aeolian beginning of a final verse, with a lower melody, reveals Frank coming to grips with her suffering. The emphasis on F major accompanies his attempts to make her comfortable, but, as the D Aeolian focus returns, he tells of her death. A brief instrumental coda seems to lay her to rest, with a subdominant-to-tonic cadence, typical of a hymn's "Amen," now in D major.

A much lighter tone is taken by "Old," in which the singer allays his fears that he is getting old by putting them in the context of larger issues. The song ultimately seems less concerned, however, with this personal debate than it is with the amusing succession of ideas that it presents. The first verse mentions Buddy Holly and "Peggy Sue," and accordingly the introduction uses

Buddy-Holly-style electric-guitar strums, which are then featured through-out the song. The song's simple harmonic vocabulary—A, D, E, and one F♯ minor chord, in the key of A, during the main portion of each verse—also recalls this style. Against this accompaniment Simon sings in a chanting style, rattling off information and glib commentary, in a way that is reminiscent of, if not quite exactly the same as, a talking blues (a storytelling style Simon used on "A Simple Desultory Philippic").

The first verse, in telling about the singer's youth, addresses not only Buddy Holly, but also the Cold War, observing that genocide remains, as does Buddy Holly, "but his catalogue was sold." The second verse talks about the singer's early experiences with drugs, rock, and joblessness, and says that his friends say that he's now "old." This key word kicks off an extension to the eight-bar verse, as the harmonic emphasis shifts to the subdominant chord, D, and then a chain of subdominants (G, C, and F) as the singer ruminates on the word. After four bars of this, though, the harmonies snap back to A and the opening A-D-A vamp returns for four bars to introduce the third verse.

This verse slams through a catalog of world religions, including Christian-ity, Buddhism, and Islam, and how "old" all of these are is described in the extension. The opening vamp is then doubled in length to allow the singer to tell his listeners to work out any disagreements. The final verse describes the great age of the human race and the universe, concludes in the extension that God is even older and that, in comparison, we're not old, and finishes by telling his listeners to disrobe, with the following terse justification: "Adam and Eve."

The title of the title track, "You're the One," seems at first blush to be a declaration of amatory devotion. The song does indeed deal with romantic relationships, but the phrase, as it turns out, is used in the chorus to accuse the partner of being responsible for the situation going wrong. Ultimately, however, the singer acknowledges that both he and his lover are to blame, and he concludes that relationships are always in peril.

The song is set against a quickly pulsing rhythm introduced by drums and guitars in the key of F, but its character is moderated by some slower singing and instrumental devices against this beat, as well as some chromatic deviations from a major scale. After the pulsing introduction, two verses are followed by an interlude and a chorus, and then two more verses are heard, each with its own chorus; the placement of this regular pattern toward the end, rather than the beginning, of the song is somewhat different from the approach of many Simon songs that set up a regular form (e.g., AABA) at the beginning and then use the components somewhat freely later.

In the first verse, accompanied by gentle electric-guitar flourishes, the singer wishes his lover safety from danger. Each of the first two four-bar phrases sandwiches a poignant B♭ minor chord, borrowed from F minor, between two F major chords. The last two four-bar phrases suggest his tender sense of protection with a Mixolydian-sounding E♭ chord and another B♭ minor harmony. In the second verse the singer chants more quickly as he describes how they could fear that things might erode and go sour "little by little." The pulsing introduction returns and leads into the interlude, in which the singer sings a slow ascending melody and a long slow descending melody telling the lover that she is "the air inside his chest"; this is lent an exotic, Indian cast by sustained accompanimental instruments and flat notes that create a "gapped" scale (one, that is, in which two consecutive scale steps are more than two half steps apart, the notes in this case being G♭ and A).

The tempo picks up for the first chorus, which uses the title line to accuse the lover of breaking the singer's heart. In the next verse, though, the singer acknowledges that the fault my be reversed. He describes a dream in which the lover is speaking, so that the following chorus uses the same words that appeared in the first one, but are now quoting her as she accuses him. The final verse sums up the inevitability of change but says that lovers don't want change, and so desire to blame each other when it occurs. The final chorus has altered words to declare that both of them are "the ones" at fault, and the song ends with an odd motion to an unresolved D5 sound.

"The Teacher" continues in the storytelling mode, and complements its exotic topic—the singer's experience with a mystical, superhuman guru— throughout with two unusual features: a meter that alternates each measure between 6/8 and 5/8, and an accompaniment that includes no regular acoustic or electric guitars, but rather pedal steel, bass, drums, percussion, bass clarinet, bamboo flute, harmonica, and French horns. After a brief instrumental introduction establishes both of these elements, the singer sings the first verse in F minor. He describes the teacher, and when the teacher speaks to tell people to follow him, the harmonies cycle through a two-measure sequence of Fm-B♭m-D♭-C, accompanying melodies that hypnotically trace similar paths. The second verse uses a different melody but works similarly against the harmonic structure: first the singer tells of himself and his parents, and then, against the cycling chords, their arduous journey over a snow-covered mountain is described.

A brief bridge cycles through more harmonies back to the dominant C chord, as the singer describes "the dreamer of love" sleeping in the stars. The original harmonic cycle then returns as he tells how cold it is, and the pedal steel and bamboo flute engage in a repetitious, echoing 16-bar duet. The third verse describes the teacher dividing in two, and the cycling chords accompany an account of his devouring forests, fields, and clouds. This is followed by a variation of the sequence that followed the second verse: the "dreamer of love" bridge returns, and then the original harmonic cycle, now with a different melody and words that tell how we can come to the end of ourselves, and how we might be overwhelmed enough to cry out. The words that are cried, imploring the teacher to "carry me home," are sung against the pedal-steel-bamboo-flute duet to bring the song to a close.

The pedal steel is also featured on "Look at That," but this is about the only thing that this song has in common with "The Teacher." Its text is a breezy, free-association romp in the tradition of "The 59th Street Bridge

Song" and "Cloudy." The song is set in an up-tempo D major with a few abrupt harmonic moves, some melodic variation, and a very unusual formal maneuver thrown in.

After the pedal steel leads a brief introduction that dwells on a pregnant Dsus4 chord (the suspended 4th that gives the chord its name also conveying a sense of needing to resolve), the singer begins the first verse with the title phrase and goes on to tell his listener to look around, try things out, and eventually to give him a hug and a kiss as he and the listener go to school. The verse is solidly in D major, but some slightly unusual harmonies keep things a bit off-balance—a bass walkdown through G, Bm/F♯, G/F, and Em to lead to a complex Bm11 chord at the end of the first line, a sudden B7-Em move toward the end of the verse, and a G/A leading to the Dsus4 at the beginning of the second verse. The melody leaps around rather freely through all this, and the pedal steel swings along in response.

The second verse is quite similar with, typically for Simon, the same chords but some significant melodic variation in its second half, as the melody glides high to depict lovers' dreams as eagles. Then the instruments chime a luminous Em9 harmony for eight bars. A B section shifts to D Mixolydian, alternating among D, C, and G chords, as the singer tells how much nerve it takes to ask someone to love one, and then sings some machine-gun-repeated nonsense syllables that lead directly into the third verse. Here similar ideas are put forth, but 12 measures are deleted from the middle of the verse before it reaches the Dsus4 harmony.

The Em9 harmony (now six measures) and B section (somewhat shortened and with different nonsense syllables) return, followed by verse material. Remarkably, though, this material mainly consists of 10 of the 12 measures that were excised from the previous appearance. This formal playfulness is punctuated with a half-spoken "you gotta go" as the G/A harmony resolves, not to a tonic D harmony, but to the Em9 music, which ends the piece with its sense of unresolved anticipation.

The very beginning of "Señorita with a Necklace of Tears" resembles that of "When Numbers Get Serious": each begins with Simon singing, unaccompanied, "I have...," with an eighth-note leap up to a B on the second beat of a 4/4 measure. It turns out that "Señorita" is in the key of E, so the B functions differently from the way it did in "Numbers" (which is in G). Nonetheless, the phrases signal a certain common interest in the two songs, in that the singer's perception of "having" something is the point of departure for a rumination on how his life fits into the ways of the world.

In "Señorita," the singer "[has] a wisdom tooth inside [his] crowded face." This offbeat observation is only conceivably related to the rest of the song in that he may be seeking to relate wisdom to his listeners. The first verse goes on, to an accompaniment dominated by gently syncopated guitar, bass, and percussion, to juxtapose a description of a "born again" friend with a reversal of generational birth order; this coincides with minor chords. A pump organ steals in midway through the verse, and the singer concludes that all this has always been the case and is what he wants; when he first says this, the music reached a deceptive cadence on C♯ minor, and then he repeats as it concludes on E.

The second verse describes a South American frog whose venom is an anti-dote for suffering (which is mentioned with the minor chords). The organ enters again, but the conclusion is abbreviated, leading to a B section in which a dobro (a guitar-like instrument with a metal resonating plate, usu-ally played by plucking the strings while sliding a metal bar along them, and often heard in bluegrass and country music contexts) accompanies the singer, along with pulsing, echoing effects from other instruments. As the chords alternate regularly between A and E, the singer describes people who are disassociated in various ways, reaching the conclusion from the first verse against these harmonies.

This song includes its title in an unusual way. In the third verse the singer says that it would be the title he would give to a song that contained "all the memories in the neck of [his] guitar"; here the significance of the minor chords comes to fruition, as they accompany the statement of the title. The tears would be sins that he has committed over the years, and, considering this, he abbreviates his conclusion a bit, omitting the idea that this is what he desires. The B section returns with a double beginning part that first describes various perspectives of other people, and then says that the singer knows who he is at the moment, but not much more. This section again fea-tures the dobro and includes the conclusion against A and E harmonies, and the syncopated guitar returns briefly to close the song.

"Love" is a moody meditation with an accompaniment dominated by reverberant electric-guitar lines and syncopated percussion. Its mood is sup-ported by both its minor mode and its tonal ambiguity: it places weight on both C minor and F minor. This is seen in the principal formal component of the song, a verse that consists of two eight-bar halves, one that fluctuates between F minor and C minor chords, ending on a C minor that sounds like a minor dominant chord in F Aeolian; and one that eventually proceeds from Fm7 through various seventh chords to a G that clearly sounds like a domi-nant chord in C minor.

When the verse first appears, its first half is a guitar solo, and in the second half, against a different guitar line, the singer pleads for solace. The same guitar lines are used in the second verse; here in the first half the singer first talks about how much he craves "it," in the second half he says "it," "the medicine," is ubiquitous and free. All of the melodic lines in the verses tend to have downward, sighing contours. The G harmony that concludes this verse leads not to a C minor chord but to a C major harmony, the bright tonality for the next section, which simply presents "its" name—"Love"—in sustained notes as the guitar repeatedly climbs C major scales.

A third verse begins, again describing our cravings and even giddy response to receiving "it." After the first half of this verse, however, the music slides into a new section in which the singer says, as the melodies gradually rise, that we fool ourselves when we think "it" is easy. Here the harmonies cycles through the standard three chords—A♭-D♭-E♭7—in A♭ major, until the last E♭7 resolves deceptively to F minor. This and a following G harmony accompany the word "why," and the G leads to the C major of the "Love" passage. A final verse bemoans the results of evil destroying love and ends by reciting images of bigotry and oppression. An instrumental coda vacillates between F minor and C minor chords, thus avoiding a sense of resolution.

As its title suggests, "Pigs, Sheep and Wolves" provides the storyteller with an opportunity to convey a message through a fable. The accompaniment here is rather simple. Drums and percussion establish a rhythm track, and featured instruments reflect the barnyard theme—a dobro lends a country flavor, and a pedal steel makes "gong" sounds that recall cowbells. An electric guitar is also in the mix, and Kumalo's sliding bass style echoes the sliding of the dobro.

The song opens with percussion and sustained C harmonies accompanying a comically spoken introductory description of the fat pig, the "barnyard thug." The song's formal simplicity mirrors its accompaniment; there are three verses, each of which contains three sections. The first section ambles along in 4/4, emphasizing tonic C chords decorated each measure with a brief F/C harmony; arpeggiated melody lines (perhaps inspired by typical dobro licks) are complemented by dobro fills. The second section shifts decisively to an F chord (as would be the case in a typical blues structure) and F and C harmonies alternate, now in 3/4 time; again, melodies are arpeggiated, and the dobro becomes more active.

The third section is accompanied by only the "pedal steel gong" and percussion; in the first two verses this section is begun by an A minor chord (approached from an F through G and E/G♯), back in 4/4, with mostly spoken text; in the third verse it remains in 3/4, uses a C chord, and more freely mixes speaking and singing.

The first verse first describes some fundamentally harmless wolves. In the second section, a sheep is described as straying from the flock, and in the third, the singer wonders where the sheep went, and then discovers that he's been killed. The second verse starts with spoken text, describing the disgusting pig and the police who pursue a wolf. This second section (sung) describes the wolf's inept attorney, and it is extended—now spoken—to quote the governor as he vindictively imposes the death penalty; the third section heralds the approach of the media.

The last verse provides connections between the fable and real life. In the first section, again spoken, the pig is described as reveling in the fact that he has gotten away with the crime. The second section says that people across the world are protesting such "animal behavior," and the third repeats this phrase and sings the title phrase three times. Finally the singer repeats once again "it's animal behavior" in exaggerated tones to make clear that he is making a necessary point about human actions beyond the song, and one last repetition of the title phrase concludes the song.

The titles of the last two songs on *You're the One*, "Hurricane Eye" and "Quiet," indicate a common theme. Remarkably, though, they take this idea of peacefulness as a point of departure in two extremely different directions—while "Hurricane Eye" is unusually active, both in its musical texture and in the degree to which it mixes styles and moods, "Quiet" closes the album by being unusually serene in the same realms—its sound is very simple, and its style is consistent throughout.

"Hurricane Eye" begins by picking up two themes from the introductory song, "That's Where I Belong." The introduction is dominated by a banjo (although played in an American folk style, rather than the style one might have expected from the island man in the earlier song), and this instrument continues to be featured in the first section. This section begins with the other reference—to storytelling—as the singer asks for a story " 'bout how it used to be."

The homespun nature of this request is supported by the banjo accompaniment, the section's division into three simple four-measure phrases in 4/4 time, and the way that the singsong melody in each of these divisions is neatly harmonized as a complete tonic-to-tonic idea in the folk-friendly key of D, using no more than the most common three chords (D, G, and A). The text, however, combines the harmless storytelling with hints of greater import, as Goldilocks is juxtaposed with "nature in the cross-hairs." The connection between these two thoughts is made as the singer reminds us of our inherent connection with the environment and suggests that only when the kind of balance that Goldilocks favored is reached will we be "home."

This word begins a section that emphasizes its desirability by shifting into a swaying 6/8 meter and featuring a different instrument, the hammered dulcimer. As the section continues, though, some uneasiness is suggested, as the texture thickens with some additional electric instruments, and some minor chords are used (although they—E minor and B minor—are still in the key of D major). As the melodic lines soar plaintively, the text acknowledges the reality of interpersonal struggles and uses the title phrase to suggest that such a balance may be fragile.

These two sections are then repeated. This time the first section presents images of an almost-silenced Native American culture colliding with the European. These ideas are said to "[lead] the spirit over the bridge of time," and with this relocation the second section commences. Now the singer describes the struggle of grappling with these ideas, wondering how to pray in the presence of "crazy angel voices." At this point, instead of incorporating the title idea in the section, he mentions "a new day," which signals a new section, as a fuzz guitar sound is featured in the unusual meter of 7/8, and "peaceful as a hurricane eye" is repeated in this context instead.

The episodic evolution of the song is still not over, as a new (and final) section begins. Shifting through 6/8 to 4/4, the music uses a melodic electric-guitar riff and a rock beat to establish a four-bar, modally flavored cycle of chords (still in D: D-A/C-G-C/G-A/D-A). This pattern continues to the end of the song, and the melodic line is almost entirely confined to the space between G and D as the singer turns cynically on the listener.

During his first three cycles, he half-speaks (again recalling a talking-blues style), asking the listener if he or she wants to be a leader, a missionary, a writer, and in each case telling him or her what such a choice would require if pursued with integrity. For the last five cycles, as instruments (including the banjo) are added to the texture, he tends more toward singing, but retains his acerbic tone, describing the listener's desire to "talk [and] squawk" about environmental issues and condescending to tell "how the story goes." In a last burst of manic energy, he returns to childhood stories and connections with the present day to say that the old woman who lived in a shoe fell asleep in a washing machine and woke up in a hurricane eye, punctuating this last thought with a hillbilly-style octave leap.

If "Hurricane Eye" brings the album full circle, winding up the storytelling by returning in some explicit ways to the opening song, "Quiet" serves as a coda. This song creates a sense of stasis with a droning accompaniment throughout that emphasizes the key of D in which "Hurricane Eye" was set. Against this Simon simply sings a series of phrases in Mixolydian mode, as various instruments occasionally provide additional melodic lines. As is the case in "The Teacher," an exotic flavor is conveyed not only by the tonal language, but also by the choice of instruments; again, no typical acoustic or electric guitar is used, but the instruments include pump reed organ, vihuela (a guitar-like instrument from medieval and Renaissance times), 96-tone harp, whirly pipe, rubbed steel bowl, upright bass, and a "tromba doo."

As Simon begins to sing, he uses key notes in the scale to establish a four-phrase pattern; the remainder of the song will be shaped by the way this pattern evolves and interacts with the text. The first phrase, in which the singer declares his goal of "a time of quiet," ascends from D through F♯ to A and descends by reversing the same path. The second ascends quickly to the C♯ that distinguishes the mode, adding poignancy to the "restlessness" that the singer is leaving, and then descends. The third follows the same path that the first did, as he again describes his coming repose, and this release is reemphasized in the fourth as it begins on the low A, leaps up to F♯, and works its way back down to D.

The second verse follows essentially the same pattern; the C♯ here colors the word "peace," and a new idea, of a "perfect circle," is introduced by a new high D in the third phrase. This circle is said in the fourth phrase to "marr[y] all beginnings and conclusions," and the melody illustrates this by ending not on D but on another A-F♯ leap; this "conclusion" becomes a "beginning" in the next verse by being repeated to start the next verse, and this "beginning" is like a "conclusion" because its phrase *does* end on D.

The third verse proceeds in typical fashion for the first two phrases, but as the text casts doubt on one's sense of self-worth, the last phrases break up and contract. They end on D, but then continue immediately with the fourth verse (previous verses were preceded by pauses in the voice part). The upright bass doubles the singer at the lower octave in this time of doubt and provides punctuations twice in the following phrases.

The fourth verse provides something of a climax, warning of ambition and greed during two normal opening phrases but inserting a digression that ascends to falsetto in the third phrase on the word "soul" (which is described as being handcuffed by these threats). After this verse winds down, a brief instrumental interlude allows the tension to dissipate. The final verse is much more serene, as the singer describes his place of quiet's remote pastoral setting: the second phrase rises only to a B rather than a C♮, although the third phrase retains the high D from the second verse (on the word "sacred," describing the water in a lake). The last phrase returns to the original A-F♯-D contour, as the accompaniment drops off to leave a single D.

SURPRISE

Paul Simon's most recent album, *Surprise*, was released in May 2006. The album cover features close-ups of a baby's face and panels of streaky blue water, and the booklet contains a wide range of images that offer various perspectives on humans and their environments. A common theme is that of water, and the printed song lyrics emphasize this typographically: words that refer to some form of water are presented in boldface type, and this is the case at least once in each song. (A few unbolded water-words are presumably inadvertent errors—one of two *clouds* in "Everything about It Is a Love Song," *cry* in "Wartime Prayers," and *Sea* and *cried* in "Beautiful.")

The 11 songs on the album comment on the state of the world with varying degrees of directness, and in doing so they draw on a wide variety of styles. In several instances, in fact, Simon juxtaposes styles within a single song, rather than developing one distinctive texture at greater length. This has the effect of forcing the listener to come to grips with the way that various sections need to be taken into account in order to make sense of the song.

For the most part, the instrumentation is relatively consistent throughout the album—most of the songs use guitars, bass, and drums. But variety in this realm is achieved not only through the varying styles that the players of these instruments produce, but also through one additional ingredient. On all of the songs but one ("Father and Daughter," which was written for *The Wild Thornberrys Movie* about four years before the other songs on the album were written), Brian Eno is credited with "electronics," which, as one may imagine, makes possible a wide variety of sounds and textures. Eno is also given a blanket credit for "sonic landscape" for the album, and shares writing credit with Simon for three of the songs, "Outrageous," "Another Galaxy," and "Once Upon a Time There Was an Ocean."

"How Can You Live in the Northeast?" is a rumination on national, ethnic, and religious heritage. Its musical form is assembled from two components. The first is a four-bar series of chords that moves from the tonic A chord to the dominant E over a descending bass line (A-Em / G-F♯m7-E); this is played with distorted electric guitar sounds, and the concluding E chord leads strongly back to the beginning A, facilitating any number of repetitions of the passage. The E chord can also be prolonged into the second component, a refrain that simply sustains an open-fifth E5 sound. The accompaniment here is more delicate, using a pattern of off-the-beat single notes, and this, along with the sustained E sound that will eventually lead to A to begin the first pattern again, conveys a need for resolution that suitably accompanies questions such as that of the title.

The song opens with two instrumental presentations of the A-to-E passage, and then, against a third, the singer introduces the national theme by singing in the first person plural about enjoying Fourth of July fireworks. He follows this with the refrain, in which phrases that begin with repeated sixteenth-note Bs and fall away ask in the second person how the listener can choose a region in which to live, or a religion. Three A-to-E passages develop the idea that everyone is born in the same way and has a chance to choose a religion, going on to ask why enlightened people can "sleep in the dark."

The refrain then uses some new text to ask how the listener can adopt specific religious, ethnic, and/or regional practices. Two A-to-E segments present first some wordless vocalizing and then return to the Fourth of July image, connecting this time with "endless skies" that lead to four soft E5 measures with vaguely "spacy" instrumental sounds. The E5 continues, accompanying a six-bar version of the refrain that replaces the single notes with smoother lines. This develops into the conclusion of the song, as first a wailing lead guitar leads the way into a brief instrumental interlude, and then the singer provides a coda, now finally in the first person singular. Against swooshing airplane-take-off electronic sounds and an E harmony, he uses melodic phrases that descend repeatedly to E, first from B and then from D, to make declarations about his heritage. The song ends on the E chord, having never arrived at a conclusive A, and thus, the singer's assertions notwithstanding, leaving its questions unanswered.

"Everything about It Is a Love Song" also uses a coda, as well as nested contrasts, to explore issues of responsibility and fallibility. The overall form is ABAcoda, but each of the A sections includes two subsections with distinct rhythmic and instrumental characteristics. A gentle introduction places guitar gestures in the foreground, but pulsing low electronics and ominous discordant melodic fragments convey a sense of unease. Against these accompanimental features, the singer begins the first A section with a melody in a relaxed shuffle rhythm, often skipping among chord tones in the key of Db. The instruments continue to add lush, exotic layers as he describes his bucolic ruminations while struggling to write a song.

In the second subsection, the basic textural foundations remain the same, but a more typical rock veneer is applied as drums enter and the rhythms become straight. Here, with a couple of brief additions of a harmony vocal, the singer uses series of repeated notes to speculate about the reckoning that would come "if [he] ever [got] back to the twentieth century" and had to face his regrets; he imagines that he would have to ponder God and await his "rescue." He concludes on the tonic D♭, and then that pitch is isolated in a rhythmic pulsing texture that leads to the B section.

An A♮ is slowly added to the texture, and the singer repeats it as he describes our "messing things up" (in an oddly casual locution) before an apology arrives, arpeggiated in an A major harmony. A similar passage dwells on the A to describe "love when it was new at a birthday party," settling this time on A minor. A third passage sarcastically tells the listener to "make a wish and close your eyes," following with the album's title, now on a D major harmony.

This harmony is retained as the opening texture returns (but now in D major rather than D♭). Now the first A subsection (with similar, but not identical, melodies) describes the singer's thoughts about the future, and the second uses various images to urge the listener to find and remember him. The coda returns to the texture of the first subsection, but without the shuffle rhythm, and harmony vocals and countermelodies accompany the singer as he presents the song's title as the conclusion that he can draw from all of these thoughts.

"Outrageous" also makes use of contrasting sections and a coda. It opens with a funky guitar-based accompaniment, cycling over a B♭ bass, B♭5-Fm / B♭-E♭ / B♭-B♭, and supporting the singer as he rants about the things that he would describe with the title. His melody moves around quite a bit, but it, too, focuses on B♭. As is the case with several other Simon protagonists (Al, Fat Charlie, Frank), though, his pugnaciousness is mixed with vulnerability, fatigue, and some confusion: he acknowledges the blessing of the rain, says that it's outrageous for him to complain, and explains that he's tired. This is apparently because he's been doing 900 situps a day; he is also, he informs the listener, "painting [his] hair the color of mud."

The refrain drops a third to emphasize a G♭ bass, and the chattering guitar drops out in favor of a dipping and diving electronic countermelody. Over this, a high harmony vocal—only occasionally heard earlier—accompanies the singer as he repeats the additionally vexing question "Who's gonna love you when your looks are gone?" The first four times the question is posed, it features repeated D♭s and finishes by descending to B♭. At the end of this section, though, the pattern repeats without pause, starting a step lower on each repetition, until it reaches the tonic G♭.

The second verse and refrain follow the same pattern, although in the verse other situations are deemed outrageous, the singer acknowledges the blessing of having the listener's love, and he now says that his compulsion to think about all this is outrageous. This time, though, the refrain is extended and followed by a chiming guitar instrumental interlude, still over G♭. Then the coda answers its question in a way that introduces a new dimension to the song.

In a series of phrases that descend from D♭ to G♭ as the harmonies alternate between D♭ and G♭ as well, the singer declares that "God will," just as he sends rain to water flowers. This development is somewhat abrupt, both because the music is new after the main verse and refrain components have been introduced and because of the close-to-literal *deus ex machina* nature of the text (whether or not it is intended to be taken at face value). Beyond this, though, Simon's style of singing, along with the harmony vocal that continues from the refrain, has now evolved into a clear imitation of Bob Dylan. The text immediately develops this, as the singer describes himself as "an ordinary player in the key of C"—both a reference to Dylan's folk-tradition associations with musical naïveté and ironic because the music is actually in G♭, the key most distant from C—and reuses the word "will" in bemoaning his "pride and...vanity." The coda continues by reiterating the refrain's question and the divine answer and concludes with the former. The listener is then left with an implied invitation to reassess the main body of the song in terms of Dylan's persona.

A continuous bass ostinato on G runs with percussion to the very end of "Sure Don't Feel Like Love," and this sets the foundation for a G Mixolydian tonality throughout. With these elements unvarying, it is left up to the text, melody, and instrumentation to shape the piece. At first it seems that this will occur in a fairly straightforward way, as a verse-refrain-verse-refrain pattern is established, but then the song proceeds into a series of new passages over the G, thus amounting to a sort of continuously evolving textual rumination with various accompanimental elaborations.

After the spare but funky accompaniment vamps for a while as an introduction, it, along with occasional harmony vocal touches, accompanies the singer in the first verse as he expresses futility over registering to vote. Much of this is done with repeated melody notes; then the refrain uses lines that descend from F natural to G to respond "so who's that conscience sticking on the sole of my shoe?" Through this and the closing title line, brief guitar punctuations and harmony vocals sound. The second verse attempts to deny the idea that fault is associated with crying, and this personal perspective is enhanced by reverb effects on the voice and electronic gestures. The same refrain again argues for attention to the conscience; its accompaniment adds some sustained electronic sounds to its texture.

The conscience idea is developed in the next section. As ominous electronic licks growl under the surface, the singer chants with repeated bursts that "it" is like an unspoken threat (and certainly not like love); he slides to some bluesy B♭s to suggest that chicken and a corn muffin are more like love. Guitar licks and chanted "Yay!"s and "Boo!"s lead to the next section, in which the texture drops back to the original bass and drums and the singer surmises in brief bursts that he might be "wrong again."

This idea develops, as various harmony vocals, along with nasty electric-guitar lines, help him to recall a few times when he might have been wrong. He concludes about the last one of these that it "didn't feel like love," and this leads to the final section. At this point the singer chants the title with a harmony vocal, first against the original bass-and-drum accompaniment, and finally (as that pattern ultimately ceases) against very unobtrusive sustained G harmonies.

Of all the songs on *Surprise,* "Wartime Prayers" draws prominently on the most accompanimental resources. In addition to using guitars, drums, bass,

Eno's electronics, and keyboards, Simon also incorporates the Jessy Dixon Singers (his collaborators, along with Phoebe Snow, on "Gone at Last") and Herbie Hancock (on piano) into the recording. These forces are used to support the song's theme: that prayers in times of war take on a special urgency and universality as people sense their need and inadequacy. This self-awareness is expressed in a refrain as a response to the points made in three successively abbreviated versions of a verse.

The introduction consists of an *obbligato* solo guitar line against atmospheric electronic sounds. This texture continues as the singer uses the first eight bars of the first verse to describe the intimacy of peacetime prayers. His melody line also includes *obbligato* features, with frequent leaps and rhythmic variety; this section begins on a B-minor chord but becomes somewhat tonally unstable, implying C and G, before reemphasizing B by ending on its dominant harmony, F#7.

The verse includes two more eight-bar sections. In the first of these, the opening texture continues for four bars, ending on a B minor harmony, as the singer says that things have changed. The next four bars—completing this second section—add an electric-guitar punctuation and a drum track as the singer alludes to C. S. Lewis's famous formulation in saying that people seeking God only "hear lunatics and liars"[5]; the section ends on a B minor that is weakened (as a tonal center) by the preceding C (which would not ordinarily precede a B minor chord in B minor).

In the final eight-bar section, the singer says that wartime prayers are spoken for every affected family around the world, and the choir joins him to support this universal reference (on "in every language spoken"). The passage implies the key of G for awhile but ultimately opens out to B *major,* ending with an electric-rock texture that alternates between B and E chords to lead into the refrain. This regular alternation continues, and a harmony voice joins the singer in regular rock rhythms for six bars to confess inadequacy and seek wisdom. The harmony voice drops away for the last line, however, and minor chords accompany the singer as he expresses a desire for personal cleansing, and the piano enters to lead the music back to B minor for the next verse.

The piano and drums continue (along with guitars and electronics) for this verse, which omits the original first eight-bar section and two bars of the G major portion near the end. With a new melody over the original chords, the singer describes attempts to endure hardship, concluding that when we reach our limit, "we wrap ourselves in prayer." The choir joins him on this line, which opens to B major and leads into the refrain as before. This time the choir accompanies the singer until the last line, when he again makes his personal statement.

In the final verse, piano, guitar, drums, and some background vocals dominate in a warm accompaniment as the singer paints an intimate picture of a mother cuddling at bedtime with her children. This verse omits the first four bars of the second verse. However, rather than abbreviating the G major section toward the end, it extends it and actually ends in G major. The ending is not resolved, however, because as the mother says her wartime prayer, the dominant harmony of D closes the song.

In "Beautiful," a straightforward instrumental texture (guitars, electronics, bass, and drums) creates a buoyant, attractive sound. The song uses static harmonies and a modified verse structure to combine whimsical images of childrearing with descriptions of babies adopted from overseas. The first verse exemplifies this, after the introduction establishes the basic instrumental pattern. First, against a constant B♭ harmony, four bars describe a deteriorating snowman; four more tell of the baby, Emily, who was brought from Bangladesh; and eight use leaps to falsetto range to describe her with the title word.

The second verse follows the same pattern, commenting humorously about the snowman, now describing a family of four, and explaining that the new baby is from China. The third verse opens with a sudden move up to a D♭ harmony. Now the singer, accompanied by a harmony vocal, describes summer activities—a go-kart, water slide, and candy stand, and frolicking in the grass. A jaw-harp sound is added to the texture, and the harmony voice spins giddily out of sync with the lead. This description, with a somewhat altered melody, fills eight bars, and eight more are now devoted to the parental perspective, in this case using a new melody to repeat a caution to watch the children in the pool.

After this expanded first half, the verse returns suddenly to the B♭ chord, repeating the opening vamp with a more active bass line before beginning the second half. Then this slightly augmented texture accompanies the third description of an adoption. This section is also extended in length; four bars tell of the baby, now from Kosovo, and then the "beautiful" music appears for eight bars while the trip and the baby are described further. Finally, the same music accompanies its original text, using a different melodic phrase to conclude as the music continues directly into the introduction to "I Don't Believe."

This song uses a simple ABABA form and a typically Simonesque variety of images to express the singer's fears that the hopeful elements of his life are chimerical illusions within a grand cosmic joke. The A and B sections, each initially 16 measures long, are distinguished from one another by their prevailing meters and rhythms, their key areas, and their instrumental textures. The introduction evolves from its beginning at the end of "Beautiful" into a 3/4 meter in E♭ with gentle, tropical-sounding guitar gestures and warm electronic sounds, and the singer uses relaxed rhythms and skips among chord tones as he builds on the preceding song's closing image to describe "acts of kindness" that act as beacons in life; the folksong nature of the song is reinforced by the simple eight-bar first half of the verse, with four bars of E♭, two of B♭7, and two of E♭.

In the second half of the verse, though, the singer uses the title phrase to express his doubts and fear; hints of slack-key guitar licks flavor the eight bars here that move through G minor and G7 chords to a C minor chord, establishing Simon's oft-favored relative minor key for the B section. Here the meter shifts as well, to 6/8, and a new guitar figure is introduced, as the singer uses more agitated rhythms in the first half to describe the "show" of the cosmos being formed. (One line, "The universe loves a drama," is credited in liner notes and sheet music to "E. B."—presumably Simon's wife, Edie Brickell—"after 2004 presidential election.") Distortion is added to the guitar licks as the second half shifts images to describe the singer receiving bad news from his broker and losing at poker, but the music then dissolves back into the gentle A section.

At this point the original first eight-bar E♭-B♭-E♭ pattern is repeated so that this verse lasts 24 measures, and the singer asks his guardian angel not to taunt him as he gracefully describes his wife and his carefree children on a beautiful summer evening. Now in the last eight bars he reverses the meaning of the title phrase, denying that life could be so full and still meaningless. But the music still goes to the minor key, and he begins the B section by questioning this conclusion and flirting with embracing "maybe." This uncertainty is reinforced by the broker's news that he was wrong, leaving questions about the singer's faith being shaken.

"Acts of kindness" return to lead back into the third A section, now 16 bars once again, but it takes a few bars this time to get back to 3/4. The texture becomes more active, including a very brief harmony vocal, as the singer retains the hopeful sense of the title phrase in this verse, denying that we are "like sheep in a flock." Nonetheless, the section moves to minor, and the distorted guitar licks of the B section return in a coda before a soft, querulous closing guitar figure is repeated against pulsing electronic sounds.

Pulsing sounds introduce and last throughout "Another Galaxy," which also moves between E♭ and its relative key, C minor. However, this song differs from "I Don't Believe" in that it develops a single image throughout: its two verses and choruses constitute a simple ballad that tells of a young woman who flees on the morning of the day on which she is to be married. The song is accompanied by the bare minimum (for this album) of guitars, electronics, bass, and drums, but a striking variety of guitar colors (all apparently produced by Simon) is used. Some of these, along with a frequently present harmony vocal, reinforce the Southwestern flavor suggested by "the border" across which she drives.

The introduction, which lasts a full minute and 25 seconds, first highlights a forebodingly reverberated electric-guitar line that emphasizes E♭ minor. Then strummed chords vacillate between E♭ *major* and C minor through G7, the dominant of C minor, before settling on a vamp in E♭; this occurs twice before the first verse begins. The two harmonies continue to compete, and they, along with the harmony vocals and a smorgasbord of emotion-laden guitar effects, add poignancy to the singer's description of the woman's flight. He concludes that "she's gone, gone, gone," and this is punctuated by a formulaic so-called falling chord progression and the vamp that immediately preceded the verse. This chord progression—D♭-A♭-E♭, or, in Roman numerals, ♭VII-IV-I—is associated with a sense of falling because it reverses the usual, classically expected pattern of root motion by descending, rather than ascending, fifths, as would be seen in Fm-B♭-E♭, or ii-V-I.

The chorus is treated in much the same way, except that a single guitar effect—a low Western-sounding reverberated line—is emphasized throughout. The singer advocates the woman's choice as "the lesser crime" (although the word "crime" seems a bit forced here in order to make a rhyme), saying in the second person that one can see "another life, another galaxy." The vamp returns, followed by the second verse, in which the melody differs from that of the first verse, but the harmonies are essentially the same, with one significant change: the beginning dwells on C minor rather than E♭. Guitar effects are less prominent at this point, and the singer describes the woman's restless dreams, in which her senses are confused—she hears clouds and sees a hurricane's eye. The pulsing subsides in the final chorus, which is otherwise quite similar to the first one, and then an instrumental coda lasts for more than a minute, including brief slide guitar licks, a lull, and then a return to the opening guitar line.

"Once Upon a Time There Was an Ocean" also uses two verses and choruses bracketed by substantial introductory and coda passages. It differs from "Another Galaxy" in that the opening and closing segments feature singing (rather than just instruments), the second verse omits some of the parts of the first verse, and the topic is quite different. In this song the singer uses the image of land masses shifting and re-forming to support his idea that his humdrum life will change. Only two chords—G and C in the key of G—are used throughout, with G present most of the time, and motions to C often accompanying the idea of change in the text.

This connection is established in the introduction, which begins with eight bars of guitar vamping on G but moves to C when the singer begins. He starts by singing the title in rather free rhythms (after an unusual "pre-echo" of the opening words), but these regularize by the end of his eight-bar segment. He concludes, against alternating C and G chords, that the ocean's change into a mountain range was inexorable, and "nothing is different, but everything's changed." At this point distorted guitars establish a rock beat, and then the first verse begins.

Against a spare guitars-bass-and-percussion texture the singer bounces among repeated chord tones to chant for eight bars about his "dead-end job" that he constantly wants to quit. He is joined by another voice for another four bars as he thinks about getting "outta here," and then the opening vamp returns for an eight-bar reference to the way that he would like to indulge himself when he "cash[es] in [his] lottery ticket." As it did in the introduction, the vamp leads into a C chord, and the chorus repeats the introduction's text with two differences: it begins with a new melody that uses regular rhythms from the start, and now the singer says that *he* is the ocean that became a mountain range.

The rock rhythm returns, and in the second verse the singer tells of moving to the city and living optimistically in humble circumstances. He says that he's never going home again, and then the eight-bar vamp section is skipped so that the music leads straight into the C chord of the chorus. Once again the melody is varied at the beginning, now describing an arresting letter from home; the chorus ends with the same text and melody that concluded the introduction and first chorus.

At this point the music subsides to a very soft, warm pulsing. A drum joins, and then a chiming guitar figure brings in the singer. Against this background, on a G harmony, he sets an entirely different scene, describing a luminously colored scene in a church. As the chord goes to C, some of the guitar figures from earlier C sections enter and the singer describes the choir singing the title line. Electronic sounds are added and blossom gloriously as he says that "old hymns and family names came fluttering down in leaves of emotion," and then they subside as the song concludes once again that "nothing is different, but everything's changed." The listener is left to draw conclusions about the relationship of this transcendent scene to the protagonist's aspirations as the song trails off to the pulsing sounds.

"That's Me" combines several typical Simon characteristics. A distinctive rhythmic figure runs throughout, although at the same time the song uses an AABA form with a significantly contrasting B section. There is extensive emphasis on a single harmony, and the text ranges through a wide variety of images as the singer invites the listener to join him as he explores his own identity.

The introduction establishes the rhythmic figure, a guitar lick that features percussive string noise against a Csus4 harmony in the key of C. This sound and harmony, which sets a dissonant fourth (F) against a C major sound, create a brash accompaniment that provides a suitable setting for the singer to use melodic lines that repeat and skip downward to tell the listener that he's going to tell about himself. Additional guitar figures enter, with brief F-chord decorations of the C harmony, as he describes a couple of scenes (as if seen in a picture album) from his youth, including "picking up a bogus degree" at graduation. A drum enters as the title phrase closes this first verse.

The texture is now rather active, with the rhythmic figure joined by various guitars and percussion figures, and a harmony vocal joins the singer as he describes his historic lack of involvement with money and says that he was like a "land-locked sailor, searching for the emerald sea." This thought is repeated in a way that, together with the harmony vocal, recalls sea-chantey style. As the second verse ends, the B section is introduced by a twirling acoustic-guitar triplet figure.

This device leads into a warmer texture, including sustained sounds and even brief hints of bagpipes (although the string-noise lick persists in the background). The harmonic palette is enriched as well, by C/E and G chords, as the singer uses slow, graceful rhythms to sing of "first love." Images of nature—a flower, a powerful black female bear in the forest, "tricky skies"—are invoked as he predicts a future of beauty and sorrow and uses the second person to wish that he and his first love could preserve their romance, if only briefly. The mood is retained in a brief instrumental interlude that continues to add lush sounds.

In the last verse the singer is again joined by a harmony vocal, but he now contemplates more profound images than those found in the first two verses. Gravity is provided by additional accompaniment in low registers as he methodically ascends a mountain and ponders constellations and the nature of memory. The title phrase finds him "in the valley of twilight" and "on the continental shelf," and finally answering an unspecified question that he himself is posing. The music then moves into a coda that consists of a series of four-bar phrases using the self-contained, monolithic chord progression C-E♭-B♭/F-C and a variety of cosmos-evoking sounds—wordless vocalizing (and a couple of reminiscent "that's me"s), low growling bass noises, high electronic swoops, and so forth.

The song that Simon had written for *The Wild Thornberrys Movie,* "Father and Daughter," concludes the album. Its form is rather simple—verse-chorus-verse-chorus-chorus, with the second verse slightly abbreviated—and the instrumentation is straightforward: guitars, bass, and drums. In the text, the singer encourages his daughter not to be frightened or anxious, says that he will watch over her, and declares his love for her. The first verse and chorus are heard in the movie as Eliza Thornberry is forced, for her safety's sake, to leave her father and the rest of her family, who are working in Africa; much of the upbeat music is heard as her plane flies through the clouds. (The entire song is heard at the beginning of the closing credits.)

In the introduction a gracefully descending electric-guitar phrase is played twice; it is then heard throughout all of the verses. Drums kick the music into a soft rock beat for the first verse. The verse consists of four pairs of four-bar phrases—the first of each pair ends on the tonic chord of E, and the second ends deceptively on C♯ minor. An ABAB rhyme scheme joins the first two pairs as the singer uses carefree rhythms and melodic contours to urge his daughter to counteract bad dreams with thoughts of the good times they have shared. Similarly structured rhymes and melodic figures in the second half of the verse accompany his declaration that "the light that shines on [her] will shine on [her] forever" (the last word is echoed by Simon's son Adrian), and that he will always watch over her.

In the chorus, the guitar hook stops and Eadd9 and Aadd9 chords (E and A major chords with ninths above the roots—F♯ and B, respectively, added) alternate as the singer is joined by a low harmony vocal to elaborate on this idea. He concludes by assuring the girl of his love as a chord progression similar to those in the verses accompanies the returning hook to lead to another deceptive cadence. The second verse includes just two phrase pairs and compensates somewhat for less frequent line-ending rhymes by including some internal ones, as the singer encourages the girl to make her way in the world without being anxious about issues that are out of her realm. The chorus returns twice (now with high and low harmony vocals), separated by a brief guitar solo. Finally, the guitar hook leads the way through an instrumental coda.

8

Identity

Paul Simon's musical career has spanned 50 years, and he has enjoyed significant popular success at three different stages: in the 1960s with Simon and Garfunkel, in the 1970s with his first three solo albums, and in the late 1980s with the *Graceland* album. It is not surprising that over such a long period of time his stylistic interests have varied and evolved, but the degree to which this has been the case, and more specifically the degree of success that he has achieved with various styles, has been remarkable. In his 1984 *Playboy* interview with Tony Schwartz, Simon addressed some of his stylistic predilections. First, with reference to the Simon and Garfunkel "folkie act," he said, "Actually, I'm a rock-'n'-roll kid. I grew up with rock-'n'-roll. My main influences in early music were Fifties R & B, Fifties doo-wop groups, Elvis Presley, and the Everly Brothers...a significant part of me just wasn't a folkie....When I began making my own albums, the songs became funkier. They were more about the streets."[1] He then went on to describe the musical explorations that informed *Paul Simon* and *There Goes Rhymin' Simon,* and said with respect to *Still Crazy After All These Years,* "I felt I was defining a real identity. Musically, I was beginning to put together a kind of New York rock, jazz influenced, with a certain kind of lyrical sophistication."[2] And these comments, of course, preceded the opening of new territory that was to take place with the *Graceland* project.

If one were seeking a common stylistic thread in Simon's work, an argument might indeed be made for rock and roll. As has been noted in the discussion of the *Graceland* project, even this album connects to this music, in that the township jive that initially appealed to Simon was reminiscent of " '50s rock 'n' roll out of the Atlantic Records school of simple three-chord pop hits,"[3] and *The Rhythm of the Saints* partially led back through Latin music to *The Capeman,* which in turn includes doo-wop and 12-bar-blues-based structures. However, while he has drawn on many styles, and while some of them may have been more formative or central than were others, the essence of Simon's compositional sensibility is not to be found in a particular style—or even in his stylistic eclecticism. Rather, these stylistic elements are one facet of a creative process that ultimately points, beyond all else, to a very traditional aesthetic instinct.

This process is *synthetic* in nature: it is characterized by identifying various musical and textual components and assembling them into a song, rather than routinely beginning with a traditional, fully integrated, tune-text combination and then adding other elements (contrasting sections, interludes, textures, and other details of arranging) to the core "song" idea. To be sure, many other songwriters also "assemble" songs in such a way, especially as large-scale changes are made during the development of a song, but in Simon's case assembly often seems to be an assumed point of departure, rather than the realization of unanticipated possibilities after a song has already gelled to a significant degree. The components that are assembled include various tracks that are layered together, text, instruments, performers, chord sequences, textures, and even styles themselves.

The discussions of individual songs in this book have frequently reflected this approach. The idea of starting with a particular rhythm track before writing a tune or text, as described with respect to "Cecilia," provides a particularly obvious case. Even more fundamental starting points are cited in Simon's discussion of the preselection of keys, tempi, and song lengths in order to fit specific positions within an album.[4] On the other hand, more elaborate ones are found in the songs that use substantial preexisting structures as bases; many instances of these, sometimes even including text, are found on the *Graceland* and *Rhythm of the Saints* albums, but "El Condor Pasa" provides a much earlier example.

Often evident at the same time as these adoptions of large-scale musical structures is the use of particular instruments, ensembles, and/or performers. This is readily observable in the instances just cited. Such distinctive performers, however, can also be used without preexisting music, but still in a way that is more organic than would be the case when, for example, a guest artist is asked to join in a duet; in the former cases the selection of one or more collaborators would be an essential part of the creation of a song. In this sense, Linda Ronstadt's participation in "Under African Skies," for example, would not constitute an essential component of the compositional process, but Stefan Grossman's work on "Paranoia Blues," the Dixie Hummingbirds' work on *There Goes Rhymin' Simon,* and Good Rockin' Dopsie and the Twisters' and Los Lobos's contributions to *Graceland* apparently would. (And, of course, the same could be said of many of the African and Brazilian performers on non-preexisting works on *Graceland* and *The Rhythm of the Saints.*)

The synthetic approach is also evident in other contexts. Just as a melody and text might be added to a preexisting rhythm/harmony track throughout an entire song, a melody in one verse might be somewhat, or even radically, different from the melody presented against the same harmonic structure in another verse of the same song. Such a procedure, of course, relates to common practices in jazz performance, in which performers routinely improvise new melodies against given sets of chord changes, but in Simon's work it occurs in both jazz and non-jazz styles. The most notable instances of this include "Save the Life of My Child," "Overs," "The Only Living Boy in New York," "Stranded in a Limousine," "René and Georgette Magritte with Their Dog after the War," "Graceland," "Born at the Right Time," "Thelma," "Time Is an Ocean," the two versions of "Killer Wants to Go to College," "Lorraine," "The Teacher," "Look at That," "Wartime Prayers," "Beautiful," "Another Galaxy," and "Once Upon a Time There Was an Ocean." Whether or not a jazz style is present, this technique reflects the fluid approach to combining various components that is under discussion here.

Another kind of example is provided by some of the alternate versions of songs, which can reveal radically different configurations of texts, melodies, formal components, and so on. One very early example of this is the reuse of text from "The Side of a Hill" in the "Canticle" portion of "Scarborough Fair/Canticle." Others include "Let Me Live in Your City" (the presumably earlier version of "Something So Right") and, later, "All Because of You" and "Spiral Highway," as compared with "Oh, Marion" and "How the Heart Approaches What It Yearns," respectively. Again, such examples of reworking are not unique to Simon, but their degree and variety are significant enough to support the notion of synthetic creation that is reflected in other ways.

Many other examples of assembling compositional components could be cited, probably none unique to Simon, but all adding up to a consistent picture of his creative approach. One final example that does bear some examination, though, is the approach to text-writing that evolved over the course of his career. "Assembly" is most readily apparent in text passages that relate somewhat uncertainly to those elsewhere in a song. These have been described occasionally in this book, including several instances in the *Graceland* album, such as the ambiguously located story in the third verse of "Gumboots," the ambiguously identified narrator in "Diamonds on the Soles of Her Shoes," the sudden appearance of transcendent images in "You Can Call Me Al," and the odd combination of images (even suggested in the title) in "All Around the World or The Myth of Fingerprints." In fact, the *Graceland* album plays a central role in a discussion that Simon had with Paul Zollo about the development of his use of language in songwriting. He says that at the time of *One-Trick Pony* and *Hearts and Bones* he was trying "to learn ... to write vernacular speech, and then intersperse it with enriched language, and then go back to vernacular."[5]

Simon's vernacular/enriched terminology seems to address primarily the level on which words communicate, rather than the degree to which they make sense together; for example, he cites the title line of "Train in the Distance" as an instance of enriched language, and the application of this metaphor to the narrative is fairly straightforward.[6] However, mixing "vernacular" with "enriched" seems often to result in a narrative disjuncture as well. Simon agrees with Zollo that the transcendent "angels in the architecture, spinning in infinity" in "You Can Call Me Al" is a good example of enriched language, and in this case the sense of the line is considerably less obvious.[7] (This particular line is something of an unusual case because, according to Simon, it indicates that Al himself is considering a different, nonmundane, level of perception.[8]) A further comment by Simon supports the notion that he is concerned to some degree with communicating on a level that is not strictly rational: in *Graceland*, "sometimes I'd increase the rhythm of the words so that they would come by you and then when a phrase was sort of different, it came by you so quickly that all you would get was a *feeling*. So I started to try and work with moving feelings around with words. Because the *sound* of the record was so good, you could move feelings."[9]

Various examples of this kind of approach can be observed throughout the latter portion of Simon's work, but the most current are a few in the most recent album, *Surprise*. While some of the album's songs use texts that seem completely integrated, others tend to combine sections with topics that are remotely related at best, along with liberal doses of "enriched language." Examples include "Everything about It Is a Love Song," with its combination of creative struggle, birthday parties, apparently unrelated regrets, reincarnation, and the title line; "Outrageous," with its railings devolving into a Dylan evocation; "Sure Don't Feel Like Love," with its variety of images; "Once Upon a Time There Was an Ocean," with its transcendent closing choir scene that may or may not resolve the struggles described earlier by the singer; and "That's Me," with its sharply contrasted brash and romantic tones that the final verse may or may not partially resolve.

These examples of stylistic, rhythmic, harmonic, instrumental, melodic, and textual approaches have suggested a distinctively synthetic approach to composition—one in which Simon selects components and assembles them as he wishes in order to create a wide variety of songs. This approach reflects a naturally analytical inclination to learn how songs can be made to work. This is consistent with the path of Simon's career, as he has repeatedly (and often very intentionally) been in a position of determining how to create within a style or genre—rock and roll, folk, American or global ethnic styles, film, musical theater. Such pursuits are necessarily practical and technical to a significant degree.

At the same time, though, these methods, and Simon's comments about them, reveal a very traditional aesthetic streak—one that is not surprising, given that he was raised in close proximity to one of the major cultural centers of the world, and that he has continued to immerse himself in various artistic milieux. It is no doubt true that much of his work has been done with a considerable level of awareness of its viability for a popular market, and it has, of course, been phenomenally successful in these terms. It is clear, however, that he has also steadily cultivated a desire to create, within the popular song format, genuine works of art—in each instance, that is, to fuse formal logic, sensuous appeal, and human experience into a compelling whole. And, as the discussions in this study have shown, Paul Simon has realized immense success in these terms as well.

Appendix: The Musical Languages of Paul Simon

TONAL LANGUAGES

In writing his songs, Paul Simon has drawn upon a wide range of musical styles. Within each style, particular harmonic and melodic devices carry specific kinds of significance. These devices can be used by a composer to convey, for example, resolution, tension, stability, motion, delay, contrast, and so on.

The musical languages in these styles are all *tonal*, meaning that a particular tone (such as C, or A♭, etc.) is central and stable, and a piece or passage can only arrive at a point of final resolution on that tone or on a harmony based on that tone. This is ordinarily designated as the *key* of the piece; keys are usually identified by this tone—called the *tonic*—and the type of scale that is used predominantly in the piece or passage. A piece in E major, then, uses a major scale and focuses on E as the tonic note.

A composer can use such a tonic note and basic scale as points of reference for creating effects such as those mentioned above. Various styles make it possible to do this with varying degrees of precision and subtlety, as will be discussed later. General examples, though, include conveying resolution and/or stability by reaching the tonic note or harmony; creating a sense of delay by dwelling on a harmony that one would expect to move to the tonic (and increasingly so by resolving that harmony to a harmony other than the tonic); establishing contrast by using different keys for different sections of a piece; expressing varying degrees of complexity with varying numbers of notes outside the predominant scale, and so on.

Major-Minor Tonality

The most highly codified and standardized of these systems is the classical major-minor tonal system, in terms of which the vast majority of European art music written in the eighteenth and nineteenth centuries can be discussed. (Sometimes music scholars use the term *tonal* to refer specifically to this system, rather than in the broader sense defined above.) Other musical languages that Simon uses often resemble this one and/or loosely adopt some of its general features, so it will be discussed first here, followed by descriptions of the ways that other styles add to and/or deviate from it. While composers' treatment of the system has varied somewhat from the eighteenth century to the present, a substantial body of norms and principles is generally accepted.[1] It is important to understand these concepts because they enable listeners to understand the significance of musical devices used by composers (such as Simon) in this system (even though the listeners are ordinarily unable to describe these ideas in technical terms).

Keys and Scales

A composition that uses this system conveys a particular major or minor scale as its basis; as indicated above, this is called its *key*. Different keys may be used at different points throughout a composition. Such variety is the norm in classical pieces of any significant length, because their forms are often partly determined by motion from key to key, achieving a sense of closure upon the return of the original key. It is quite common for a popular or folk song to use only a single key—the form is usually most fundamentally determined by a text-based scheme, such as a succession of verses or an alternation of verses and choruses. But such a song might also use more than one key to reinforce its textual form—verses might be in one key and choruses in another, or the B section of an AABA form might imply a key other than that of the A sections.

Each major scale includes 7 different pitches. These are selected from the total of 12 possible pitches, and they form a pattern of *half steps* (where two successive pitches are included) and *whole steps* (where one of the 12 available pitches is skipped). This pattern is called "diatonic," and is illustrated by the white keys on a piano: all 12 pitches form a repeating pattern of white and black keys, and the black keys are the pitches that are skipped. The pattern is also illustrated in sound by "Do-Re-Mi," the song that Maria sings in *The Sound of Music* in order to teach the von Trapp children how to sing.

The pattern of half- and whole steps in the major scale lets the listener know which of the notes is the tonic note; each other note is a different distance from the tonic and thus has a unique identity.[2] In theoretical discussions, each of these scale steps is assigned a name (such as "tonic"); in music pedagogy, students are often taught to connect these scale-step identities with the sounds of the notes by assigning a syllable to each note, and Maria's

Table A.1
Scale Step Names, Syllables, Intervals, and Notes in Various Major Keys

Scale step	Name	Syllable	Interval	C Major	G Major	D Major	Ab Major
1st	Tonic	do	Whole step	C	G	D	Ab
7th	Leading tone	ti	Half step	B	F#	C#	G
6th	Submediant	la	Whole step	A	E	B	F
5th	Dominant	sol	Whole step	G	D	A	Eb
4th	Subdominant	fa	Whole step	F	C	G	Db
3rd	Mediant	mi	Half step	E	B	F#	C
2nd	Supertonic	re	Whole step	D	A	E	Bb
1st	Tonic	do	Whole step	C	G	D	Ab

song exemplifies this process. For example, Maria's *do* is the tonic note, and the note immediately (a half-step) below the tonic note—Maria's *ti*—is ordinarily expected to lead melodically to the tonic and is thus called the *leading tone*.[3] The note a whole step above the tonic note (Maria's *re*) is called the *supertonic*. Table A.1 shows the name and syllable for each note of the scale, along with the interval to the note above it, with some examples in four different keys. The sharped and flatted notes—black keys on the piano—are necessary in order to preserve the proper pattern of half- and whole steps in relation to each tonic note. If all white keys are used—no sharps or flats—the tonic is C major.

HARMONIES AND "PROGRESSIONS" IN CLASSICAL MUSIC

The simplest harmonies that are found in classical music—and most folk and popular music—are "triads," each of which consists of three notes that sound together in the texture of a piece: the *root* (by which it is identified), the *third* (two scale steps above the root) and the *fifth* (two steps above the third). For example, the tonic harmony includes the tonic note, the mediant, and the dominant (C-E-G in C major, or Ab-C-Eb in Ab major). This harmony is considered to be stable and occurs often, notably conveying stability at the end of a piece, where the melody will usually have arrived on the tonic note.

The harmony that is next most prominent (after the tonic harmony) in major-minor tonal music is the *dominant* harmony, composed of the dominant note, the leading tone, and the supertonic (G-B-D in C major, or Eb-G-Bb in Ab major). Forward motion from one harmony to another is called a *progression,* and just as the leading tone is expected to lead melodically to the tonic note, the dominant harmony is expected to *progress* to the tonic harmony. This dominant-to-tonic motion is considered the strongest progression in major-minor tonality, and it includes a strong motion in individual *voices* within the chords. These can include motion in the melody from the leading tone in the dominant chord to the tonic note, or from the supertonic to the tonic. Very often, especially at the end of a musical section, they will also include motion in the lowest voice from the dominant to the tonic. This *root motion* (so called because it involves the root of each chord) by a descending *fifth* (distance reckoned by the total number of scale steps from dominant down to tonic) is considered essential to the strong harmonic motion between the chords.

Musical phrases in classical music are ended with harmonic progressions called *cadences*. Most of these consist of either this dominant-to-tonic progression, which is called an *authentic cadence*, or with a progression to a dominant harmony, which is called a *half cadence*, implying that further closure with an authentic cadence will eventually arrive at the end of a subsequent phrase. (This pattern of a half cadence followed by an authentic cadence is found, for example, in "He Was My Brother," "Wednesday Morning, 3 A.M.," the acoustic version of "A Simple Desultory Philippic," "Soft Parachutes," and "Train in the Distance.") When either of these is a significant event in a classical piece, the dominant harmony may often be preceded by a tonic harmony with the dominant note (the fifth of the tonic chord) in the lowest voice. Examples of this in Simon's music include the C/G chord toward the end of the A sections of "American Tune" and the E♭/B♭ chord in the repeated chord pattern in "Under African Skies."

A third kind of cadence, far less common than these two but far more common than any other in classical music, is the *deceptive* cadence; here the dominant harmony, rather than resolving to the stable tonic harmony at the end of a phrase, moves to the submediant harmony. The effect, as one might expect, is one of deviation from an expected resolution, with the listener anticipating a more satisfactory conclusion later. Simon uses this device at the end of the first two verses of "The Side of a Hill" and in the middle of verses of "Father and Daughter," and he uses it to set up the repetition of verse- or section-ending lines in "Still Crazy after All These Years," "Señorita with a Necklace of Tears," and "Bridge over Troubled Water"; it actually concludes "That's Where I Belong," helping the song to lead to the remainder of *You're the One*.

A triad can be built on any of the scale steps. Each of these triads has a particular sound *quality*, determined by the distances between its notes. If root-to-third includes two whole steps, and third-to-fifth a whole step and a half step, as is the case with the tonic, dominant, and subdominant harmonies in a major key, the triad is *major*. Conversely, if root-to-third includes a whole step and a half step, and third-to-fifth includes two whole steps (as is the case with the tonic harmony in a minor key (and three of the harmonies in a major key), the triad is *minor*. The seventh harmony in a major key, built on the leading tone, has a whole step and a half step between root and third, and between third and fifth; it thus encompasses one less half step overall than do the major and minor triads, and its quality is *diminished*. Each triad is commonly identified not only by its root (*tonic harmony, dominant harmony, submediant harmony*), but also by a Roman numeral indicating its root's scale step, with the quality indicated by upper-case letters for major (I, IV, V), lower-case for minor (ii, iii, vi), and lower case with a superscript circle for diminished (vii°).

In classical music, some progressions among these diatonic harmonies are quite common, and thus their familiarity to the listener signals normal forward motion. (Music-theory students typically perform *Roman-numeral analyses,* showing how a harmonic progression fits the listener's expectations.) Other progressions are extremely uncommon, and in the rare cases in which they occur, an analyst would ordinarily feel obligated to explain what consideration or effect is overriding normal expectations. Besides the dominant-to-tonic (or V-I) motion already discussed, two of the most typical diatonic progressions are the approach to the dominant chord from the subdominant (IV) or supertonic (ii) harmony. When they act in this way, they are often identified as "predominant" chords. Motion from ii to V mimics the descending-fifth root movement of the strong V-I progression (good examples of this are the Em-A7-D motion at the end of the choruses in "Baby Driver" and the Bm-E motion at the midpoint of the verses of "Think Too Much (a)"). The tonic harmony can lead to any other, so a very basic phrase might progress I-IV-V-I or I-ii-V-I; the submediant (vi) harmony might commonly precede IV or ii (creating, perhaps, I-vi-IV-V-I or I-vi-ii-V-I).

While in classical music the dominant harmony usually leads to the tonic harmony, and the others usually move toward the dominant harmony (although the subdominant might also move more softly back to tonic), diatonic phrases may still involve considerably longer sequences of harmonies than are shown in these examples, because the appearance of the tonic harmony does not necessarily indicate the end of a phrase. For example, a phrase might use the progression I-V-I-vi-IV-ii-V-vi-ii-V-I, or a host of other possibilities. However, as indicated above, some progressions simply do not fit the classical mold. For example, V rarely moves to ii or IV, and vi and ii rarely move to I. The vii° chord ordinarily moves to I, but not to IV or ii; the ii harmony rarely progresses to vi or IV; and the iii harmony does not often appear, but when it does it often moves to vi (this can initiate a chain, or *circle,* of descending-fifth-root motions—iii-vi-ii-V-I). Finally, any of these triads can be supplemented with a fourth note—a *seventh* can be added to create a dissonance that reinforces forward motion by resolving as one harmony progresses to the next. (These harmonies are called *seventh chords* rather than *triads*; since the practice is associated with forward motion, it is not often applied to the stable tonic chord.)

MINOR KEYS IN CLASSICAL MUSIC

The preceding discussion has focused on common practices in the major-minor system in the case of major keys. Similar principles apply to minor keys, with the following adjustments. First, minor keys do not focus as clearly on seven-note diatonic scales as do major keys. Table A.2 shows how various

Table A.2
Scale Step Names, Syllables, Intervals, and Notes in Various Minor Keys

Scale step	Name	Syllable	Interval	A minor	E minor	B minor	F minor
1st	Tonic	do	Whole step	A	E	B	F
7th	Subtonic	te	Whole step	G	D	A	E♭
6th	Submediant	le	Whole step	F	C	G	D♭
5th	Dominant	sol	Half step	E	B	F♯	C
4th	Subdominant	fa	Whole step	D	A	E	B♭
3rd	Mediant	me	Whole step	C	G	D	A♭
2nd	Supertonic	re	Half step	B	F♯	C♯	G
1st	Tonic	do	Whole step	A	E	B	F

minor keys often use diatonic scales—the notes in each scale are the same as they were in the preceding table, but the tonic note is located differently within the pattern of half- and whole steps. (Systems for applying syllables to minor scales vary, so the syllables included in Table A.2 represent just one possible approach.)

These differences in interval patterns result in different qualities for triads—for example, the tonic and subdominant triads (i and iv) are now minor, and the mediant and submediant triads (III and VI) are now major. However, in actual practice, classical music invariably alters this scheme, specifically with reference to the sixth and seventh scale steps. When the seventh scale step leads to tonic, it is raised a half-step (to G♯ in A minor, for example) so as to move strongly as it does in a major key. (When this happens, the note is called the leading tone; when it does not move to the tonic note and is not raised, it is called the subtonic as shown in the table.) Accordingly, whenever a dominant harmony moves to tonic (as it usually does), the triad becomes major (E-G♯-B in A minor—V), rather than minor (E-G-B—v). The sixth scale step is often similarly raised if it is moving melodically up through the leading tone to tonic; this could, for example, make the subdominant chord major (D-F♯-A in A minor—IV), rather than minor (D-F-A—iv).

Most of the harmonies in a minor key are expected to move in similar ways to those described above for major keys. Phrases usually end with authentic (V-i) or half (V) cadences but can also end with deceptive cadences (V-VI). Important dominant harmonies are often approached by iv or ii° harmonies, which might in turn be approached by VI. The V chord does not ordinarily move to ii° or iv, and ii° and VI do not ordinarily go to i. When the seventh step is raised to create a leading-tone triad (vii°), it usually moves to i but not to ii° or iv. However, III is somewhat more common in minor than is iii in major; III in minor commonly moves by fifth-root-motion to VI, and it can be preceded by similar motion from VII, the subtonic chord created when the seventh scale step is *not* raised (this chord does not exist in the major mode). Finally, again, sevenths can be added to triads in minor keys, and these dissonances help to propel the music forward.

CHROMATICISM AND MODULATION

The foregoing discussion describes common diatonic practices in major-minor tonal music. However, very few classical compositions, and probably none of any significant length, restrict themselves to a single major or minor scale. When other notes, called *chromatic* notes, are used, they create additional interesting sounds and harmonies. More importantly, though, they emphasize various notes in the key by leading strongly toward them or even treating them somewhat like tonic notes. In the key of C, for example, a G♯ might lead to an A, acting for a moment as a leading tone would in the key of A minor.

This idea of using notes outside a key—chromatic notes rather than diatonic ones—can go one step further: if a new collection of notes is retained, the listener can perceive that the music has *modulated*, or moved to a new key. A piece can modulate to a key that is closely related to the original key or more distantly related. Proximity of keys is reflected by the number of pitches that they share: the more pitches that are common to the two keys, the more closely related the keys are. Because relatively few pitches change, modulation to a closely related key is usually less abrupt for a listener than is modulation to a more distant key. Commonly, key relations are considered "close" if the two keys share at least six of the seven diatonic pitches. This occurs between any key and the keys that correspond to the major and minor triads in that key. (For example, as one can see by making triads with Table A.1, for C major these would be D minor, E minor, F major, G major, and A minor. In Table A.2, closely related keys for B minor would be D major, E minor, F♯ minor, G major, and A major.)

Motion to closely related keys is more common in concert music than is motion to more distantly related keys, especially early in the major-minor tonal period. (One particularly important relationship in classical instrumental music is that between a major key and the key based on its dominant note.) Theoretically, a major key is most closely related to the minor key based on its submediant note, since these two keys share all pitches, apart from modifications to the sixth and seventh steps of the minor scale. Such keys are called "relative major and minor" keys, and these relationships are shown in the columns of Tables A.1 and A.2 that share the same pitches—A minor is C major's relative minor key, C major is A minor's relative major, E minor is G major's relative minor, and so forth. While much folk music stays in a single key, using relative major and minor keys to distinguish contrasting sections is not uncommon (two familiar examples, although not folk songs, are the Christmas hymn "We Three Kings," and "Feed the Birds" from *Mary Poppins*, both of which use minor verses and choruses in the relative major key).

Simon uses this key relationship often. His predilection for the use of the submediant *chord* in a major key has been noted in print; two examples include his interview with Paul Zollo and his comments on Ray Phiri's work on "Graceland" in the liner notes to *Graceland*.[4] But this inclination is also seen often on a broader scale as he juxtaposes a major key with the key that corresponds to its submediant chord. Various approaches to this technique are found (in chronological order) in "The Sound of Silence," "April, Come She Will," "A Poem on the Underground Wall," "El Condor Pasa," "The Boxer," "Song for the Asking," "Mother and Child Reunion," "Run that Body Down," "Peace Like a River," "Something So Right," "50 Ways to Leave Your Lover," "Slip Slidin' Away," "Think Too Much (b)," "Thelma," "Born in Puerto Rico," "Can I Forgive Him," "Darling Lorraine," "I Don't Believe," and "Another Galaxy."

Even apart from this particular key relationship, most of Simon's songs that move among keys use keys that are fairly closely related. Some, however, explore more distant relationships; these include "Fakin' It," "Everything Put Together Falls Apart," "I Do It for Your Love," "When Numbers Get Serious," "Outrageous," and "Beautiful." The reader may find it interesting to compare the effects of these various key juxtapositions, particularly insofar as they relate to the texts of the songs.

PRINCIPLES OF MAJOR-MINOR TONALITY AND SIMON'S MUSICAL STYLES

This overview of the major-minor tonal system that applies to the vast majority of concert music of the baroque, classical, and romantic eras includes several important elements: the establishment of a pitch as tonal center; the establishment of a collection of pitches—a scale—as essential to a piece or passage, with other pitches playing special roles with respect to those; specific expectations and significance for particular harmonies and successions of harmonies; and the possibility of moving from one key to another key. Hardly any, if any, of Simon's songs use all of these elements of classical major-minor tonality throughout. But the principles are important to understand, because a great deal of Simon's music (a) uses some of them; (b) uses elements that can be easily understood with these as a backdrop; and/or (c) accomplishes similar ends with somewhat different means. These possibilities can be illustrated by surveying some of the general styles upon which Simon draws.

As Simon's music illustrates, clear lines cannot be drawn to distinguish such styles as folk, blues, rock, and jazz from one another. Not only does each of these labels include many different and distinct stylistic types, but many songs include more than one distinct style, or use a style that combines elements so as to be more properly identified, for instance, as folk blues, jazz rock, and so on. This discussion, then, is not intended to define particular styles as though each of Simon's songs could be cleanly categorized in this way, but rather to focus on some musical elements associated with the folk, blues, jazz, and rock traditions, so that these elements may be understood as they are encountered in his music.

"THREE-CHORD" SONGS

Many of the songs in the urban folk movement that so strongly influenced Simon and Garfunkel as they were first achieving widespread popularity are very purely diatonic, that is, containing no notes outside the scale of the key. Perhaps the stereotypical epitome of this is the so-called "three-chord" song—if, for example, this involved a singer and a guitar, all of the sung notes would ordinarily be diatonic, within a major scale, and the three chords would be the tonic, subdominant, and dominant harmonies in that key. In a major key, all three chords would be major. They would be drawn from those easily played on a guitar: F, C, G, D, A, and E, which would accommodate the keys of C, G, D, and A major.

Such a premise does not lend itself to sophisticated harmonic structures, but this is not the same as saying that sophisticated and elegant musical structure is not possible. The composer of the song can use combinations of melodic rise and fall, registral placement, important roles of melodic notes, and common functional implications of the three chords (stability for tonic, strong inclination to move to tonic for dominant, and motion toward dominant or relaxed respite from tonic for subdominant) as they interact with one another and with important features of the text, toward these ends.

The three-chord characterization is also sometimes applied to rock music, especially 1950s-vintage rock and roll. Simon himself substantiates this, for example when he uses the Bobettes' "Mr. Lee" and Laverne Baker's "Jim Dandy" as points of comparison for the township jive music that originally directed his attention toward South Africa for the *Graceland* album.[5] The three chords in this sort of scheme were again the tonic, subdominant, and dominant chords in a major key. One strong influence on these early rock and roll songs was blues music, which had already flourished for decades. This influence took many forms, but one that relates specifically to harmonic issues is the common 12-bar blues progression. While there are quite a few variants of this scheme (and many blues songs do not use it at all), it would typically deploy the chords over its 12 measures as follows (with common alternate choices in parentheses): I-I-I (IV)-I-IV-IV-I-I-V-IV (V)-I-I (V).

Many 1950s rock and roll songs directly adopted this plan (two examples among hundreds are "Rock around the Clock" by Bill Haley and the Comets and Chuck Berry's "Johnny B. Goode), and many others used the same chords in other orders. Simon uses the 12-bar blues scheme, or some variation of or reference to it, in "Keep the Customer Satisfied," "Baby Driver," "Armistice Day," "Paranoia Blues," "You're Kind," "Late in the Evening," "One-Trick Pony," "Satin Summer Nights," "Shoplifting Clothes," and "Pigs, Sheep, and Wolves." He also uses the three chords in something of a rock context in many other songs, including (as he has said) several on *Graceland*. Furthermore, the 12-bar scheme provides a good example of the way that understanding the style of a song is crucial when interpreting its harmonic structure, since motion from V to IV in a classical song would create a distinctive effect because it is so unusual, but it would not be distinctive when it occurs normatively in the ninth and tenth bars of a 12-bar blues scheme.

The three-chord stereotype notwithstanding, most folk and rock music makes use of more than the tonic, subdominant, and dominant chords. These harmonic resources might be divided into four categories: other diatonic chords, *modal* chords, *classical* chromatic chords, and other chromatic chords.

Additional Diatonic Harmonies

The three chords in major keys—I, IV, and V—are all major triads. The three minor triads—ii, iii, and vi—are often used to contribute other harmonic flavors to urban folk songs. (The diminished vii° chord is less common.) In C major, the minor chords (D minor, E minor, and A minor) are all easy to play on guitar. Among other common major folk keys (G, D, A, and E), these harmonies include increasing numbers of barre chords. These chords (B minor, F♯ minor, C♯ minor, and G♯ minor in these keys) are a bit more difficult to play than are non-barre chords, because they require the player to use the index finger of the left hand as a "bar" across all six strings, while the remaining fingers (other than the thumb) additionally stop some of the strings. In addition to being more difficult to play, the barre chords offer less opportunity for adding interesting melodic figures, because the index finger is occupied in providing the bar, and its rigid position limits the motion of the other fingers. Although many performers could either play these chords or use non-barre partial fingerings to accommodate them, it is fair to say that the more of them that a key requires, the less likely it is that a song will use a lot of them—Bm chords are quite common in the key of D and somewhat common in G, F♯m chords are occasionally heard in songs in D and A, and C♯m and G♯m chords are fairly uncommon.

In Simon's urban-folk-influenced songs, it is interesting to see the degree to which his desire for maximum expressive possibilities while remaining within the key may be reflected by how many of the six major and minor chords he uses. As the discussion of these songs shows, he often employs all six. (Examples include "The Side of a Hill," "A Church Is Burning," "Bleecker Street," "Wednesday Morning, 3 A.M.," "Kathy's Song," "I Am a Rock," and "Old Friends," which also includes one nondiatonic chord.) As is typical in this style, the progressions draw freely on classical major-minor norms: while there is no expectation that progressions will always conform to these norms, they often use the most fundamental features, such as half, authentic, and deceptive cadences, and the stable and unstable roles of tonic and dominant harmonies, respectively, for the same ends to which classical style puts them.

Modal Harmonies

A *mode* is a particular scale within a specified system; for example, within major-minor tonality, the major and minor scales are considered different modes. The term has been more distinctively applied to many different musical styles, including (1) music of ancient Greece, (2) monophonic (single-voice-part) liturgical music of the Middle Ages, (3) the polyphonic (multiple-voice-part) music that followed that repertoire in the Middle Ages and Renaissance, (4) concert music of the late nineteenth century and later that sought tonal alternatives to the major-minor tonal system, (5) Anglo and Anglo-American folk song, and (6) various so-called synthetic scales explored by composers such as Olivier Messiaen, among others.[6] The second through fifth categories are all related to one another historically and structurally, but it is the fifth, the Anglo and Anglo-American folk-song tradition, to which the term "modal" refers most primarily within this book.

In this system, a mode is a diatonic scale—that is, having the same pattern of half- and whole steps as the major scale, or the white keys on a piano—with one of its notes identified as the tonal center. Defined in this way, there are seven modes, one for each possible tonal center. If the white keys—no sharps or flats—are used, and C is the tonal center, the mode is called *Ionian*; if D, *Dorian*; E, *Phrygian*; F, *Lydian*; G, *Mixolydian*; A, *Aeolian*; and B, *Locrian* (these names are drawn from ancient Greek music theory). The half- and whole-step pattern is arranged differently with respect to the tonal center, or tonic, in each mode, and this creates a unique sound for each. (Any diatonic pattern other than the white keys—that is, the notes from any major scale—could also be used, in which case the tonal center associated with each mode would shift so as to maintain the same relationship to the pattern; thus the mode's distinctive sound would remain, but the whole scheme would simply be pitched higher or lower.)

The Ionian mode is identical to the major scale. Technically, a piece could be said to be in Ionian rather than major if it used this scale but did not use the harmonic patterns common to major-minor tonality. In practice, though, when a song that uses this mode is being discussed, such distinctions are rarely made, and the term "major" is usually used; such a song is not ordinarily considered to sound particularly "modal."

The three modes that are most commonly used in Anglo-based folk song are Aeolian, Mixolydian, and Dorian, and the distinctive feature that these share is the interval of a whole step between the tonic and the seventh scale degree, the note below the tonic. While the Aeolian scale is that same as the *natural minor* scale, this feature constitutes a much stronger distinction than is found between the Ionian mode and the major scale. If a song using this scale raises the seventh scale degree (to a leading tone) to lead to the tonic note, it is acting like a classical minor song, but if it leads to the tonic from the unraised (subtonic) seventh scale degree, it is acting modally. Two songs that use both of these approaches to some degree are "We've

Got a Groovey Thing Goin'" and "Hazy Shade of Winter"; others that use the Aeolian mode to varying degrees are "Sparrow," "Sound of Silence," "Patterns," "Peace Like a River," "Allergies," "Thelma," "Sweet Lorraine," and "Love." In these songs (which draw on both folk and rock styles), one can often see how modal harmonic progressions substitute for major-minor ones; for example, i-VII-VI-VII-i motions show how VII, rather than V, can lead to i in "Sparrow," "Patterns," and "Thelma," and i-VII-i acts similarly in "Patterns" and "Peace Like a River" (which also uses i-v-i).

The Mixolydian scale is identical to the major scale, except that its seventh step is lowered. Songs that draw on this pattern are "He Was My Brother," "For Emily, Wherever I May Find Her," and "You're the One" (all of which also use the major-scale options); and "The Rhythm of the Saints," "Sweet Lorraine," "Look at This," "Quiet," and "Sure Don't Feel Like Love." The Dorian mode is less common than is the Aeolian mode and differs from it by having a higher sixth scale degree; it is famously used in "Scarborough Fair" (although this tune is not Simon's original composition) and also appears in "The Boy in the Bubble." More generally, because of the distinctive lowered-seventh-scale-degree sound of these commonly used modal scales, songs that use the lowered seventh scale degree are often said to have something of a modal sound. Others, again including folk- and rock-flavored examples, that do this in some way include "A Church Is Burning," "Leaves that Are Green," "Richard Cory," "Big Bright Green Pleasure Machine," "Duncan," "Learn How to Fall," "The Obvious Child," "Proof," and "Hurricane Eye." (The three diatonic modes other than Ionian, Aeolian, Mixolydian, and Dorian appear less commonly in Anglo folk song, presumably because their distinctive features—lowered second scale step for Phrygian, raised fourth for Lydian, and lowered second and fifth for Locrian, were relatively unpalatable for performers and/or listeners; although they are sometimes heard in certain rock and jazz contexts, they do not figure prominently in Simon's music either.)

CHROMATIC HARMONIES

Sometimes Simon uses chromatic chords—those that include notes outside the key or mode—as they would be used in a classical major-minor context. Such situations would obviously include introducing new pitches in order to modulate to a different key. Short of this, however, they would most commonly include *secondary dominants* and *modal borrowing*. Secondary dominants are harmonies that would be dominant chords in the key of a diatonic triad other than the tonic chord. For example, in the first line of "Why Don't You Write Me?" in the key of E♭, the second chord is F7, which includes A♮, rather than the diatonic Fm7, which would include an A♭. The F7 chord acts like a dominant chord in the key of B♭, the harmony that follows, and thus leads more strongly to it than the Fm7 chord would have (the A♮ acts like a leading tone). In "Papa Hobo," in the line "Got a left-handed way of makin' a man sign up on that automotive dream, oh yeah," in the key of C, an E7/B chord, with a chromatic G♯, acts like a dominant to the following A-minor chord, and a D/F♯ chord leads in the same way to a G chord. These kinds of patterns can also be applied to the strong *circle-of-fifths* progression described before: while diatonic versions of this occur at the beginning of "Run That Body Down" and in "American Tune," secondary-dominant-type versions occur at the beginnings of verses in "Mrs. Robinson," in the bridge of "The Only Living Boy in New York," in the A section of "Learn How to Fall," and in the ragtime-influenced "Hobo's Blues" and "Stranded in a Limousine." (The pattern is extended to large-scale tonal motion in "Papa Hobo," which travels among closely related *keys,* not just harmonies, along a circle of fifths, and on the first side of *Still Crazy after All These Years,* as Kaminsky noted with relation to the introduction of the title song.)

Modal borrowing in this context refers not to the diatonic modes just discussed, but rather to the major and minor "modes." In major-minor tonality the term usually refers to the use in a major key of harmonies from the *parallel* minor key, that is, the key with the same tonic note. (For example, whereas C major and A minor are *relative* major and minor keys, C major and *C* minor are parallel major and minor keys.) As was discussed earlier, the quality of the triad built on each scale step is different in minor from its quality in major—i is minor rather than major, ii° is diminished rather than minor, and so on. Using chords from the minor scale while in a major key produces a somewhat different sound, sometimes creating a particular emotional cast—perhaps a poignancy or sadness—and often emphasizing motion of the lowered sixth scale step to the fifth. Examples in Simon's music include an A-minor chord borrowed from the minor mode of E in "Trailways Bus" and "Old Friends" (in the actual sounding key), and a B♭-minor chord borrowed from the minor mode of F in "You're the One"; these use the lowered sixth scale steps of C♮ and D♭, respectively. The idea of vacillating between major and minor is explored at greater length at the end of "Silent Eyes."

While these uses of chromaticism follow classical procedures fairly closely, it is more often the case that Simon uses chromatic chords simply to provide particular colors and sounds that he wants. Sometimes these are common devices in popular, ethnic, and/or jazz styles, and in other situations they seem more custom-devised for a particular situation. Simon's ventures into jazz harmonies make broad use of chromaticism and dissonant harmonies such as seventh, ninth, and eleventh chords. Some of the harmonic motion in these cases is loosely based on classical procedures (such as circle-of-fifths motion), and some follows fairly common jazz formulas, but much of it fits into a less systematized jazz tradition.

In either case, Simon's uses of jazz styles usually reinforce textual interests in significant and transparent ways. As one might imagine, though, given the wide emotional range that can be expressed in various jazz styles, the specific textual implications vary from situation to situation. In "Cloudy" and "Punky's Dilemma," the jazz materials reinforce two slightly different easygoing moods. In "Overs," "So Long, Frank Lloyd Wright," "Everything Put Together Falls Apart," "Congratulations," "St. Judy's Comet," and "I Do it for Your Love," a mellow, gentle tone is created that relates to the text with varying degrees of irony. The jazz materials imply a certain degree of emotional intensity or complexity in some of the songs on side one of *Still Crazy after All These Years* (such as the title track and "50 Ways to Leave Your Lover") and on *The Rhythm of the Saints* (such as "Further to Fly" and "Cool, Cool River"). In some songs an implication established by a jazz style is set in contrast to another perspective; this is seen in the soft contrast established in "Learn How to Fall," the accentuation of unexpected occurrences in "That's Why God Made the Movies," and the emotional intensity created in "The Late Great Johnny Ace." Finally, Simon presents an interesting insight in this regard with respect to "Jonah" when he opines in retrospect that the Brazilian-jazz-flavored music is too sophisticated for the folksingers described in the text (although he doesn't in this instance address the issue of whether the music-text combination might still be appropriate for its dramatic function when it appears in the context of *One-Trick Pony*).[7]

There are many examples of chromatic harmonies in Simon's music, and in a generally chromatic jazz context or an ethnically based song, for example, these can most importantly be simply establishing an overall sound environment. (An obvious example is provided by some of the songs in *The Capeman*, which connect with the cultural setting appropriate to the narrative, but similar examples can be found in stand-alone songs that similarly create the appropriate setting for their miniature narrative.) It was observed above, though, that jazz harmonies can provide contrasts within songs, and it is interesting to conclude this discussion by noting some of the ways that nonjazz-related chromatic passages can also create contrast within generally diatonic contexts. Some widely varied examples include the A major chord that accompanies new characters in "Sparrow"; the A♭ and G7 chords that accompany the climactic melodic sequence in "The Dangling Conversation"; and the G♭, C♭, and D♭ chords that lend a sense of expansiveness to "this whole wide world" in "Nobody." It is hoped that the reader may use these instances, and the discussions of various musical languages and styles that have preceded them, as a basis for further exploration.

Discography of Discussed Albums and Songs

Note: This list provides the original album appearance (or appearances, where more than one version is considered) of each of the songs discussed in the book. The albums are listed in chronological order of their original release. In addition to indicating the songs as they are addressed in the book, this list includes some songs not written or cowritten by Simon, set in brackets, and demos and the like included as extras on album rereleases.

Wednesday Morning, 3 A.M. Columbia CS 9049 (Mono CL 2249), 1964
- ["You Can Tell the World"]
- ["Last Night I Had the Strangest Dream"]
- "Bleecker Street"
- "Sparrow"
- "Benedictus" (arranged with Garfunkel)
- "The Sound of Silence"
- "He Was My Brother" (by Simon as "Paul Kane")
- ["Peggy-O"]
- ["Go Tell It on the Mountain"]
- ["The Sun Is Burning"]
- ["The Times They Are A-Changin'"]
- "Wednesday Morning, 3 A.M."

The Paul Simon Songbook CBS 62579, 1965
- "I Am a Rock"
- "Leaves That Are Green"
- "A Church Is Burning"
- "April, Come She Will"

"The Sound of Silence"
"A Most Peculiar Man"
"He Was My Brother" (Simon as "Paul Kane")
"Kathy's Song"
"The Side of a Hill"
"A Simple Desultory Philippic"
"Flowers Never Bend with the Rainfall"
"Patterns"

Sounds of Silence Columbia 9269, 1966

"The Sound of Silence"
"Leaves That Are Green"
"Blessed"
"Kathy's Song"
"Somewhere They Can't Find Me"
["Anji"]
"Richard Cory"
"A Most Peculiar Man"
"April, Come She Will"
"We've Got a Groovey Thing Goin'"
"I Am a Rock"

Parsley, Sage, Rosemary and Thyme Columbia 9363, 1966

"Scarborough Fair/Canticle" (Simon and Garfunkel)
"Patterns"
"Cloudy"
"Homeward Bound"
"The Big Bright Green Pleasure Machine"
"The 59th Street Bridge Song"
"The Dangling Conversation"
"Flowers Never Bend with the Rainfall"
"A Simple Desultory Philippic"
"For Emily, Whenever I May Find Her"
"A Poem on the Underground Wall"
"7 O' Clock News/Silent Night"

The Graduate Columbia 3180, 1968

"The Sound of Silence"
"Mrs. Robinson"
"Scarborough Fair/Canticle" (Simon and Garfunkel)
"April, Come She Will"
"The Big Bright Green Pleasure Machine"
(also includes incidental music for the film written by Dave Grusin)

Bookends Columbia CK-9529, 1968

"Bookends Theme"
"Save the Life of My Child"

"America"
"Overs"
"Voices of Old People" (Simon and Garfunkel)
"Old Friends"
"Bookends Theme" (reprise)
"Fakin' It"
"Punky's Dilemma"
"Mrs. Robinson"
"A Hazy Shade of Winter"
"At the Zoo"

Bridge over Troubled Water Columbia PC 9914, 1970

"Bridge over Troubled Water"
"El Condor Pasa" (Simon, Jorge Milchberg, and Daniel Robles)
"Cecilia"
"Keep the Customer Satisfied"
"So Long, Frank Lloyd Wright"
"The Boxer"
"Baby Driver"
"The Only Living Boy in New York"
"Why Don't You Write Me?"
["Bye Bye Love"]
"Song for the Asking"

Paul Simon Columbia KC 30750, 1972

"Mother and Child Reunion"
"Duncan"
"Everything Put Together Falls Apart"
"Run That Body Down"
"Armistice Day"
"Me and Julio Down by the Schoolyard"
"Peace Like a River"
"Papa Hobo"
"Hobo's Blues" (Simon and Stefane Grappelli)
"Paranoia Blues"
"Congratulations"
Included on 2004 rerelease:
(demos of "Me and Julio Down by the Schoolyard" and "Duncan," and an
alternate take of "Paranoia Blues")

There Goes Rhymin' Simon Columbia KC 32280 1973

"Kodachrome"
"Tenderness"
"Take Me to the Mardi Gras"
"Something So Right"
"One Man's Ceiling Is Another Man's Floor"

"American Tune"
"Was a Sunny Day"
"Learn How to Fall"
"St. Judy's Comet"
"Loves Me Like a Rock"
Included on 2004 rerelease:
"Let Me Live in Your City" ("Work-in-Progress")
(also unfinished demo of "American Tune" and acoustic demos of "Take Me to the Mardi Gras" and "Loves Me Like a Rock")

Still Crazy after All These Years Columbia PC 33540, 1975

"Still Crazy after All These Years"
"My Little Town"
"I Do It for Your Love"
"50 Ways to Leave Your Lover"
"Night Game"
"Gone at Last"
"Some Folks' Lives Roll Easy"
"Have a Good Time"
"You're Kind"
"Silent Eyes"
Included on 2004 rerelease:
demos of "Slip Slidin' Away" and "Gone at Last"

Greatest Hits, Etc. CBS JC 35032, 1977

includes previously released material, but also the initial album releases of:
"Slip Slidin' Away"
"Stranded in a Limousine"

One-Trick Pony Warner Brothers HS 3472, 1980 (video is Warner Brothers 1045)

"Late in the Evening"
"That's Why God Made the Movies"
"One-Trick Pony"
"How the Heart Approaches What It Yearns"
"Oh, Marion"
"Ace in the Hole"
"Nobody"
"Jonah"
"God Bless the Absentee"
"Long, Long Day"
Included on 2004 rerelease:
"Soft Parachutes"
"All Because of You" (out-take)
"Spiral Highway"
"Stranded in a Limousine"

Hearts and Bones LP Warner Brothers 9 23942–1, CD Warner Brothers 9 23942–2, 1983

"Allergies"
"Hearts and Bones"
"When Numbers Get Serious"
"Think Too Much (b)"
"Song about the Moon"
"Think Too Much (a)"
"Train in the Distance"
"René and Georgette Magritte with Their Dog after the War"
"Cars Are Cars"
"The Late, Great Johnny Ace" (with coda by Philip Glass)
Included on 2004 rerelease:
"Shelter of Your Arms" ("Work-in-Progress")
(also acoustic demos of "Train in the Distance," "René and Georgette Magritte with Their Dog after the War," and "The Late, Great Johnny Ace")

Graceland LP Warner Brothers 25447–1, CD Warner Brothers W2 25447, 1983

"The Boy in the Bubble" (Simon and Forere Motloheloa)
"Graceland"
"I Know What I Know" (Simon and General M. D. Shirinda)
"Gumboots" (Simon, Jonhjon Mkhalali, and Lulu Masilela)
"Diamonds on the Soles of Her Shoes" (Simon and Joseph Shabalala)
"You Can Call Me Al"
"Under African Skies"
"Homeless" (Simon and Joseph Shabalala)
"Crazy Love, Vol. II"
"That Was Your Mother"
"All around the World or The Myth of Fingerprints"
Included on 2004 rerelease:
(demo of "Homeless," unreleased version of "Diamonds on the Soles of Her Shoes," and early version of "All Around the World or The Myth of Fingerprints")

The Rhythm of the Saints Warner Brothers 26098, 1990

"The Obvious Child"
"Can't Run But"
"The Coast" (Simon and Vincent Nguini)
"Proof"
"Further to Fly"
"She Moves On"
"Born at the Right Time"
"The Cool, Cool River"
"Spirit Voices" (Simon and Milton Nascimento)

"The Rhythm of the Saints"
Included on 2004 re-release:
"Thelma" (outtake)
(also demo of "Born at the Right Time" and working tapes of "The Coast"
and "Spirit Voices")

Songs from The Capeman (lyrics written with Derek Walcott) Warner Brothers
46814, 1997

"Adios Hermanos"
"Born in Puerto Rico"
"Satin Summer Nights"
"Bernadette"
"The Vampires"
"Quality"
"Can I Forgive Him"
"Sunday Afternoon"
"Killer Wants to Go to College"
"Time Is an Ocean"
"Virgil"
"Killer Wants to Go to College II"
"Trailways Bus"
Included on 2004 rerelease:
"Shoplifting Clothes"
(also demos of "Born in Puerto Rico" and "Can I Forgive Him")

You're the One Warner Brothers 9 47844–2, 2000

"That's Where I Belong"
"Darling Lorraine"
"Old"
"You're the One"
"The Teacher"
"Look at That"
"Señorita with a Necklace of Tears"
"Love"
"Pigs, Sheep and Wolves"
"Hurricane Eye"
"Quiet"

Surprise Warner Brothers 49982–2, 2006

"How Can You Live in the Northeast?"
"Everything about It Is a Love Song"
"Outrageous" (Simon and Brian Eno)
"Sure Don't Feel Like Love"
"Wartime Prayers"
"Beautiful"

"I Don't Believe"
"Another Galaxy" (Simon and Brian Eno)
"Once Upon a Time There Was an Ocean" (Simon and Brian Eno)
"That's Me"
"Father and Daughter"

Notes

INTRODUCTION

1. My discussion of these factors focuses on the effect of these elements that are apparent to the listener and thus most pertinent to the listening experience, and it is not an attempt to describe accurately all of the subtle ingredients and techniques that may have been incorporated into the studio production process.

CHAPTER 1

1. Several of Simon's songwriting efforts from that time are commercially available now; for example, the CD *Before the Fame* (Alchemy Entertainment, Ltd. BFTF182, 2003) contains 15 songs, including, "Hey Schoolgirl" and the novelty number, "The Lone Teen Ranger."

2. The song also appears on the soundtrack album for *The Graduate*.

3. Information about order of composition of six of the songs discussed in this chapter is drawn from an interview with Art Garfunkel in "Garfunkel," by Paul Zollo in *SongTalk*, Spring 1990, reprinted in *The Paul Simon Companion: Four Decades of Commentary*, ed. Stacey Luftig (New York: Schirmer Books, 1997), pp. 42–43. (The seventh song, "A Church is Burning," is not mentioned in the interview.)

4. Tony Schwartz, "*Playboy* Interview: Paul Simon," *Playboy*, February 1984, p. 168.

5. Arthur Garfunkel, liner notes for *Wednesday Morning, 3 A.M.*, Columbia CS 9049, 1964. (The comments on "He Was My Brother" are also included in the liner notes for *The Paul Simon Songbook* (CBS 62579, 1965).)

6. The song actually sounds in the key of E♭ major on *Songbook* and E major on *Wednesday*, but Simon plays it with D fingerings, presumably using a capo to raise

the key to the recorded level. (The capo may have been at the second fret on both occasions, resulting in different keys because Simon's guitar was probably tuned a half-step low during the *Songbook* sessions.) In this book, unless otherwise noted, all discussions of guitar-based songs in which a distinction is made between the key of the guitar chords and the actual sounding key that results from the use of a capo will specify both keys and then consistently refer to chords, melody notes, and so on, in the fingered guitar key; also, the fret location of a capo will assume a guitar tuned at concert pitch. Finally, "fractionally" named chords, such as the Bm/F♯ in the present example, indicate a harmony and the bass note that sounds with it; in this case the harmony is B minor and the bass note is F♯.

7. Patrick Humphries, *The Boy in the Bubble* (London: Sidgwick and Jackson Ltd., 1988), p. 27.

8. John Swenson, *Simon and Garfunkel* (London: W. H. Allen and Co., 1984), pp. 65–66.

9. Garfunkel, liner notes for *Wednesday Morning, 3 A.M.*

CHAPTER 2

1. Simon's interest in developing his guitar-playing skills was probably greater than that of many of his contemporaries, and "Anji" was apparently a favorite of his. Its inclusion on the *Sounds of Silence* album is sometimes described as something of a favor to Graham—see, for example, Patrick Humphries, *The Boy in the Bubble: A Biography of Paul Simon* (London: Sidgwick and Jackson Limited, 1988), p. 56—who was apparently in poor financial straits at the time and would have benefited greatly from the royalties generated by what Simon could have anticipated would be substantial sales.

2. According to Judith Piepe, as quoted in Humphries, *The Boy in the Bubble*, p. 56.

3. Interview with Zollo, in Stacey Luftig, *The Paul Simon Companion: Four Decades of Commentary* (New York: Schirmer Books, 1997), p. 50.

4. Interview with Paul Zollo in *SongTalk* (Spring and Fall 1990), excerpted and reprinted in Paul Zollo, *Songwriters on Songwriting*, expanded edition (New York: Da Capo Press, 1997), p. 108 (this interview, excerpted differently, is also included in Luftig, *The Paul Simon Companion*, pp. 207–41). This was a point of contention for a while, as Carthy objected to the fact that the song was not acknowledged on *Parsley, Sage, Rosemary and Thyme* as being a traditional song, but rather appeared to be Simon's original composition (as reported, for example, in Humphries, *The Boy in the Bubble*, pp. 46–47).

5. Zollo interview with Garfunkel, Luftig, *The Paul Simon Companion*, pp. 47–48.

6. Tony Schwartz, "*Playboy* Interview: Paul Simon," *Playboy* (February 1984), p. 51; reprinted in Luftig, *The Paul Simon Companion*, p. 144.

7. Humphries, *The Boy in the Bubble*, pp. 42–44.

8. Zollo interview with Garfunkel, in Luftig, *The Paul Simon Companion*, p. 45.

9. Because of the capo, the ostinato actually sounds as E♭-D-C-B♭, and this bass line is E♭-D-C; the important point is that the same pitches are used in each song.

10. See, for example, Judith Piepe's comment as quoted in Humphries, *The Boy in the Bubble*, p. 39.

CHAPTER 3

1. Jay Cocks, "Songs of a Thinking Man," *Time,* November 12, 1990, p. 114; reprinted in Stacey Luftig, *The Paul Simon Companion: Four Decades of Commentary* (New York: Schirmer Books, 1997), p. 201.

2. Tony Schwartz, "*Playboy* Interview: Paul Simon." *Playboy* (February 1984), p. 170.

3. The young woman is presumably, as mentioned earlier, named after Kathy Chitty.

4. Jon Landau, "The *Rolling Stone* Interview with Paul Simon," *Rolling Stone* 113 (July 20, 1972), p. 33, reprinted in Luftig, *The Paul Simon Companion,* p. 86.

5. Paul Zollo, interview with Garfunkel, in Luftig, *The Paul Simon Companion,* pp. 50–51.

6. Landau, "*Rolling Stone* Interview," p. 33 (Luftig, *The Paul Simon Companion,* p. 84).

7. Zollo interview with Garfunkel, in Luftig, *The Paul Simon Companion,* p. 57.

8. Schwartz, "*Playboy* Interview," p. 170.

9. Ibid., p. 172.

10. As was common for the duo's recordings by this time, great freedom was employed in terms of overdubs and the like—it is not possible to tell exactly where additional guitar work or vocals have been added subtly to the mix. As suggested in an earlier note, this discussion concerns itself with the instrumental and vocal elements that are clearly evident in shaping the song and is not scrupulous about all details that might augment these elements—for example, whether this opening verse uses one guitar, or bits and pieces of four guitar tracks, etc.

11. Simon has said that the song is "very much about the twelve-string," Paul Zollo interview with Simon in Zollo, *Songwriters on Songwriting* (New York: Da Capo Press, 1997), p. 107.

12. Landau, "*Rolling Stone* Interview," p. 34 (Luftig, *The Paul Simon Companion,* p. 93).

13. John Swenson, *Simon and Garfunkel* (London: W. H. Allen and Co., 1984), p. 113.

14. Landau, "*Rolling Stone* Interview, p. 34 (Luftig, *The Paul Simon Companion,* pp. 88–89).

CHAPTER 4

1. Jon Landau, "The *Rolling Stone* Interview with Paul Simon," *Rolling Stone* 113 (July 20, 1972), p. 33; and Tony Schwartz, "*Playboy* Interview: Paul Simon," *Playboy* (February 1984), p. 172.

2. John Swenson, *Simon and Garfunkel* (London: W. H. Allen and Co., 1984), pp. 128–29.

3. This elegant device is based on the symmetrical structure of the F#+ chord. Ordinarily, the F# dominant chord that would lead to a B minor chord would be spelled as a major triad: F#-A#-C#. A jazzier sounding version of this chord is an augmented triad (indicated by the + symbol); this replaces the C# with a C double-sharp (C##), but the chord still leads to a B harmony. However, C## is the same note as D, and so the chord can also be heard as a D-F#-A# harmony. This would be a

D+ chord, which leads to G just as F#+ leads to B. Simon takes advantage of this double possibility in this passage by variously proceeding from the chord to B minor, B major, and G chords.

4. Landau, "*Rolling Stone* Interview," p. 34 (Stacey Luftig, *The Paul Simon Companion: Four Decades of Commentary* (New York: Schirmer Books, 1997), p. 91).

5. Swenson, *Simon and Garfunkel*, p. 128.

6. Jon Landau, "Paul Simon: Everything Put Together Falls Apart," *Rolling Stone* 103 (March 2, 1972), p. 56. Simon has mentioned this kind of approach in the course of lamenting critics' usual attention to the text to the exclusion of the music: "Most of the time, though, what I'm writing is about music, not about lyrics, and critics pay scant attention to the music. I mean, if you're saying something with music *and* words—if you're saying one thing with words and the opposite with music and you're creating a sense of irony...that's lost...." Quoted in "Paul Simon: Survivor from the Sixties," by Bruce Pollock, in *Saturday Review,* June 12, 1976, pp. 43–44+ (Luftig, *The Paul Simon Companion,* p. 124).

7. Patrick Humphries, *The Boy in the Bubble: A Biography of Paul Simon* (London: Sidgwick and Jackson Limited, 1988), p. 89, and Joseph Morella and Patricia Barey, *Simon and Garfunkel: Old Friends* (New York: Birch Lane Press, 1991), pp. 99–100.

8. Swenson, *Simon and Garfunkel*, p. 139.

9. Paul Zollo interview with Simon in Luftig, *The Paul Simon Companion,* pp. 227–28. This approach might seem odd if one assumes that the basic textual idea of a song would be an initial impulse in its composition, but it is consistent with the ways that many of Simon's songs, even well before *The Rhythm of the Saints,* were "assembled" from various points of departure, such as a rhythm track. On the other hand, ironically, the sequence of songs on *The Rhythm of the Saints* underwent a wholesale revision after this interview, and the song Simon was describing, "Thelma," was not included. (It is now available, however, as a bonus track on that album as well as on the collection *Paul Simon 1964/1993.*)

10. Peter Kaminsky, "The Popular Album As Song Cycle: Paul Simon's *Still Crazy after All These Years,*" *College Music Symposium* 32 (1992): 38–54.

11. Ibid., pp. 43–44.

12. Ibid., pp. 42, 45–48.

13. Ibid., pp. 48–51.

14. Ibid., pp. 51–54.

15. Swenson, *Simon and Garfunkel*, p. 161.

16. Kaminsky, "The Popular Album As Song Cycle," p. 43.

17. Ibid.

18. Simon credits Chuck Israels with the suggestion for this modulation in his interview with Paul Zollo in Zollo's *Songwriters on Songwriting* (New York: Da Capo Press, 1997), pp. 102–3.

19. Swenson, *Simon and Garfunkel*, p. 159.

20. Ibid., p. 162.

21. Kaminsky, "The Popular Album As Song Cycle," pp. 43n and 43.

22. Ibid., p. 45n.

23. Ibid., p. 49.

24. Ibid., pp. 49–51.

25. Ibid., pp. 49, 51.

Chapter 5

1. *Dr. Strangelove or: How I Learned to Stop Worrying and Love the Bomb,* Hawk Films Ltd., released January 29, 1964.

2. *Desperate Housewives,* Season One, Episode 8, "Guilty," first aired November 28, 2004.

3. Kunelian is played by rocker Lou Reed in a somewhat ironic bit of casting, since Reed, known for his thorough involvement in the production of his own music, here portrays a character who attempts to lead Jonah to compromise his work. Kunelian was first seen as Fox's assistant in Jonah's initial meeting with Fox, but he is here introduced to Jonah as if for the first time; it is unclear whether this is an editing gaffe or Fox is intended to be communicating in this way.

4. Simon comments on this in Tony Schwartz, "*Playboy* Interview: Paul Simon," *Playboy* (February 1984), pp. 50–51; also in Stacey Luftig, *The Paul Simon Companion: Four Decades of Commentary* (New York: Schirmer Books, 1997), 139–41.

5. Simon makes this point with reference to the song "Hearts and Bones" in his interview with Paul Zollo, in *Songwriters on Songwriting* (New York: Da Capo Press, 1997), p. 110.

6. Zollo interview with Simon in *Songwriters on Songwriting,* p. 98.

7. Schwartz, "*Playboy* Interview," p. 166.

8. Ibid., and Joseph Morella and Patricia Barey, *Simon and Garfunkel: Old Friends* (New York: Birch Lane Press, 1991), pp. 94, 96.

9. The second verse includes a linguistic gag. The listener expects the last syllable of the doo-wop insertion to set up a rhyme with the word "war" that will come at the end of the fourth phrase. For example, in the first verse this syllable was the word "for." However, the syllable in the second verse is the word "air." All is well, however, as Simon (soon after a reference to laughter!) replaces "after the war" with the French "*après la guerre.*"

Chapter 6

1. Paul Simon, liner notes for *Graceland,* Warner Bros. 9 25447–2 (1986), p. 4.

2. Paul Zollo interview with Simon in *Songwriters on Songwriting* (New York: Da Capo Press, 1997), p. 110.

3. An extended discussion of these ideas is found in James Bennighof, "Fluidity in Paul Simon's 'Graceland': On Text and Music in a Popular Song," *College Music Symposium* 33/34 (1993/1994): 212–36.

4. At least one sheet music source, *The Definitive Paul Simon Songbook* (New York: Amsco Publications, 2005), pp. 182–83, places barlines differently, so that the four beats of D are split and thus one bar consists of two beats of D and two of G, and the next includes two beats of A and two of D. However, it is much easier to hear the strongest beats of measures as falling on the initial D harmony (as the point of arrival after the dominant A harmony), rather than on the third beat of D, and on the G harmony (as the initial departure from the tonic D), rather than on the A harmony.

5. Simon, liner notes for *Graceland,* p. 3.

6. Ibid.

7. Ibid., p. 4.

8. Zollo interview with Simon in *Songwriters on Songwriting,* p. 101.

9. Jon Landau, "The *Rolling Stone* Interview with Paul Simon." *Rolling Stone* 113 (July 20, 1972), p. 34; also in Stacey Luftig, *The Paul Simon Companion: Four Decades of Commentary* (New York: Schirmer Books, 1997), p. 92.

10. Simon, liner notes for *Graceland,* p. 4.

11. Zollo interview with Simon in *Songwriters on Songwriting,* p. 93.

12. Some acoustic guitar parts are played with a capo on the second fret, but this song will be described at the pitch level at which it actually sounds.

13. His idea of living in his car recalls part of "Cars Are Cars"; however, although the two songs share a certain ruminative sense, they are generally unrelated otherwise.

14. See Chapter 4, note 8.

15. Zollo interview with Simon, in Luftig, *The Paul Simon Companion,* pp. 227–28.

CHAPTER 7

1. Paul Simon, liner notes for *Songs from* The Capeman, Warner Brothers R2 78906, p. 3.

2. In an interesting echo of the preceding album, "the setting sun…bounces off the avenue" here as "the sun hits off the runway" in "She Moves On." (In a third strikingly related line, "gravity leaps like a knife off the pavement" in "Song about the moon.")

3. Simon describes his father teaching him this progression in his interview with Paul Zollo in *Songwriters on Songwriting* (New York: Da Capo Press, 1997), p. 91.

4. The song is apparently played in the key of E minor on a guitar that is tuned down a whole step to sound in D minor; here the song will be discussed in the key in which it sounds, D minor.

5. Lewis argued in *Mere Christianity* (London: Geoffrey Bles, 1952, more recently issued several times, including London: HarperCollins, 2001), on p. 52 of the 2001 edition, that one could only interpret the claims of Jesus to conclude that he was the Son of God, a lunatic, or "the Devil of Hell" (the implication being that identifying him merely as a nondivine "good man," great prophet, or the like is not a viable option); sometimes known as "the Trilemma," these alternatives have since been commonly stated alliteratively as "liar, lunatic, or Lord."

CHAPTER 8

1. Tony Schwartz, "*Playboy* Interview: Paul Simon," *Playboy* (February 1984), p. 51.

2. Ibid., p. 172.

3. Paul Simon, liner notes for *Graceland,* p. 2.

4. Paul Zollo interview with Simon, in Stacey Luftig, *The Paul Simon Companion: Four Decades of Commentary* (New York: Schirmer Books, 1997), pp. 227–28.

5. Paul Zollo interview with Simon, in *Songwriters on Songwriting* (New York: Da Capo Press, 1997), p. 98.

6. Ibid., p. 99.

7. Ibid.

8. Ibid, p. 100.

9. Ibid., p. 99 (italics in Zollo's transcription).

APPENDIX

1. This is reflected by the fact that these concepts form the basis for most academic music theory curricula.

2. Related issues are discussed in Richmond Browne, "Tonal Implications of the Diatonic Set," *In Theory Only* 5/6–7 (July–August 1981), pp. 3–21.

3. Most of Maria's syllables have been used for centuries.

4. Zollo interview with Simon, in Stacey Luftig, *The Paul Simon Companion: Four Decades of Commentary* (New York: Schirmer Books, 1997), pp. 215–16; and Paul Simon, liner notes to *Graceland,* p. 3. (It is interesting to note that both of these sources reveal a distinction between highly experienced songwriters and music theorists, in that both Zollo and Simon use the term "relative minor" to refer to the submediant *chord,* whereas the accepted usage in the academic realm would only apply this term to a *key*—a distinction also made in the present discussion.)

5. Simon, liner notes for *Graceland,* p. 2.

6. A detailed discussion of these ideas and more can be found in Don Randel, ed., *The New Harvard Dictionary of Music* (Cambridge, MA: The Belknap Press of Harvard University Press, 1986), s.v. "mode," pp. 499–502; a very extensive discussion can be found in Harold S. Powers, Frans Wiering, James Porter, James Cowdery, Richard Widdess, Ruth Davies, Marc Perlman, Stephen Jones, and Allan Marett, s.v. "mode" in *The New Grove Dictionary of Music and Musicians,* 2nd ed., vol. 16, ed. Stanley Sadie (London: Macmillan Publishers Limited, 2001), pp. 775–860.

7. Paul Zollo interview with Simon in *Songwriters on Songwriting* (New York: Da Capo Press, 1997), p. 116.

Bibliography

Bennighof, James. "Fluidity in Paul Simon's 'Graceland': On Text and Music in a Popular Song." *College Music Symposium* 33/34 (1993/1994): 212–36.

Browne, Richmond. "Tonal Implications of the Diatonic Set." *In Theory Only* 5/6–7 (July–August 1981): 3–21.

Cocks, Jay. "Songs of a Thinking Man." *Time* (November 12, 1990): 112–14; reprinted in Stacey Luftig, *The Paul Simon Companion: Four Decades of Commentary*. New York: Schirmer Books, 1997, pp. 198–202.

Garfunkel, Arthur. Linear notes from *Wednesday Morning, 3 A.M.* Columbia CS 9049, 1964.

Humphries, Patrick. *The Boy in the Bubble: A Biography of Paul Simon*. London: Sidgwick and Jackson Limited, 1988.

Kaminsky, Peter. "The Popular Album as Song Cycle: Paul Simon's *Still Crazy after All These Years*." *College Music Symposium* 32 (1992): 38–54.

Landau, Jon. "Paul Simon: Everything Put Together Falls Apart" (review of *Paul Simon*). *Rolling Stone* 103 (March 2, 1972): 56.

———. "The *Rolling Stone* Interview with Paul Simon." *Rolling Stone* 113 (July 20, 1972): 33; much of this interview is reprinted in Luftig, pp. 79–107.

Lewis, Clive Staples. *Mere Christianity*. London: Geoffrey Bles, 1952. (More recently issued several times, including London: HarperCollins 2001.)

Luftig, Stacey. *The Paul Simon Companion: Four Decades of Commentary*. New York: Schirmer Books, 1997.

Matthew-Walker, Robert. *Simon and Garfunkel*. New York: Hippocrene Books, Inc., 1984.

Morella, Joseph, and Patricia Barey. *Simon and Garfunkel: Old Friends*. New York: Birch Lane Press, 1991.

Perone, James E. *Paul Simon: A Bio-bibliography*. Westport, CT: Greenwood Press, 2000.

Pollock, Bruce. "Paul Simon: Survivor from the Sixties." *Saturday Review* (June 12, 1976): 43–44+; reprinted in Luftig, pp. 121–25 (although erroneously cited from *Stereo Review*).

Powers, Harold S., Frans Wiering, James Porter, James Cowdery, Richard Widdess, Ruth Davies, Marc Perlman, Stephen Jones, and Allan Marett. S.v. "mode." In *The New Grove Dictionary of Music and Musicians.* Vol. 16, 2nd ed., ed. Stanley Sadie, pp. 775–860. London: Macmillan Publishers Limited, 2001.

Randel, Don, ed. S.v. "mode." *The New Harvard Dictionary of Music,* pp. 499–502. Cambridge, MA: The Belknap Press of Harvard University Press, 1986.

Schwartz, Tony. "*Playboy* Interview: Paul Simon." *Playboy* (February 1984): 49–51, 163–74.

Simon, Paul. *The Definitive Paul Simon Songbook.* New York: Amsco Publications, 2005.

———. Liner notes for *Graceland*. Warner Bros. 9 25447–2, 1986.

———. Liner notes for *Songs from* The Capeman. Warner Brothers R2 78906, 1997.

———. *Surprise* (sheet music). New York: Amsco Publications, 2006.

Simon, Paul, Judith Piepe, and Arthur Garfunkel. Liner notes for *The Paul Simon Songbook*. CBS 62579, 1965.

Swenson, John. *Simon and Garfunkel*. London: W. H. Allen and Co., 1984.

Zollo, Paul. "Interview with Paul Simon." Part I published in *SongTalk* (Spring 1990); Part II published in *SongTalk* (Fall 1990).

———. *Songwriters on Songwriting,* expanded version. New York: Da Capo Press, 1997, pp. 87–122; a differently selected excerpt appears in Luftig, pp. 207–41.

———. "Interview with Art Garfunkel." *SongTalk* (Spring 1990); reprinted in Luftig, pp. 42–43.

Index

About the Author

JAMES BENNIGHOF is Professor of Music Theory and Vice Provost for Academic Administration at Baylor University. He has presented numerous articles and papers in leading scholarly journals and conferences on music theory and analysis, including studies of American vernacular music by Scott Joplin, Robert Johnson, Artie Matthews, Janis Joplin, and Paul Simon. He has also composed both text and music for some three-dozen choral works, several of which are published by Oxford University Press.